*After You, Marco Polo*

# After You,
# MARCO POLO

*by Jean Bowie Shor*

**McGRAW-HILL BOOK COMPANY, INC.**
*New York   Toronto   London*

*I wish to express my appreciation to the National Geographic Society for permission to reprint certain portions of this story which appeared earlier, in different form, in the Society's magazine.*

Library of Congress Catalog Card Number: 55-10413

Published by the McGraw-Hill Book Company, Inc.
Printed in the United States of America

FOR FRANC SHOR
*who humored my whims*

# ILLUSTRATIONS

ix

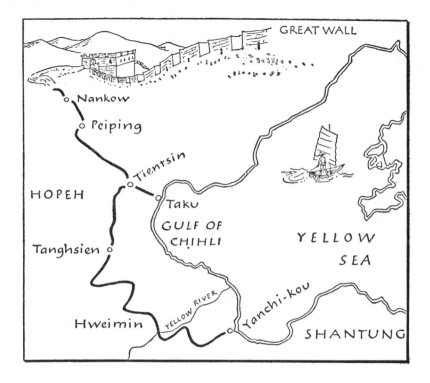

# *I*

# AMARILLO TO SHANGHAI

THERE IS A PASS across the High Pamirs, in the region called Wakhan. It is dangerous, and eerie, and awful. Marco Polo crossed that pass, and so did I. And one night I stood watch in a rude rock shelter on a snow field under the 20,000-foot summit while my husband, Franc, raved in fever.

I knew that he was probably dying, and in his lucid moments he knew it too. In an atmosphere so thin that every movement required painful exertion of will and body, I gathered yak dung for our guttering fire. I melted snow and cajoled him to drink, and I bathed his parched skin.

The candle, flickering low, was our last. I adjusted it so the light would not shine in Franc's eyes, but would be reflected on the broad, brooding faces of our Kirghiz yak pullers. The military escort provided by the King of Afghanistan had deserted us. Only the tribesmen remained, and they were no longer reliable. For three days we had had almost nothing to eat. Now, when I forced medicine down Franc's throat, they suspected that I fed him from a secret store. They gave me no help, only watched intently. I knew they were waiting for Franc to die, hoping he would die quickly, so that they could desert us.

Franc's temperature passed 105, almost certainly fatal at such an altitude. He became delirious and struggled to get out of his sleeping bag. He said he was going back to the pass. He is a big man, but I tied him in the bag, and sat on him until he slept.

At dawn, exhausted, I crawled through the door of the abandoned sheep fold in which we had found refuge, and looked out upon the march of ice-helmeted stone giants ringing us, and asked myself a question. I asked it aloud:

"Jean Bowie Shor, what are you doing here?"

My heart knew the answer. I had persuaded my husband to embark with me upon an impossible adventure. I had dreamed of following the footsteps of Marco Polo, for many years a hero to me, on his immortal journey from Venice to China. I wanted to follow Marco Polo's footsteps exactly, across the Middle East, Central Asia, and the Roof of the World.

Everyone had said that we couldn't make it, not in the middle years of the twentieth century. Travel had been simpler in the thirteenth century, when visas were unnecessary and there wasn't so much suspicion and fear on the border roads between East and West. In Marco Polo's day, people were more hospitable to strangers. Marco Polo had traveled with the blessings of a pope, the sanction of princes, and under the protection of the Golden Tablet of Kublai Khan. We possessed a plain American passport, in a day when Americans were not everywhere welcome.

The expedition seemed impossible for a physical reason as well —what geographers call the Pamir Knot. Imagine that a giant confined inside the earth in Central Asia had struck an angry blow against his round prison, so that his fist raised a great plateau, and his knuckles twisted peaks. In this convulsion were created the Hindu Kush and the Karakoram, to jostle the mighty Himalayas. Here is the Pamir Knot. Here Russia, Afghanistan, China, and Pakistan meet but do not merge.

Struggling toward Cathay, Marco Polo had traversed the Wakhan to reach the Pamirs. Franc had talked with awe of this treacherous corridor. Few Europeans, and no woman, had ever attempted it. If we crossed successfully, we would be the first Westerners to go through the Wakhan in 110 years. Expeditions backed by governments, possessing elaborate equipment and unlimited funds, had been turned back. The odds were forbiddingly heavy against our succeeding.

I had been stubborn, insistent. The responsibility was mine. My fault that we were trapped in this savage place. I was afraid, and more than afraid. I was guilty.

If I wanted to indulge in wild rationalization, I might suggest that the person chiefly responsible for my predicament that night in the Wakhan was not me at all, but my grandfather, George Morland Bowie, who died when I was young. He was a restless Scottish schoolteacher who started for China in the seventies. He crossed the Atlantic, took the train to St. Louis, and then set out on horseback for San Francisco, where he hoped to board a Shanghai bound packet. He never made it. In central Texas he met a girl, and that was as far on the road west as Grandfather Bowie ever traveled. He settled down, married, started a family, and founded a prosperous lumber business.

My grandfather Bowie was a courageous man, for he wore his kilt and plaid in Texas. He was bald and of medium height, but I was always awed by his enormous dignity, his formal manner, and by his beautiful white beard.

His questing spirit refused to be confined to the town of Weatherford, Texas. Whenever he could get away from business he journeyed to Europe, Mexico, Central and South America. And he bought travel books, and stories of adventure, and histories by the hundreds. In those days, sets of books were sold from door to door, and in Texas from ranch to distant ranch, by dusty book

peddlers in weathered buckboards. These plains-hardened traveling salesmen seldom stopped at the Bowies' without making a
sale.

Grandfather Bowie never did get to China, but as Tennyson
said of Marco Polo, he was "always hunting with a hungry heart."
This wanderlust was his special legacy to me, a heritage which
many years after his death drove my husband and me to the
pass in the High Pamirs.

My career as a nomad began, I believe, at the age of five. I
loaded my little red wagon with apples, cookies, and my favorite
doll, and found my way to the house of a relative, ten unfamiliar
blocks away. Our Negro cook commented sagely, "That Miss
Jean, she sure got her foot in the path!" When I started to read,
I skipped the books that little girls usually like, and began early
to concentrate on the far places. I soon discovered *The National
Geographic Magazine,* with its fascinating maps and pictures.
Grandfather had been one of the earliest members of the National
Geographic Society, and he had saved each issue. Then, through
Rotary International, I corresponded madly with children in Hol-
land, Czechoslovakia, Greece, and Poland, who wanted to hear
from American "cousins." I learned a good deal—mostly about
Texas. My correspondents on the other side of the Atlantic had
a thousand questions to ask, and I had to do considerable research
to answer them.

In the cool Texas evenings, I sailed off to India, to the South
Seas, or to England with Kipling and Maugham and Robert Louis
Stevenson. I accompanied the caravans of Harold Lamb, and read
every history of Asia and Europe I could lay my hands on. With
wonder, I consumed Mark Twain's *Innocents Abroad,* and Sven
Hedin's accounts of his travels in Asia. I read Cellini, Leonardo
da Vinci, and the history of the Borgias. But above all else, I was
enthralled by the adventures of Marco Polo. The itinerary of
Marco Polo I could recite like a train schedule, and it was Marco
Polo who taught me respect for maps.

I dreamed of becoming an explorer, and seeking out the unknown places of the earth. In my dreams the purple sunsets became Oriental battlements, and the tiny twisters we call dust

devils took human shape and pursued me across the plains. Right in Texas, I have fled the Mongol hordes of Tamerlane and Genghis Khan.

Eventually, those dreams began to come true. I became familiar with Europe, and saw war, and witnessed the creeping conquest of China. I was captured by Communists and subjected to brainwashing, when the term, and the ordeal, was a novelty to Americans. I hitchhiked across the Gobi Desert, and looked upon the Caves of the Thousand Buddhas and the tomb of Genghis Khan. Finally, I followed Marco Polo's path east, from Venice to China.

My first trip abroad was a wonderful carefree, prewar unconducted tour. An aunt from Connecticut—everyone should have one!—sent me a check for $1,000 with a note saying that "it is about time you see Europe." I left a week later while the family was still trying to decide if it was all right for me to go alone. The summer and autumn of 1938, I stretched that $1,000 to the vanishing point, begrudgingly parting with my pennies in London's Soho, in Paris where I discovered *lapin* meant rabbit and you could eat it, in Berlin where I caught a frightening glimpse of Hitler meeting Admiral Horthy in a city eerily floodlit in green. I stretched it through Hungary and Italy and Holland. My pocketbook and my feet took an awful beating. Everywhere I traveled third class, or no class at all, wide-eyed, incredulous, and certain that I had found my profession, traveling.

As it turned out, the U.S. Government took the responsibility for my second safari out of my aunt's hands. Soon after the United States entered World War II, I joined the American Red Cross and asked for overseas duty. My life in far-off places began—with a vengeance.

I was assigned to the 306th Fighter Wing of the 15th Air Force, based on the Adriatic side of Italy. The mission of the wing was to protect the heavy bombers that struck each day into Germany and Central Europe. My mission was to command a clubmobile, and serve doughnuts and coffee to the fighter pilots and their ground crews on two adjoining airfields.

I saw the first missions off before dawn every morning, and welcomed the last ones home in late afternoon. I delivered and dis-

tributed some three thousand doughnuts a day on the bases, altogether handing out more than a million. One morning, suffering
from doughnut fatigue, I inadvertently mixed soap powder into
the batter, and the next day most of the Fourth Squadron of the
52d Fighter Group were immobilized. (Perhaps, come to think
of it, immobilized is not precisely the word!) Yet, on the whole,
the doughnut business must have seemed worth while because
whenever the mix ran low the wing loaned me a B-17 heavy
bomber—complete with crew, of course—and I rode to Florence
or Bari in high style for more lard and flour from the Red Cross
depot.

When a mission was expected back, I'd drive out to the field
in either an old ambulance or an equally old command car, un-
limber a big camp stove, and make coffee in twenty-gallon lots,
boiling my water in GI cans. I'd lay out trays of cups hammered
from old tin cans, a ten-pound sack of sugar, punctured cans of
milk, and doughnuts by the hundreds. Then I'd ring a gas alarm
bell or honk my horn for customers. Business was fine. There never
was a slack season.

For months the home of our five-girl unit was the little town
of San Severo where we occupied a two-room apartment over a
wine press. San Severo's red-light district was down our street
some six blocks and was often a source of bewildering amusement
and some annoyance. One day a misdirected and happily inebri-
ated GI knocked on our door, and I answered. "Howdy, Sig-
norinie," he said politely, listing a bit to starboard, and added a
few more phrases in bad Italian.

"I'm sorry," I said, "but I don't understand you. What do you
want?"

His eyes lit up. "Gee!" he said. "They speak English, too!"

We straightened him out, not without difficulty, and sent him
on his way.

I won't forget the unfailing politeness and consideration of the
GIs. Occasionally I'd stay on the airfield after dark for a movie.
You haven't heard descriptive language until you've sat through
a Lana Turner or Rita Hayworth film attended by several hun-

dred appreciative airmen and soldiers shouting advice, opinions, and ad lib dialogue. So before the start of a feature, invariably some alert GI would stand up and make an announcement. "Watch your language, you bums," he'd say. "Jean's here tonight." I'm afraid I spoiled their fun.

After V-E Day I traded a case of fruit juice to a British flying officer for a bottle of Scotch, and swapped the Scotch with a homeward-bound American sergeant for a "liberated" Volkswagen. I filled its tank with army gasoline, loaded PX supplies aboard, and toured Italy at leisure. Most of the countryside was in the same battered condition as my car. A firsthand look at war's bleak aftermath should be part of everyone's education. If you haven't seen the effects of war you cannot understand it. Even those who have seen it forget quickly, as they forget pain. They prefer to recall leaves in Paris and Wiesbaden rather than numbing days at the front and starving children in ruined villages and bodies piled like cordwood in concentration camps.

WHEN THE WAR was over on both fronts, I resigned from the Red Cross, but by then my foot was definitely "in the path." The world of Marco Polo lay to the east, in Asia. In 1946 I took a job with UNRRA in China and went to work as an administrative assistant in Shanghai.

Postwar Shanghai was the world's most wicked city—and proud of it. Its fabled White Russian women were at once its courtesans and entrepreneurs. Its black marketeers traded in dollars and gold and diamonds, canned food and morphine, silks and bodies, and in the secrets of any country. It was jammed with Jewish refugees, and American troops, and rich Chinese fugitives from the areas already overrun by the Communists, and people without "visible means of support" who might rightfully be called international adventurers.

It was a city of skyrocketing prices and worthless currency and chain cocktail parties and wild rumors. Incredible luxury and unbelievable squalor lived side by side. Everyone assured everyone else that Shanghai's future was bright, that things were going to be all right, but nobody really believed it. The shadow of doom lay over the city.

Yet I loved my years in Shanghai. I loved the crowded streets and the luxurious hotels, the little shops where ivory and bronze and jade were piled in careless profusion, the men who sold sesame seeds on the curbs, the ricksha coolies who jauntily risked their lives in front of speeding cars. I loved sluggish Soochow Creek, and the ancient junks which covered its slimy surface, and the families who spent their lives and made their living on these junks and raised innumerable children to play in the filthy water. Shanghai was wicked and riddled with graft, but it was alive and vibrant, and there was no boredom there.

The next year, in 1947, I was transferred briefly to Peiping, and the old capital, so rich in history, was a relief from Shanghai's pace. Yet Peiping was like a city resting in the eye of a hurricane, for in the north the Communist guerrilla bands crept ever closer. While the merchants and officials of Peiping ardently talked the Nationalist cause, they felt the first breath of the red storm upon their necks. Later, when the Communists marched in, many were to switch their allegiance, just as the wind shifts after the eye of the hurricane passes on.

I tried to do my job and keep out of political discussions, for UNRRA was an international agency employing citizens of every country. I knew that our task, attempting to dole out relief to both sides, Nationalist and Communist, was almost hopeless. Bringing relief to graft-ridden, divided China was like pouring sugar into the sea.

Peiping is one of the oldest cities continuously inhabited by man, founded in 3000 B.C., according to legend. It is, to me, the most beautiful spot in the world. I tramped through the Forbidden City where the Manchus ruled, and looked upon the Temple of Heaven, and inspected the Ming tombs, and passed between the kneeling stone camels of the Alley of Animals. I walked the wide, shaded avenues, brushing elbows with the tall northern Chinese. In Tartar City restaurants, I ate *hwa gwa* Mongolian meals, which you cook yourself over a brazier. The older Chinese restaurants were tall buildings surrounding courtyards. At the end of the meal, after receiving his tip, the waiter would go to the balcony and announce the amount to everyone in the establishment. If you left a big tip, you descended the stairs to a buzz of approval. If it was small, the silence made the passage painful.

Standing in the main bazaar of the Thieves Market one afternoon, I looked up to see a long camel caravan just entering the Great Western Gate. The shaggy Bactrian camels, with deep-toned bells hanging from their necks, led by traders in tattered sheepskins and leather leggings, suddenly typified for me all the mystery of the desert and the ageless romance of the East.

My mind skipped quickly to another ageless trademark of China's past and, then and there, I determined to see it—the Great Wall.

The Americans in Peiping advised me not to try. The Great Wall is not far from the city, at Nankow Pass, perhaps four hours by train, but all the railroads in North China were now in danger. The Communist bands blew up a train or trestle almost every night. Wise travelers rode the trains only in the daylight hours.

Not long afterward, I met a Chinese named Chou, a slight and delicate man of dignified expression and courtly manners. Chou had been a guide for Thomas Cook, and therefore possessed great face among all the guides of Peiping. He lamented that now there were no more American or British tourists, and that it was well known that the Russian tourists were not really tourists at all. His fortunes had declined, and he feared they would decline still further. Having long been associated with a famous capitalist organization, he hinted delicately that soon he might even cease to exist entirely.

This was an opportunity too good to be missed. "How would you like to escort me on a Cook's tour?" I asked.

"Where would you like to go?" he said, beaming.

"To the Great Wall."

Mr. Chou came only to my shoulder, and at five seven I am not exactly an Amazon. Now he seemed to shrink even smaller. "Once—" he said wistfully. "But now, you know it is impossible. The Reds—the bandits—they keep blowing up the train."

"Chou," I said, "are you not a guide of Thomas Cook, and is not a guide of Thomas Cook capable of taking one anywhere?"

"It is true," he agreed. "But Thomas Cook would not think of endangering the lives of its clients."

But I refused to give up. Chou was the only person who could take me. So I played my best card. "I would pay very well," I said. He stood quietly for a moment. I could see him weighing the danger against the need of rice for his table. I might be the last American tourist he would ever see; yet this innocent sight-seeing jaunt might end in sudden death.

Without a change of expression he made his decision. "There is a work train that daily goes beyond the Wall at Nankow," he said. "The bandits do not blow it up because they do not consider it worthwhile, or perhaps because some of their own kind ride it, disguised as laborers. If you meet me at three o'clock in the morning at the station—"

I met him at the station at this furtive hour, looking as rugged as I could manage in suntan khaki shirt and trousers, and GI shoes. Chou wore a long blue silk gown and a pith helmet, and on his tiny feet were soft black wool slippers. We each carried our lunch, his wrapped in a white silk handkerchief, mine in a paper carton.

Soon a string of flatcars was shoved up the track. "This is our train," Chou announced. "Please board, missy." On our car, their legs dangling over the side, were some twenty blue-clad laborers, friendly and inquisitive gents who inspected me curiously and smiled. They were pleased, Chou told me, that I would go to the trouble to ride the work train to see the Wall, which remained an impressive giant even to these laborers who saw it daily.

We rode the train to where the railroad penetrates the Great Wall, at Nankow Pass, jumped off at the summit of the pass, and climbed to the top section of the Wall running west, Chou all the while pretending his feet didn't hurt in his soft slippers. It was bright morning when we reached a secluded, crumbling watch-tower. In every direction the view was awesome and lonely.

The wall snaked across the gray earth and blue rocks as far as we could see. I scrambled over several miles of its broad top, examined stairways and sentry boxes, skinned my hands and knees, and congratulated myself that I had been lucky enough to see the most monumental work ever conceived by man. The Great Wall makes the Pyramids, as well as such modern pygmies as Boulder Dam and the Empire State Building, seem undersized and puny indeed. With all its turns and loops, its length is over 1,500 miles.

It was started, some say, five hundred years before the birth of Christ and it was generations a-building. In 220 B.C. all its works were linked by the Emperor Ch'in Shih Huang, who, Chou told me, expended the lives of 500,000 criminals and prisoners of war in the process. Later construction was done in the Ming dynasty (A.D. 1368–1644). Cathay was protected by this single fortification from the Yellow Sea to the great deserts beyond Yumen in Kansu. Watchers were stationed on every turret and tower, day and night. They used a code of smoke signals to summon help when the savage horsemen of Mongolia massed against the Wall. So, for a time, the barbarians were held off, but in the end the Great Wall proved about as useful as its pathetic latter-day imitator, the Maginot Line.

We had our picnic on the Wall, Chou and I. He ate dainty strips of sweet-and-sour pork and chicken, and candied kumquats, while I munched away on K-ration cheese on crackers, and Spam-on-rye. Chou talked of the Wall and its history. It would stand a long time, he said, for it was cemented by blood. "For each block of stone, count one life."

We were back at the pass well before the train was due. Farmers with baskets of garlic waited along the track. We would have more passengers going back to Peiping than coming out. Then a whisper ran through the farmers lining the track and was heard by Chou. "Our train," he explained calmly, "has been blown up on the other side of the pass."

My sudden change of expression must have shown Chou that this sort of thing was not part of my normal routine. Before I had a chance to worry over it, he smiled and said, "It is really not so serious, missy. It was a mistake. The bandits undoubtedly in-

tended to blow up an express train, but unfortunately the express
train was delayed. So the work train ran over the explosives instead. I am sure they regret the error."

"What's not so serious about that?" I asked.

"The engine itself will not have been hurt, for it always pushes
several empty flatcars ahead, as a safety measure against just such
a stupid mistake. Surely another work train is being assembled
north of the pass, and the tracks have been repaired. It will arrive
presently."

"Are you sure?" I said.

"Remember," said Chou, "that I am a guide of Thomas Cook.
It is the business of a guide to know everything dealing with
transportation."

I said, "Yes, Mr. Chou." I was impressed. I wondered how much
of Mr. Chou's calmness the station master at Grand Central might
have mustered on hearing that a string of freight cars had been
blown sky-high just outside of Scarsdale.

There was a Nationalist sentry box, a cubicle of stone surmounted by a watchtower, at the pass, and we were allowed to
nap in this shelter when night came. I slept with my head on a
bag of garlic. There were worse odors in that place.

"Presently," in Chinese, can mean almost any length of time
short of a century, and it was almost dawn when the new work
train chugged up the pass and wheezed to a stop.

The ride back to Peiping was uneventful. Mr. Chou came to
my house a few nights later and very formally presented me with
a heavy sheet of Chinese paper, lined vertically. Written in beautiful Chinese characters, it established my bona fides: "This is
to certify that Miss Jean Bowie has made a visit to the Great Wall
of China, escorted by Guide Precious North Chou, formerly of
Thomas Cook." Perhaps Chou felt that since there were no post-
card peddlers or itinerant photographers to snap us leaning on
the Wall in the best tourist tradition, he must supply a memento.

I have it still. I doubt that Mr. Chou ever escorted another
tourist. Indeed, I may have been the last Western tourist to visit
the Great Wall for a long, long time, as we measure time, but not
as time is measured by the Great Wall.

DAY BY DAY, conditions got worse. The war between the Nationalists and Communists grew more open and the fighting crept closer.

It was the duty of UNRRA to distribute relief supplies to both Nationalists and Communists, in proportion to the population of the areas devastated by the Japanese. At that time eighty per cent of the population was in areas controlled by the Nationalists, and so they received eighty per cent of all relief supplies. Since the Nationalists controlled all the ports, they could screen supplies destined for the Communists. Quite rightly, they insisted that no supplies which might be converted to military use be sent the Communists. Somehow, almost everything, from sewing machines to dentists' drills, developed a military potential.

Nevertheless, it was the duty of UNRRA to see that the Communists received their share, or as much of their share as could be convoyed to them. It was not up to us to decide policy. Our job was to carry out the orders of the governments, including the United States, that framed the UNRRA Charter.

Since there was constant fighting in the north, every shipment that went into Communist areas required the equivalent of a private treaty between the two forces and had to be accompanied by Nationalist and Communist liaison officers, and UNRRA personnel. I wanted desperately to make a trip on one of these convoys, to see what life was like on the other side of the lines. In 1947, the shape of the enemy was still hazy. I begged and pleaded to go into Communist territory with an UNRRA team. Finally, my superiors were worn down, and they granted permission.

I found out the nature of the enemy, all right. Firsthand.

The convoy to which I was assigned formed up at Tientsin. It was to carry relief supplies down the Grand Canal, by barge, to the destitute millions in the Communist-held areas of Hopeh and Shantung Provinces. In the group were four UNRRA representatives besides myself, three newspaper correspondents, and the Nationalist and Communist liaison officers, two young men who maintained a precise degree of politeness to everyone, but managed not to be aware of each other's presence.

From Tientsin we went a day's ride south by train, transferred to jeeps, and drove another day to the town of Tsangshien where we boarded the barges. The barges were loaded with useless sewing-machine treadles, dried-soup powder, tinned British biscuits, and dental plaster of Paris. I was too accustomed to such insanity to ask any questions.

Twenty coolies, dressed in faded blue cotton and straw hats big as parasols, pulled each barge. They chanted as they tugged, each with a long rope biting into his shoulders. The countryside seemed oddly peaceful, despite soldiers on the move, deserted slit trenches, and isolated pillboxes, some of them scorched. I was told that whenever an UNRRA team passed through the lines, both sides declared a local truce. No trouble was anticipated. Other convoys had preceded us.

That afternoon I heard what sounded like a thunderstorm behind us, although the sky was not clouded. In the evening, just before we tied up at a small squalid village, the thunder was accompanied by flashes of lightning. The Nationalist liaison officer, who had become quieter with every additional mile we penetrated into Communist territory, now seemed downright frightened. My thunder and lightning was a battle in progress back in Tsangshien.

There was a reception committee on the bank to greet us, headed by a tall, wide-shouldered, handsome man wearing a military jacket and trousers of tan homespun cotton. He was the local commissar, and he made a speech. He was delighted, he said, to have us as his guests. Unfortunately, it would be dangerous for us to go on. There might be fighting ahead.

We asked whether it would be all right for us to go back. It was obvious that something had gone very wrong. Unfortunately, said the commissar, we could not go back either. At that moment a battle was in progress for Tsangshien. If we were allowed to return, it was possible that some of us might report the troop dispositions of the People's Army. He looked pointedly at our Nationalist officer. However, he was sure our stay in the village would be pleasant. He would be host at a feast that night, and we would be comfortably billeted in a motor-pool compound.

True to his word, the commissar gave us a banquet. It was the most elaborate meal I ever had in China, with fifteen courses washed down by cups of hot yellow wine, and including whole roast suckling pigs, duck, fish, roast chicken, and interspersed with such delicacies as melon soup, shark-fin soup, ancient buried eggs, and glutinous rice pudding. This was no spur-of-the-moment cookery—obviously, we had been expected for dinner.

We were, literally, fat and complacent that night when suddenly the party line changed. A squad of armed soldiers entered the compound. They said not a word, but moved ominously into our huts. I had a battery radio which a soldier savagely bayoneted. After a brief and violent search, they took away one of the correspondents, a photographer, while maintaining a guard over the rest of us. A propaganda trial was held in the torchlit village square, and the photographer was denounced as a tool of the capitalistic imperialists before a crowd of school children and illiterate farmers. His film was confiscated, and he was returned to the compound a very subdued young man. None of us was exactly happy.

The whole performance was crazy and illogical. We were bringing them supplies—not what they wanted, to be sure, but still all we could manage—and as a reward we were being treated like criminals. Gathering our wits and our nerve, we threatened to report the matter to the United Nations. We would bring the wrath of the American embassy down on their heads. We demanded to speak to the commissar, who only a few hours before had been so friendly. Now, he would not see us.

In the morning we were loaded aboard trucks, at gun muzzle, and driven south, deeper into Hopeh. We bounced along a dusty road all day, and in the evening came to the village of Hsiao Wang Chang. I climbed out of the truck, stretched, and looked up into the face of a hulking red-haired man whose eyes shone with excitement and contempt. This was my introduction to Dr. Frey, an Austrian physician, a Jewish refugee from the Nazis who had fled to China before the war. He had lived in the interior with his Chinese wife, there joining Mao Tse Tung, and becoming one of the foreign political advisers to the Chinese Communists in what he termed the "liberated areas."

We would, Dr. Frey informed us in perfect English, be under his control so long as we remained in Hsiao Wang Chang.

"How long will that be?" I asked.

"It depends," he said. "But perhaps while you are here, I can add something to your education."

I shrugged. This would be a new type of "education." The man was obviously a fanatic.

In the village lived twenty farm families, each in a mud, thatch-roofed house, fenced off from one another by rude compound walls. Around the settlement stretched wheat fields. There were a few water buffalo and chickens, but most of the families had pigpens. Throughout our stay, the villagers were unfailingly curious and friendly, not comprehending the increasing friction between great powers that had brought us, prisoners, to this remote place.

The tenants of one of the compounds were evicted so we could be housed. The house consisted of one large room, its floor a hardened paste of ox blood and mud. Along one side of the room was a large *kang*, or built-in bed. This is simply a mud platform raised above floor level. A flue from an outdoor fireplace is buried under it, so that in winter the *kang* is heated. This Chinese equivalent of an electric blanket plus radiant heat is crude, but it works.

All ten of us slept in this one room. While it is considered most improper for a lady to sleep in the same room with one man not her husband, no one seems to worry when there are nine.

There was a single outdoor latrine, in disreputable condition, with a rotting floor and a broken door. Modern plumbing is hard to find in the backwoods of China, and I have seen worse than this before and since. I have slept in huts where an out-of-the-way pigsty, complete with pig, was used as a privy. A girl traveling in Asia requires good kidneys, a stopped-up nose, and elastic views on modesty.

Dr. Frey assigned a personal guard to each of us. They were army cadets and called themselves "Red Devils." My particular Red Devil was a bandy-legged boy who wore a charm bracelet of grenades around his waist and was named, I believe, Ruh Shui. The first half dozen times I called him, he came running with hot water. Then I realized that Ruh Shui is very close to the Chinese expression for hot water. In my Texas accent, that is.

Our food, I must admit, was exotic. Our principal protein was goldfish—I mean real fishbowl goldfish—and we ate them every day. In northern China, their original home, goldfish are netted by the thousands, like sardines. I must admit to a growing fondness for them, deep-fried in soybean oil and piled high in bowls garnished with greens. They were crisp and tasty, and reminded me of French-fried potatoes. We ate them whole, heads, insides and all. I ate so many that whenever I see a bowl of goldfish at the home of a friend, I get hungry.

After the first week, each day dragged by like a month, and I had the horrible feeling that we had never been missed by UNRRA and were destined to live on in that village compound forever.

Every night the towering Dr. Frey favored us with a political lecture. At first we tried to argue with this mind locked in Communist dogma, but he automatically rejected even the simplest and best-known facts of history. He could, however, be needled. "Is it true," I asked innocently one night, "that Stalin and Chiang are about to sign a nonaggression pact?"

His whole face turned the color of his hair, as he denounced the rumor as impossible.

"Well," one of the correspondents joined in the game, "Stalin signed a pact with Hitler, didn't he?"

And Dr. Frey became apoplectic, as we tried not to laugh aloud.

He hated us, and particularly he seemed to hate me, although we were all equally unafraid of his blustering tantrums. When he called me a filthy capitalist, I admitted to being filthy, all right, but I wasn't by any means a capitalist. A capitalist would have had ways and means of buying his way out of such a predicament. When he called the photographer a tool of Wall Street, he was promptly reminded of lend-lease, and asked where the Russians would be without it.

After a time the political lectures and the baiting of Dr. Frey began to grow tiresome, and when he spoke of Wall Street we wouldn't answer. Instead my mind would wander on over to Fifth

Avenue and the chic girls in front of Saks's or Bonwit Teller's. How strange I would have looked to them! . . . Frey had begun to beat us down, by constant ranting, and we knew that answering only made him rage and scream the longer.

Now we call this technique, developed to a finer science, "brain-washing," and we know that when carried on for months or years it can pound to a jelly even the mind of a courageous and stubborn person. Dr. Frey didn't have that long to work on us, but even if he had, I prefer to think that his verbal bludgeoning would not have been effective. He was a bitter man, so filled with poison and hatred that his infection was plain. He hated everyone, including, no doubt, himself.

One day, after two weeks, I decided it was my duty, being the only woman in our party, to clean house. This was a considerable job, for many years had passed since anyone had bothered to so much as sweep the dirt floor. I felt more like an archeologist than a house cleaner, burrowing through layer after layer of grime and dirt with a shovel. Then, in a corner, I unearthed artifacts more valuable than Ming vases—three ancient copies of the *Reader's Digest*. First the issue for April, 1946, which was in pretty good condition. Then, one layer down, I discovered the February, 1938, issue, plainly stamped, "Do not take from library." It failed to say what library. Deep in the debris was an issue of March, 1932, stained and dog-eared, but still readable.

My male compatriots had been jibing at me for being house-wifey. Now, starved for diversion, they changed their tune. I appointed myself librarian, put our library into circulation, and reserved the 1932 volume, so old that it sounded fresh and new, for myself. That was a wonderful year, 1932, even if there seemed to be a bit of a depression going on. In 1932 there were no wars anywhere in the world, although that was the year that a group of Shanghai gangsters murdered a Japanese Buddhist priest, the first of a series of incidents that led to the Japanese invasion of China. Yet, fifteen years later, crouched on the mud floor of a hut in Communist China, I read nostalgically of peaceful, old-fashioned 1932.

In our third week of captivity we were told that negotiations were under way for our release. UNRRA had not forgotten us! A few days later we knew the party line had switched again. Our guards became jolly and polite. Dr. Frey smiled, for the first time, and announced that the Communist governor was to entertain us at dinner. We knew that UNRRA must have reached some agreement with the Communist hierarchy.

The governor's banquet was held at a military post near the village. My hands appeared so coarse and the dirt was so deeply ingrained that I hesitated to touch the linen napkins or the tablecloth. The beautiful silver seemed difficult to manipulate after a month of chopsticks. Surprisingly, we were served a complete Western-style dinner, cooked and served by the governor's kitchen staff, brought a hundred miles for the occasion.

The governor sat at the head of the table, and he placed me at his right. An aide told me that the governor was somewhat deaf and spoke no English in any case, so the table conversation was carried on through a shouting interpreter.

Brandy was brought in after dinner, and one of the governor's aides said, "His Excellency would be honored if you would play the finger game with him." Unlike "footsie," which is played under the table, the finger game is played topside. It is, so they assured me, an old Chinese custom. Each player unclenches his fist, suddenly extending any number of fingers on one hand and shouting his guess of the total. If you guess correctly, your opponent drains his glass of brandy at a single draught. The idea seems to be for everyone to get tight in a hurry. It does loosen up a party.

I explained to the aide that I was very poor at the finger game, and besides how could I play it with His Excellency? I spoke little Chinese, and he no English, and in addition His Excellency was deaf.

At this point His Excellency leaned toward me and whispered, "But I do speak English, and I would very much like to play the finger game with you."

I jumped in my chair; he must have overheard some choice remarks about our stay, I said. His Excellency laughed hilariously and I couldn't help joining him. I agreed to play the finger game, but added, "Not for long." This amused him even more, and when I observed that he was a "wily Oriental," he courteously agreed.

During the course of the conversation that night we heard the first news in a month of what had been going on in the world outside our village prison. For one thing, the United States was supplying new arms to the Nationalists. One of the Communist officers observed, "That is a very good thing. We will capture it all very quickly."

I couldn't guess that his prediction would prove so right, so soon, and that our own guns would be turned against us in Korea.


AFTER FIVE NIGHTS of traveling in an American six-by-six truck which already had fallen into Communist hands, we arrived at the coastal city of Yanchi-kou. An LST, converted to an UNRRA supply ship, was on the way, we were told. The LST could not enter the shallow harbor, but we would go out in junks and meet it.

Robinson Crusoe did not await a ship with more anxiety than we.

Two days later we were told that the LST was approaching the coast. We rushed down to the wharf, where motor junks waited to carry us to our rendezvous. Slowly the superstructure of our ship arose out of the sea. Then we heard a disquieting sound—heavy machine guns, far off. Three planes fell out of the sky like plummeting hawks to attack our ship. The LST turned broadside to us, and then it put on speed and fled.

We sat on the wharf for a long time, stunned, before our Communist guards herded us back to our room. "You see," they said, "the treacherous running dogs of Chiang Kai-shek have attacked your UNRRA ship."

We did not believe it, then, but later discovered it was true. While the Nationalists had agreed, in principle, to allow certain UNRRA supplies to reach the Communists, they did everything possible to see that this didn't happen. On three different occasions to my knowledge, LSTs operated by the international relief agency were attacked by Nationalist planes.

Fortunately, the Nationalists were not as yet skilled in air warfare. Usually their bombs and bullets missed, as they did on this occasion. Yet this knowledge offered little comfort; I had that sinking feeling again that we would never get out of our bug-ridden room in Yanchi-kou.

It was now necessary, as we later found out, to reopen negotiations for our delivery all over again. Several days later we were again escorted to the docks. Once more we saw an LST approach, but this time it anchored far off shore. We boarded the junks, which for some reason were loaded with bales of cotton, and dripping and shivering from the spray that broke over the heavily laden craft, we at last climbed up cargo nets to the deck of the LST. (The cotton was unloaded, right after us. What sort of a private deal took place I'll never know.) That first night at sea, while we were eating supper aboard, someone ransacked my cabin and stole most of my clothes and all my money. I returned to Tientsin penniless and ragged and bug-bitten as any refugee.

But I had learned about the Chinese Communists—the hard way.


UNRRA REASSIGNED ME to Shanghai, where I lived in luxury (that means, in a room by myself, without nine male escorts, and with an utterly private white tile bath) at the Hotel Metropole, my windows overlooking the busy Whangpoo River, until the agency was disbanded. Then I took a job as executive assistant to Dr. Chang Kia-Gnau, president of the Central Bank of China. The title sounded formidable, but mostly I ghosted the speeches he delivered before gatherings of American businessmen in Shanghai, and drafted the replies to his English-language correspondence.

On the evening of March 24, a date I have no trouble remembering, I attended a large party at the home of Evert Barger, the distinguished British archeologist and geographer. There too was Franc Shor, China correspondent of the *Reader's Digest,* and formerly executive officer for UNRRA in China. I had met him before, of course, as had practically everyone else in Shanghai. He was a tall, big-boned, wide-shouldered ex-newspaperman and mag-

azine writer. Fiorello La Guardia, at one time a director general
of UNRRA, had found in Franc a talent for administration, and
had sent him to China to straighten out what was a considerable
tangle. I had watched and admired the way he had gone about
it, and his own absolute integrity. He had ruthlessly fired the black
marketeers and weeded out the incompetents. He never could get
rid of them all, but he did his best.

Franc elbowed his way through the crowd. "Come have a drink
with me," he called, "it's my birthday."

"You're in good company," I answered. "It's my birthday, too."

He showed marvelous tact and didn't ask my age. Having been
in charge of all UNRRA personnel, he probably knew it anyway.
He simply said, "Naturally we'll have to celebrate."

So we did, and all over Shanghai. By the time he took me back
to the Metropole, at first light, I had learned a lot about Shanghai
cabarets and night clubs and a great deal more about Franc Shor.

"Franc" was his way of shortening Francis Marion Luther Shor
to distinguish himself from numerous Franks already in his family.
His father had been a newspaper editor in Boston and Philadel-
phia and New York and Franc had followed on a journalistic career. He left the newspaper business for the Army the day after
Pearl Harbor, and had seen service in New Guinea, in India and
in Burma, and behind the Japanese lines in South China.

I found Franc relaxed, and relaxing. When he smiled he did
it as if he meant it. But it is hard to describe your husband, and
harder to explain what it is about him that attracts you. I have
made the attempt before, and each time I feel like someone trying to finish the sentence "I like Franc Shor because . . ." in
twenty-five words or less and win a trip to Europe. Besides, I've
had a trip to Europe.

After that, we saw each other almost every night. We had much
in common—mutual friends, similar interests, enthusiasm for our
life abroad, and most of all a desire to travel. Franc had seen more
of the world than I, and gallantly offered to fill in the gaps in my
education. He spoke fluent Chinese, some French and German,
and bits and pieces of Turkish, Turki, and Pashto. I spoke some
Spanish, and was extremely fluent in sign language. We decided

to merge our wanderlusts and our resources, and see the world. In short, we fell in love and got married.

The wedding, which was a Chinese ceremony, was arranged by Jimmy Wei, a Chinese government official and one of Franc's best friends, and was held in his home one evening. It was as if the ceremony took place at a happy reception, rather than in a church. We sat in lacquered red chairs at one end of a long room. Red is the good-luck color of China, and bowls of red gladioli repeated the color. There were tables of food all around the room, and servants pouring tea and drinks. A Chinese jurist, Henry Ai, performed the rite. While he was speaking, there was a constant chatter among the guests, and glasses were raised and toasts shouted. The noise didn't bother Henry Ai, for the more noise there was, the better luck and the finer the wedding.

I couldn't understand Ai in any case. Jimmy Wei interpreted for me, and I made my responses in English which were then repeated in Chinese. As I remember, the promises to love, honor, and cherish were just as in our Episcopal ceremony. But I don't recall anything about "obey."

When it was over, Henry Ai presented us with the beautiful marriage scrolls elaborately painted with Chinese characters and enclosed in red cylinders that looked like giant firecrackers. Patterns of birds, fish, flowers, and animals bordered the script. We signed the certificates with our Chinese and English names; it was witnessed and signed by two guests. The document in translation was lovely too. It wished us long life and great happiness, and hoped that we would age "gracefully like the maple trees turning golden in autumn, and bring forth fruit like the blossoming apple trees in the spring."

I moved into Franc's house in the beautiful suburb of Hungjao the day after the ceremony, and immediately appointed myself manager of the household. "Just let Ah Tsung, the number one boy, take care of everything," Franc advised. "He does all the buying and pays all the servants, and I've never known him to gyp me out of a nickel. Let him alone, and the house will run itself." Privately I doubted that Ah Tsung could do it as economically as I.

In talking to friends in Shanghai, who for years had managed homes in the Orient, I had heard a good deal about Chinese number one boys, and their private payoffs and squeeze. At bridge parties and teas I had listened for hours to the intricate problems you faced when running a household in China.

"From now on," I told Franc vigorously, "I'll keep the books, and Ah Tsung will account for every penny he draws."

"He is a very sensitive man," Franc said. "Please don't upset him."

"If my guess is right, this will probably be the first case in history where two actually lived cheaper than one." Then I asked Franc how many servants there were, in addition to Ah Tsung.

He looked vague, and then began counting on his fingers. "Well, there's Tung Sen the chauffeur, and Hwang the cook, and his wife, Mei Li, who is the amah, and Fong the coolie, and Sing the gardener. Oh yes, there's the gateman and the gateman's wife. Seems to me I've seen some others. I'm not sure."

"Where do they all live?"

"Why, in the servants' quarters. Of course the gateman and his wife live in the gatehouse."

The next day I took a census, not without opposition. Franc's and Ah Tsung's. The place was as overpopulated as the Black Hole of Calcutta.

"The gatehouse," I reported smugly to Franc, "is occupied not only by the gateman and his wife, but by their two unemployed sons. One of these sons has a wife, and the other has two children. In addition, a stranger seems to be renting floor space. Tung Sen, the chauffeur, has his wife and three children living over the garage. Hwang, the cook, and Mei Li have four children living with them in the servants' quarters. Since Mei Li is too busy here, being our wash amah, *she* has an amah. The amah's amah has a baby. Ah Tsung himself doesn't have any children, but his father and mother share his room. Fong, the coolie, is planning to marry, and bring his wife to live with us. Presently, his cousin from Foochow is a visitor and sleeping in the hall."

"Well, we have to be hospitable," Franc muttered.

"But that isn't all. Tung Sen, the chauffeur, not only has his wife and children over the garage, but keeps a concubine in a cardboard room behind the gasoline barrels. She's certainly a fire hazard. I'm not sure, but I think the concubine has an amah. In addition, some unidentified young men sometimes bed down in the garden. I believe they pay the gardener for the privilege."

"Where do all these people eat?" asked Franc.

"Hospitable old you," I told him; "they eat off us!"

That night we cut down the population, but stopped short of firing Ah Tsung. A number one boy comes with the house. He has peculiar privileges, and can hardly be considered a servant. Say, rather, that he shares the house with his master. Besides, Franc assured me, Ah Tsung made superb martinis.

I did keep accounts, however. With the loss of our excess boarders, I was confident expenses would be cut at least a third. At the end of a month I proudly took my accounts to Franc. He looked at the total. Then, silently, he brought his old account books from his desk. He showed me the figure for the previous month, when Ah Tsung had had a free hand. It was just forty per cent less than under my stewardship. The next day, losing considerable face, missy handed the bookkeeping chores back to Ah Tsung.

We decided not to take a honeymoon until the pressure of Franc's writing eased. We had been married several months before Franc announced that he could get away. "Any place in China you'd like to go!" he said expansively. "Just pick it! Take a look at the map. Plenty of wonderful places within a day's flight— Peiping, Hongkong, Hangchow. State your pleasure."

He looked bewildered when I stated my pleasure. "Franc, let's cross the Gobi Desert!"

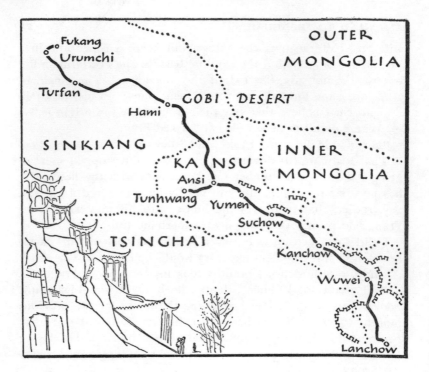

# 2

# HITCHHIKE ACROSS THE GOBI

I CHOSE THE GOBI for our honeymoon for many reasons, none of them very sensible.

Deserts had always fascinated me, and the Gobi is the mother of deserts. It lies across Central Asia like an enormous scimitar, 3,000 miles long and 1,200 miles broad, pocked by unpeopled depressions and warty with corroded mountains. Out of the Gobi came the Turkis, ancestors of the Hungarians, the Finns, and the Turks. The Gobi spawned the Mongol hordes that rallied to Genghis Khan. The Gobi bred conquerors who nourished on its shale, boulders, and shifting sands.

Few Americans or Western Europeans have crossed the Gobi, and I knew that if I were ever to make the journey it must be then, for the darkness of Communism was closing in over all of China. We would not be the first Americans to cross the Gobi, but we might be the last for a long time.

Finally, Marco Polo, seeking the palaces of Kublai Khan in Cathay, had crossed the Gobi. I recalled what he had written about its wonders:

"It is a well-known fact that the desert is the abode of many evil spirits who amuse travelers to their destruction with most extraordinary illusions . . . If any person fall behind on the road, they unexpectedly hear themselves called by their names, and are lured from the direct road, and not knowing in what direction to advance, are left to perish . . . The spirits of the deserts at times fill the air with sounds of musical instruments and drums and the clash of arms, and compel the travelers to close their ranks . . . excessive troubles and dangers must unavoidably be encountered."

I wished to challenge Marco Polo's spirits and spooks.

Franc and I decided to fly as far into Central Asia as we could, then return overland, using whatever transportation was available. To put it bluntly, we would hitchhike back. This was perhaps possible, said our Chinese friends who knew the Gobi, although such an enterprise was obviously a form of insanity. We would have to ride camels, horses, and the itinerant trucks that plied the ancient caravan routes. On occasion, we might have to walk. It was conceivable that we would meet bandits and be killed or kidnaped. Or we might simply become ill, hundreds of miles from any doctor, and die.

Packing for such a honeymoon was most simple. My trousseau for the trip consisted of army surplus GI uniforms. Our luggage included a barracks bag, sleeping sacks, musette bags, a carbine, shotgun and cameras. In a pinch, we could carry everything ourselves.

A war-weary C-46, with meat-grinder motors, made the run to Urumchi, the capital of Sinkiang Province (Chinese Turkestan) in extreme northwest China. Urumchi was the end of the line;

beyond Urumchi lay Russia's land of the Kazaks. The air route skirted the Mongolian People's Republic.

This was a flight I am not likely to forget. We left Shanghai at four A.M. The plane's heating system wasn't working, nor was there so much as a cup of hot coffee aboard. Our pilot was a Canadian-born Chinese who had difficulty in understanding his Chinese passengers and called on Franc occasionally to interpret for him.

Two hundred miles west of Shanghai we bumped down at Nanking to pick up some Chinese officials, including a stiff backed general who occupied the bucket seat opposite me. For eight hundred miles we flew northwest for a gas stop at Sian, then twelve hundred miles due west to put down at Lanchow.

There a Turki family came aboard. The Turkis are the remnants of the Mongol tribes that followed the great khans and swept across all of Asia and much of Europe. Even today, they retain their distinctive dress and manners. The men, hard-faced and straight and proud, wear round black skullcaps. The women dress in baggy trousers, long overblouses, and big head scarves. They are devout Moslems, but live peaceably alongside their Buddhist neighbors.

Ignoring the vacant seats, the Turki family spread blankets on the floor near the tail and squatted down among their bundles and baskets. The center of their attention was a tiny, fragile old lady whom they had carefully laid on a limp pallet. Obviously she was very ill, probably dying of some wasting disease. Why, I wondered, were they flying her into the heart of the continent, when all medical aid lay toward the east?

Our next leg took us a thousand miles straight across the desert. The plane became colder and colder, and over the twisted rocks of the Black Gobi we were bounced around by frightening air currents. Motion sickness is not only contagious but it seems to be a national characteristic of the Chinese. One official, seated near the front of the plane, became ill. One by one the other passengers succumbed. The plane was a mess.

Franc and I held out, and so did the stiff-backed general, although the general's face grew gray and his eyes glazed. By then it was late afternoon and we were starved. We opened our lunch basket and examined the delicacies. Our cook had packed a wonderful lunch—turkey and chicken sandwiches, salad, stuffed eggs, fruit and champagne. The general's eyes were fixed on us. It hardly seemed polite to eat while he had nothing, so I arranged a couple of sandwiches, a helping of salad, and a stuffed egg on a paper plate. I offered it to the general across the aisle.

This was a ghastly mistake. The general took a long, shuddering look at the heaped plate, his head rolled to one side, and he gave up. He gave up everything. We saw him several times after that in Urumchi, but he never spoke to us. I had caused him to lose much face.

During the entire rough trip, the Turki husband knelt close to his sick wife, trying to ease her pain, and every few minutes lowering his beard to his chest in prayer. Their married daughter tried to calm her two squalling babies, frequently nursing both at once.

As we approached Urumchi, Franc spoke to the Turki husband, offering to help lift the sick woman after the plane landed. Franc asked why they were bringing her so far.

"My wife has been to all the hospitals in Kansu Province," the husband said, "and to many modern doctors. None can save her. But in Urumchi is a healer of the Faith, and now we must put our trust in him."

IT WAS DEEP dusk when we bounced down on the tiny unlighted airfield at Urumchi, a city of 25,000, the hub of caravan routes and communications in that part of Asia. It possessed inns of a sort, of course, but we had been advised that G. Hall Paxton, the American consul, might put us up. At the consulate compound we were welcomed like old friends unexpectedly come to visit, although neither the consul nor his wife had ever seen us before.

Hall Paxton was the son of missionaries, and a Yale graduate. This slight, thin-haired, quiet and scholarly man had encountered more than his share of adventures in Asia. He had been aboard the gunboat *Panay* when the Japanese bombed and sank it in

1937. His wife, Vincoe, had been a medical missionary, and became an army nurse during the war. Like us they had met and married in China.

In Urumchi the Paxtons found themselves in another hot spot. There were more than a hundred officials, armed with ample funds, in the Russian consulate, aggressively spreading their doctrine. To oppose them, Vincoe taught a language school and maintained a clinic. Hall entertained the provincial officials with his small allowance. Bob Driessen, his vice-consul, distributed American literature and news to those who could read it. But they were three against a hundred, and their situation hopeless.

The Paxtons assigned us their largest bedroom. In it we were dumfounded to find the tombstone of a British vice-consul who had died in Urumchi ten years before. Although he had been buried properly, I was glad to learn, the tombstone had been delivered to the American consulate as the British office was temporarily out of business. During the war it had been stored in the bedroom and since then so much had been happening in Urumchi that nobody ever found time to cart it out to the graveyard. The British seemed to have forgotten about the marker, and the Americans were too busy keeping track of the Russians. Rather ghoulish décor, I thought.

In the consulate was one tin bathtub, screened by a short curtain in the main hallway. When you took a bath it was necessary to make a general announcement beforehand. Still, so far as I know, it was the only bathtub in all of Sinkiang Province, an area twice as large as Texas, with a population of 3,500,000. Nearly 3,000,000 are Uigurs, a Turkic tribe sprung from the Gobi. There are 300,000 nomad Kazaks, and the rest are Tajiks, Chinese, a handful of Manchus, and a few frightened and despondent White Russians.

Each morning in Urumchi we were awakened by the sonorous melody of camel bells as the great caravans from Peiping and Lanchow and Kashgar plodded into the city. Each evening the temple bells and the bronze gongs tolled their call to prayer. And all day the air was filled with a melodious humming and whistling, which at first we thought must be the fault of our ears, the

result of the plane trip or the change in altitude. Then we noticed
pigeons spiraling down out of the cobalt sky, bringing the whistling with them. It was a local custom to attach tiny whistles to
the legs of the pigeons, so that all day the air was filled with music.

Urumchi was a pleasant city, little changed by the centuries,
and the people were friendly. Flowers were everywhere. Giant
cosmos, dahlias, and sunflowers glowed in the consulate compound. In the distance we could see some of the highest mountain
ranges in the world, and to the east was the glacier-clad peak of
Bogdo Ula, the sacred mountain of Turkestan.

There were no taxicabs in Urumchi, but the city had a rapid
transit system that probably existed in Marco Polo's time. Buckboards drawn by shaggy ponies clattered along the cobbled streets
from dawn until dark. You trotted alongside, bargained with the
driver, and jumped aboard. When you reached a place that looked
interesting, or which was near your destination, you jumped off.
The trotting trolleys always followed the same route, as if on
rails.

The streets were filled with venders of spicy meats and exotic
fruits. For lunch we would stop at a *shashlik* stand, and squat in
the dust beside long-robed Turki traders, blue-gowned Chinese,
and Kazak tribesmen in sheepskin cloaks. The Kazaks were fascinating, their dress right out of ancient Oriental history books.
I particularly admired their pale silk bonnets, lined with soft
fur and topped with a sprig of eagle feathers. For a few cents we
ate crisply roasted nuggets of lamb, sprinkled with cumin, on long
skewers; dried dates and raisins, and saucer-shaped loaves of Turki
bread. For dessert we would buy a melon, a big one.

The melons of Turkestan are deservedly the most famous in
the world. They are piled in tall pyramids on every street corner
—yellow and green and striped and spotted and gray. They are
sweet and rich with juice. The melon was our canteen, not only
in Urumchi but on the whole journey back across the Gobi. Where
melons are plentiful, it is hardly necessary to carry water.

A foreigner expects to be gypped when he shops in China, but
not so in Urumchi. In the shops of Shanghai and Canton crowds
will gather to chortle at the sight of a foreigner being fleeced.

Urumchi had seen very few Americans, and the legend that all such are laden with gold, and eager to throw it away, had not penetrated this far. A friendly group always followed us on our shopping tours, and they saw to it that we weren't cheated. When a merchant named his first price, the crowd would howl for his head. A delegation would take over the bargaining on our behalf. They would decide upon a fair price, and the irritated merchant would be forced to accept.

THE LAKE of Heaven, halfway up the side of the sacred mountain, Bogda Ula, is perhaps the most beautiful spot in all of Turkestan. There Franc and I honeymooned in the idyllic and traditional sense.

We set out for the mountain in a battered Russian copy of a 1938 Ford panel truck. The road ended seven hours later at an encampment of Kazak tribesmen, their felt *yurts* pitched beside a glacial stream and their camels grazing untended nearby. The Kazaks loaned us horses, and provided an escort. We were joined by two Chinese geologists who were making a mineral survey of the mountain. China is very poor in minerals, except tungsten, but the geologists talked hopefully of uranium.

One of the earnest young scientists, Mr. Wong, had never ridden a horse, but he closely examined the animal and reached a mathematical conclusion concerning the art of riding. The further his rear was separated from the saddle, he decided, the better off he would be. Against our advice, he had his servant pile all his bedding on the saddle, after which he managed to climb to his precarious perch on top.

Mr. Wong teetered there a moment, and then ordered the horse to proceed, at the same time maintaining his balance by pulling hard on the reins. The horse backed, and Mr. Wong fell off.

"Mr. Shor," he complained to Franc, "this animal has a defect."

Franc explained about reins, and the servant helped him aboard again. A few minutes later our path led through trees, and ultimately a low branch brushed Mr. Wong rudely from his perch. Thereafter he walked.

The trail climbed steadily, until the rest of us had to dismount. On the steep ridges we clung to the tails of our horses, and allowed them to drag us upward. The atmosphere was so clear that it seemed as if I could reach out and touch the austere tip of Bogda Ula, 22,000 feet high. At dusk we reached the Lake of Heaven, 10,000 feet above sea level. Two miles long and half a mile wide, it curved around a spur of the mountain like a new moon. The lake, fed by Bogda Ula's glacier, was a brighter blue than the Mediterranean. As we panted up the last slope we saw, perfectly reflected on its mirror-smooth surface, the ancient Buddhist temple where we were to camp.

For a week we spread our bedding in a monk's cell in that temple on the banks of the Lake of Heaven. We ate rainbow trout Franc caught in the lake, and red-leg partridge he shot on the side of the mountain. The monastery itself was inoperative; its priests had long since abandoned the place. Sometimes we dined with Chinese soldiers, and sometimes with the geologists, and once or twice with visiting Kazak horsemen. We were the only Westerners. The lake and the temple seemed the common domain of all.

Each day two happy Tungan bakers supplied the visitors with steamed bread, called *mon-tow*. Franc and I liked to sit in the bakery and watch them as they kneaded the dough with the steady rhythm of oarsmen. "What they need," I suggested, "is a song. Why don't you teach them one?"

Franc considered this problem for a while, and then made his contribution to the dissemination of American culture. He taught them an old radio commercial which goes, "Yo-ho, Yo-ho . . . we are the bakers of Wonder Bread." We pictured the bewilderment of the next American—an anthropologist, we hoped—to come to the Lake of Heaven, trying to trace the source of this chant.

One day a Chinese was kicked by his horse, and came to us for treatment, for in remote Central Asia all foreigners are expected to be doctors. Fortunately, there were no broken bones, so we could offer aspirin with a clear conscience. I think aspirin, like air-sickness, is contagious. By afternoon, everybody in the temple, and from miles around, had come to us, pleading imaginary ills, clutching leg or head or stomach, and begging for medicine. I gave each two aspirins until our supply ran low. Then I switched to salt tablets. I think they preferred the salt because it tasted worse. We made them swallow the pills in our presence, otherwise they would have sold them to the local herb doctor. By the end of the afternoon, dozens of Asiatic pill fanciers hailed us as people of great wisdom and powerful medicine. I have never doubted psychosomatic illness since.

One morning we were awakened by the tinkling of bells and the sound of a conch horn. In the courtyard stood an ancient, wizened Buddhist monk, dressed in a saffron robe. He entered the disused temple, and moved about for an hour, chanting singsong prayers, tapping the dusty gongs, and sounding long, wailing blasts from the horn. For a small space of time the temple lived again.

"I was a novitiate here," he told Franc in Chinese, "and for forty years I served the Holy One in the temple. When the government ordered it closed, I moved to a monastery near Fu Kong, fifty miles from here. But every year I walk back to my Temple of Heaven, for here is where my heart lies. I say one service. In this way this place remains holy, and the spirits of the departed ones remain in peace. It will be thus while I have strength."

Every night a bonfire was lighted in the stone-paved temple courtyard, and sections of fir trees, fifteen feet long, were burned in a tall pyramid. The blaze, roaring high, seemed to cast its golden glow over the whole lake. Around the fire gathered all the day's visitors, enjoying the warmth of the flames—for each night grew colder—and the beauty of the clear night sky. The Tungan bakers—Tungans are Moslem Chinese—sang folk songs, the Chinese soldiers chanted marching songs, and a Turki colonel did a wild and sensuous dance, his round cap pushed forward at a rakish angle, to the rhythm of clapping hands and stamping feet. Franc sang "Blues in the Night" in Chinese. Since I can't carry a tune even with the help of a choir, I remained in the shadows, an appreciative listener.

Every night the snow line crept closer down the mountain.

The Chinese soldiers warned us that it was time to leave. With each succeeding day, the path back would become more dangerous. One morning the snow was at the temple gates, and we knew we must depart. I packed reluctantly. When I chose the Gobi, I never dreamed of finding such an idyllic spot of beauty and tranquillity for a belated honeymoon.

As we rode our horses through the temple gates snow began to fall, a chill suggestion that the trip down might be hazardous. Perhaps I was still bemused by the beauty I had left. Certainly I grew careless, for in a single instant the treacherous trail down Bogda Ula betrayed me. In that second my honeymoon, and my life, almost came to an end.

With our escort of Chinese cavalry we were crossing a turbulent, glacier-fed stream coursing down a steep ravine. My pony was cautiously stepping between the stones, with the swift water above his knees, when without warning he stepped into a deep hole and was swept off his feet. I remember frantically fighting to free my boots from the stirrups as the water came up to meet me. Then I was rolling downstream on the icy bottom.

The water was so cold that it felt as if my hands were manacled, my legs in chains. I could neither move nor get my head up to breathe. That narrow stream was of a sudden a giant that twisted me, pummeled me, dragged me along its bottom, holding me under and beating the life from me.

Then a heavy weight fell on top of me, and my rolling stopped. A hand groped for my collar and I was yanked to my feet, sobbing for air. I could only gasp and shake, I couldn't speak. A soldier had leaped from his horse and had stopped me simply by standing on me. Then he and Franc had dragged me to the bank. The pony struggled ashore a hundred yards downstream.

I am afraid that instead of being grateful, I was furious. I had never literally been stepped on before. To add to my humiliation, Franc unceremoniously dumped me on the bank and pulled off my boots. Ice water ran up my legs. I shouted at him to stop, but he paid no attention whatsoever. He grappled with the buttons of my trench coat, and a gallon of water cascaded out of each pocket. I wailed, not in self-pity, but at what I saw tumble out of those pockets—the two cameras and our exposed film rolls. The film packets were sodden, and we had lost almost every picture we made at the Lake of Heaven.

Franc buttoned me back into my trench coat, and wrestled the boots back on my feet. He made me mount the wet pony, astride a soaking saddle rapidly rimming with ice. We rode on in the snowstorm.

Through chattering teeth I demanded that we stop and build a fire. I had to get warm, and rest, and put on dry clothes.

"Keep riding," Franc said. "Only exercise will keep you from freezing." He had served in the cavalry and knew what he was doing.

I was so mad I couldn't speak. Anger helped warm me a bit, however.

From the bottom of his musette bag Franc brought a bottle of Napoleon brandy, reserved for celebrations and emergencies. All the way down to the Kazak camp I nipped at that bottle. When my fingers froze to the glass, I licked them loose. But I warmed inside, and by the time we reached the camp site I was almost dry.

The Kazaks came to the door of their *yurt,* and when they heard of my mishap they insisted that I come inside for a bowl of hot salt tea. Franc, riding a mare, trotted up behind me, and I could read my dear ex-cavalryman's mind. "These people are horsemen," he was thinking. "I'll dismount smartly and show 'em how it's done in the U.S. Cavalry."

What he didn't notice was a foal, barely weaned, which ran up to nuzzle the homecoming mare. As Cavalryman Shor swung his right leg off the saddle, it hit the colt, which reared in fright, upsetting Franc's balance. He slammed over backward on the ground in a three-point landing, his carbine flopping off his shoulder and whacking him on the head. Despite my congealed features, I roared with laughter, and the Kazaks, who had been politely hiding their grins, joined me. They laughed until tears ran down their flat cheeks, and we had a merry session in their warm and friendly *yurt.* Franc laughed about it six months later.

THE NEXT MORNING, warm and dry back at the Paxtons' in Urumchi, I discovered that our cameras, Franc's Rolleiflex and my
Perfex, were literally junk. Mine was a mass of rust from its
dunking, and the fall had broken a delicate gear in Franc's. Since
the nearest camera repair shop was roughly two thousand miles
away, this was disaster. We had talked confidently of selling
articles, with pictures, on the Gobi. Even if the photographs were
never published, they were to be the record of our honeymoon.
Crossing the Gobi without cameras was like going big-game hunting without guns.

The Paxtons were sympathetic, but they doubted that in all
Turkestan was there anyone acquainted with the insides of a
camera. However, they did have a Czech mechanic named Irving
on their staff. He kept the consulate car in shape, fixed the
plumbing, and tinkered with the wiring when the electricity
failed. Irving had escaped from a German prison during the war,
and later from a Russian internment center. Somehow he had
made his way across Siberia, crossed the Russian border into
China, and had found protection and service with the Americans
in Urumchi.

We found Irving in the garage. I noted hopefully that it was
neat and clean, that his tools were hung in neat rows on the
walls, that there was a much-used workbench. But I was asking
for a miracle. Garage mechanics tinker with car parts one hundred times the size of camera parts. Irving was a stocky man with
a wide, smiling face, blue eyes, and sandy hair.

"What do you know about cameras?" Franc asked.

"Nothing at all," said Irving. "I have never been inside one."

"Ours are broken." I was carrying them by the straps. They
seemed heavy and lifeless. I had an unhappy vision of Irving trying to climb into my camera the way he might go under the hood
of a car.

"So I have heard," said Irving. He took the cameras in his
broad, strong hands and examined them thoughtfully. "Their insides are broken," he said, "so there is probably nothing I can do,
except remove the rust."

"Would you try?" If he only cleaned and oiled them they might be worth salvaging after we returned to Shanghai.

He shrugged noncommittally and agreed to try.

Irving was a mechanical genius. In twenty-four hours he took apart those strange, complicated mechanisms, studied their operation, dried and cleaned every delicate lens and tiny part, and put them together again, as good as new. With a file and a piece of scrap aluminum, he fashioned an exact replica of the Rollei's broken gear. The camera is still in use, working perfectly with its ersatz gear made in Turkestan.

It was the wildest chance that brought the talented Irving and our two broken cameras together in Urumchi, from opposite ends of the earth. I often wonder what we'd be doing now if it weren't for Irving. For having those cameras in working condition changed the whole course of our lives.

Franc wanted to spend a few days shooting ibex and wild boar in the mountains before we started across the Gobi. I shooed him off, for I sought a few days of solitude to browse through the Paxtons' impressive library, which included a fine collection of books on Asian exploration. I read the works of Peter Fleming, Georges le Fevre, Sir Eric Teichman, and Aurel Stein. I read Sven Hedin's thrilling account of the buried cities of Chinese Turkestan, and a book on the Caves of the Thousand Buddhas by Paul Pelliot, the Frenchman. I began to realize what a fabulous area we were in, and how little we had seen!

By the time Franc returned from his hunting I was more fired up than ever about the return journey across the Gobi. We would have to make a side trip to visit the caves, I told him, and we would have to pause in Lanchow to find the grave of Genghis Khan. And— I paused.

"And?" Franc eyed me good-humoredly.

"Did you know that Marco Polo passed through Sinkiang and Kansu on his way to Peiping?"

"Do we have to find his grave too?"

"Perhaps later." I showed off my vastly superior knowledge of history. "He was buried in Venice."

"Can't you enjoy the trip you're on," Franc said grinning, "unless you're planning the next one?" Thus Franc showed his vastly superior knowledge of me.

THE ANCIENT CARAVAN route that Marco Polo followed across the Gobi to Lanchow had been pounded and widened into a road. It was pocked with holes and cluttered with small-sized boulders, but usable. This arm of the Great Silk Road had linked two imperial civilizations, Persia and Cathay, while Europe was clambering out of barbarism and slumbering in the Dark Ages. Along this route, in Polo's time, were camel stations at regular intervals. Most of these were now ruins, or in disrepair, for silk no longer traveled west on ships of the desert. Although camel caravans still hauled much of the freight along this road, travelers were accommodated by a haphazard truck line operated by the provincial government. At odd intervals, mail and army trucks bumped over its rough surface.

On the morning of September 29, the Paxtons drove us to the Urumchi central motor compound and bade us good-by. As a farewell gift, they presented us with chopsticks, rice bowls, a packet of tea, and a teapot. "I think you will use these before you reach Lanchow," Hall said. It was the understatement of the year. We used them every day.

Our vehicle was a battered Studebaker truck, of wartime vintage, a survivor of the Burma Road. Since we were friends of the American consul, our stocky Chinese driver, Mr. Li, graciously invited us to ride in the cab, with the honored mail. We found space for our barracks and musette bags on top of the cab. The gun case, trench coats, teapot, cameras, and the bag of mail we held on our laps. Under our feet was the crank, tool box, and Mr. Li's suitcase. The back of the truck was loaded with freight, gas and oil drums, and luggage, surmounted by six Chinese passengers and Mr. Kao, our mechanic. Our departure resembled in miniature the sailing of the *Queen Elizabeth*. Relatives and friends of the passengers crowded alongside the truck, laughing, weeping, and wishing us safe journey.

Finally the driver jumped inside the cab to the accompaniment

of resounding cheers from the throng. He majestically motioned
to the spindly, worried Mr. Kao. Mr. Kao turned the crank several times to build up compression. Mr. Li turned the switch,
and shouted the Chinese equivalent of "contact." Mr. Kao leaped
into the air, came down with all his 110 pounds on the crank,
and spun it madly. The motor coughed, the truck shook, and
Mr. Kao scrambled up to the top of the cab, sitting there in
triumph, his pipestem legs dangling down over the windshield.
The gears grated, and we were off.

A mile beyond Urumchi, and out of sight of officialdom, the
truck ground to a stop and we were introduced to the Chinese
custom of the "yellow fish." Gathered at the side of the road were
fourteen new passengers, including a family of eight traveling
with all its possessions. The "yellow fish" were those who preferred to pay the driver rather than the government ticket agent.
This way the cost of the trip was less, and with a little extra
squeeze they might even obtain the de luxe accommodations in
the cab.

Mr. Li bargained with the "yellow fish," and when agreement
was reached permitted them to pile their possessions and luggage
aboard. I watched in amazement as they jammed two squealing
pigs, a crate of chickens, and an assortment of bundles and bales
upon the already overloaded truck. Then one man produced a
bamboo ladder, constructed especially for this purpose, and they
climbed to the top of the mound, jostling the legal customers
into an indignant human mash behind the cab.

The road swung into a defile that dropped steeply downward
into the Turfan Depression, one of the lowest and most barren
regions on earth. A few weeks before, a Chinese pilot had buzzed
Turfan, thus achieving the dubious honor of having flown below
sea level. The defile was called the Valley of the Demons. Thousands of small skeletons lined the road—the skeletons of donkeys.

In all the 125 miles between Urumchi and Turfan there is no
oasis, no waterhole. Rain is unknown. But the area surrounding
the town of Turfan itself is fantastically fertile, the land watered
by springs rising from underground rivers. These originate in the

snows of the mountains ringing Urumchi, and in the glacier of
the Bogdo Ula. They pass far beneath the Valley of the Demons,
and issue in crystal loveliness and cold purity at Turfan.

In Turfan are grown the sweetest white grapes in the world,
and there—where rain clouds are unknown although spring water
is plentiful—drying raisins is no problem. For centuries the lus-
cious white raisins have been carried by donkeys to Urumchi,
the crossroads of caravans, and then distributed throughout Central Asia, and shipped to the West. Because there is no water on
the trail, the laden donkeys leave Turfan in the cool evening,
and are driven without food or rest all the way to Urumchi.
Many perish on the trail, their bones a monument to the white
raisin.

We were chugging along at a steady 25-miles-an-hour when I
noticed Mr. Li frowning at the ammeter. It was charging perfectly, I saw, but Mr. Li stopped the truck. Everyone disem-
barked, and Mr. Li and Mr. Kao raised the hood and took out
the generator, which the Chinese call the "send-out-electricity-
machine." They disassembled it, with flourishes, wiped each part,
and then painstakingly put it back together. The passengers
watched in awe. When Mr. Li frowned, they grew apprehensive.
When he smiled, they chattered and showered him with congratu-
lations.

This performance was repeated twice more on the road to
Turfan, and the third time Franc grasped what was going on.
Mr. Li and Mr. Kao were giving an exhibition of their mechanical skill, thus gaining much face with the passengers, and pre-
sumably with us. There was nothing at all wrong with the generator.

We came finally to the Flame Hills, the northern guardian of
the oasis of Turfan. The hills were bare brown stone, scoured
smooth by the blowing sands. During the cloudless days they
absorb the sun's heat, and in the evening the warm air rises from
the heated rock, shimmering, so that the rays of the sinking sun
set the hills afire.

When the road topped the Flame Hills, an astonishing spectacle lay below. A few miles ahead our arid sea lapped at the

shores of a verdant island, the oasis of Turfan. Soon we were
driving through its famous vineyards.

Though fine for grapes, Turfan was bad for people. Because
it lies in the bottom of an immense bowl unblessed by rain, the
temperature rises to 130 degrees every day in summer. In these
hottest months the populace, mostly Turki Moslems, live in caves
underground, close to the cooling waters of the subterranean
rivers. The streets are shaded by leafy arcades, but most business
is conducted in the late evening. In winter the temperature drops
to zero.

The truck stopped at a roadside inn, which in no way resembled Ye Olde Cozy Motel on Route 66, and we engaged a room
in a mud compound for the night. This was the first in a long
series of *lui-gwans,* the Chinese word for caravansary, which were
to be our desert lodgings. Each tiny room has a raised *kang* of
baked mud, for sleeping, and windows of oiled rice paper. A
burning twist of lamb's wool, floating in a flat dish of oil, furnished the only light. All these comforts are available for a few
cents a night.

After washing in a teapot of hot water, we went for a walk on
the main street, seeking food. On one corner children were selling stewed chicken from an iron pot, but a Chinese officer ahead
of us dipped into the pot with his chopsticks, and delicately
tasted each piece before making his selection. We decided against
chicken, buying instead a loaf of Turki bread, dried raisins, and
a juicy melon. We sat on a curb to eat it and watch the people
of Turfan, who were watching us. It was a case of mutual curiosity.

We had been warned by the Paxtons and others against giant
scorpions, and a myriad of other vicious insects which might creep
into our shoes, clothing and bags during the night. All the ver-
min of the desert migrate to Turfan, bug heaven of the Gobi.
That night we sprinkled a wall of louse powder around our tarpaulin, and laid the sleeping bags in the middle. Like Western
cowboys with their ropes coiled in a circle around them to ward
off snakes, we had taken all possible precautions against the
buggy terrors of our first night in the Gobi.

We were awakened at four the next morning and ate *jyawdz*—
a dumpling full of meat. They were steamed and about the size
of my clenched fist. On this desert trip we often ate as many as
eight apiece for breakfast. These, with tea, or a glass of hot potent
grain distillate called *baigar,* if it was a very cold morning, lasted
us through a long hard day.

When the truck left before dawn, we were not too surprised to
find that we had lost our seats in the cab to an affluent "yellow
fish." The influence of the American consul, it seemed, had its
boundaries. Sitting high on the back, I discovered, after many
bumpy miles, that the best place to ride on a Gobi truck was atop
the heap of freight and luggage, with your feet dangling over the
side. It was too windy toward the front, too dusty over the back,
and too rough over the wheels.

That evening we came to the town of Hami, which Marco Polo
had found an oasis of strange customs, much discussed when the
account of his travels first apprised Europe of the wonders of the
East. In our *lui-gwan* that night, I read aloud to Franc from my
trusty Everyman's Library edition of Polo's travels.

"The men [of Hami]," Marco Polo wrote, "are addicted to
pleasure, and attend to little else than playing upon instruments,
singing, dancing, and the pursuit, in short, of every kind of
amusement. When strangers arrive and desire to have lodging
and accommodation in their house, it affords them the highest
gratification. They give positive orders to their wives, daughters,
sisters, and other female relations to indulge their guests in every
wish, while they themselves leave their homes . . . the women
are in truth very handsome, very sensual, and fully disposed to
conform in this respect to the injunction of their husbands."

I looked inquiringly at Franc. My husband is a man with normal impulses and excessive curiosity.

"Well?" I said.

"I believe I'll investigate." He didn't make a move. "I'll find
the mayor, and tell him that according to Marco Polo I am en-
titled to the pick of the females in his household."

"Have you seen the females of Hami?"

"Yes," he sighed, "I have looked upon the females of Hami.

Either the travelers of Marco Polo's day had very bad taste, or the standards of beauty have changed."

Our hut in Hami had the usual glazed-paper windows. Not long after Franc had so summarily turned down the favors of every wench in Hami, I heard a sharp popping sound, and looked up to see a finger poking into our room. Then an eye appeared in place of the finger. The eye saw that I saw and promptly vanished. This was repeated by other fingers and other inquisitive eyes.

A few minutes later there was a knock on the door. A girl, perhaps eighteen, stood outside, her head humbly bent. She wished to offer ten thousand apologies for this intrusion by unworthy self upon the illustrious visitors. She bowed deeply, and folded her hands against her breasts, as if inviting a scourge of words.

I asked what she wanted. Franc translated our Chinese-English conversation.

Her aged and revered grandmother, she said, had learned that a foreign woman had come to Hami. Her grandmother had heard strange tales of white foreign women, but in all her eighty-five years she herself had never beheld one. Was it possible that she could bring her grandmother to view the honored visitor?

I said certainly. I felt pleased and flattered.

An hour later the girl returned with the grandmother, a tiny woman, withered to little more than four feet, and weighing perhaps eighty pounds. Her hair was snowy white, pulled back to a neat bun, and her bright, alert, birdlike eyes were very black. She used a cane and her walk was a painful hobble. I looked down and saw that her feet were bound, the custom of Chinese ladies of quality of the last century.

Her satin shoes were no longer than my fist, indeed the toes were curled under the sole to make a fist, the arch broken and irrevocably deformed. Such feet were called "lily feet." It was fashionable until the end of the Manchu dynasty to bind the feet of infant girls thus, to indicate that they need never walk like common people, but always would be carried in sedan chairs by servants and slaves. Fortunate was the husband who could afford a wife with "lily feet," for she was a treasure, like fragile porce-lain, and proof of her husband's wealth and position.

The old Chinese lady came closer to me with timid, painful steps. She looked up at me, towering above her, and laughed with delight, beckoning for me to bend my head. I did, and she felt my hair, and made remarks about it. "She marvels," Franc inter-preted, "that it is real." Then she noticed my feet. My feet are just average American female feet, but I was wearing GI shoes, so that they seemed considerably enlarged. She shook her head, astonished and unbelieving. "How wonderful!" she said. "How wonderful!"

It is strange how you can forget cathedrals and museums and whole cities when you travel, but an old lady with "lily feet," you never forget.

We didn't leave on schedule the next morning, for Mr. Li and Mr. Kao apparently had discovered some Marco-Polo-like hospi-tality. They turned up, red-eyed and seedy, at noon. The truck, they explained, was in a government garage for overhaul and we would be delayed a day or two. They were sure that the sights of Hami would prove interesting.

"All I want in Hami," I said, "is a bath. Is it possible to find a bath?"

Mr. Li and Mr. Kao called Captain Hwang, one of our fellow passengers, into consultation. Hwang beckoned to an elderly Chinese gentleman, and asked for further guidance. Several others joined the group, all talking excitedly. At length Captain Hwang addressed me. Yes, he said, there was a public bathhouse in Hami. Unfortunately, it was for men only. If women felt it necessary to bathe, they bathed at home. However, since so few foreign women ever visited Hami, the bathhouse proprietor would be asked to make an exception.

We had an entourage of at least fifty Chinese, Turkis, and Kazaks when we reached the bathhouse, a one-story frame struc-ture shielded by bamboo fences. The entire retinue tried to jam its way into the office with us.

The proprietor, fat and prosperous, listened patiently to our proposal, although he was obviously shocked. A woman, he replied firmly, could not be allowed in a bathhouse. The reputation of his establishment would be ruined!

Our friends became indignant. A fierce Turki chieftain, wearing a sheepskin coat and fox fur hat, spoke menacingly to the proprietor. A Chinese elder added his support in dignified tones, then turned and appealed to the crowd. Our followers muttered and became insistent. A couple of tall Turkis moved toward the unhappy owner. He held firm for a final moment, then public pressure grew too great and he scurried into the bathhouse. The regular customers began to emerge, still damp, and very startled, clutching their disordered clothes around them.

Within a few minutes I had the establishment to myself, with a bench, table, buckets of hot water, even a pot of tea. The crowd stood guard outside, protecting the reputation of both the establishment and me, and Franc stood guard over the crowd. It was a marvelous bath, and I made the most of it, guessing that it would be a long time before I enjoyed another. The harried proprietor refused pay, but Franc left a pile of Chinese currency on his desk.

That night a forty-camel caravan carrying coal from the west shuffled into Hami, sounding like a hundred old men wearing carpet slippers. The music of their deep bells filled the compound as they knelt for the night.

As WE LEFT Hami three days later, a businessman climbed on top with a huge set of wapiti antlers still in the velvet. Franc made a joking offer to buy them, and was quietly informed that the price was $3,000! The businessman explained the Chinese regard for powdered wapiti horn as a powerful aphrodisiac, and that the antlers would fetch a good deal more than $3,000 if he could get them safely to Shanghai. Franc muttered into the wind, "Why didn't I hunt elk, instead of ibex!"

That night, at the camel station of Lo To Chan, the bedbugs penetrated our Maginot Line of DDT and we picked up our sleeping bags and fled to the desert. Just after midnight the wind rose and began to howl, and black clouds blotted out the stars. Soon our bags were covered with six inches of sand and pebbles, and we staggered back into the inn where we slept on the mud floor under the kitchen table. The wind made a noise like giant sheets of sandpaper being rubbed together, and streams of grit poured into the room as rain is driven by a hurricane. When we awoke at dawn the truck wheels were buried a foot deep in the Gobi.

We made good time that day, crossing the barren pebble plains where even the sight of a clump of Asiatic sage would have been welcome. At nightfall we came to the Inn of the Seven-cornered Well, which could not have changed much since the area fell to Jagatai, third son of Genghis Khan. There were four small tables in the kitchen and overhead swung elongated lamps, with wicks of sheep wool and fuel of soybean oil. They reminded me of the fable of Aladdin; lamps have been shaped thus for three thousand years.

We were half through our meal of noodles and pork with hot red peppers when a Chinese major came to our table. He addressed Franc, and Franc turned to me, repeating each sentence of this choice conversation, which is the only reason I am able to remember it almost exactly.

I was wearing my old GI flight jacket from Italy, with the insignia of the American Red Cross still on one sleeve. "I have noticed," the major began, looking at me, "that your wife is a Red Ten-character Association Woman." (The Chinese character for ten is a cross.)

"Well, she was," Franc said warily.

"My wife's mother," the major said, "is quite ill back at the *lui-gwan,* where she has been attending to my honorable first-born. Please ask your wife, when she has finished dinner, to call upon my humble wife's unworthy mother, and see if she can assist."

"I am terribly sorry," Franc said, "but while my wife was a Red Ten-character Association Woman during the war, she is not a Look-at-Disease Woman."

The major looked again at the patch on my arm, bewildered.

"How can she be a Red Ten-character Association Woman and not be a Look-at-Disease Woman?" he asked. "In Burma I saw one such, and she was a Look-at-Disease Woman."

Franc cleared his throat, sparring for time. "Yes, that is true," he said. "In the American Army there are two kinds of Red Ten-character Association Women. One kind is a Look-at-Disease Woman, but the others entertain the troops."

"Ah, I see!" the major said, smiling so hard I thought his face would split. "It is the same in our army. But we call the second kind troop-comforting women." The major inspected me again, in a different manner. I believe that it can be said that he leered. Anyway, I knew what he had said, and what was meant, without Franc's translation. My husband claimed later that he really tried his best to explain, but was handicapped by his hysterical laughter. Never having been mistaken for a troop-comforting woman before, I was decidedly annoyed. Later I went to the *lui-gwan* and presented an aspirin to the unworthy mother of the major's humble wife. She recovered immediately, and I regained my reputation. Then I ripped that patch off my arm.

Ever since the snow advanced upon the temple of the Lake of Heaven, winter had been stalking us. Winter moves swiftly in northwestern China, and we were shivering when we left the *lui-gwan* at the Inn of the Seven-cornered Well. Near our truck was a vender of hot baked potatoes. Franc and I bought one, split and ate it. Then, on inspiration, we bought four more, put them in our trench-coat pockets, and enjoyed them as excellent hand-warmers.

Eighteen hours later, after a freezing ride through a treeless wilderness of shale, sand, and eroded stone called Land of the Wind, we came to Ansi, tucked into the farthest corner of China proper, in northwest Kansu Province, where we bade good-by to Mr. Li and Mr. Kao. Here we were to swing south seventy miles, if we could find transportation, to the dying metropolis of Tunhwang, and the Caves of the Thousand Buddhas.

Centuries before the birth of Christ, traders discovered an oasis at Tunhwang. Sometimes it rained, and on occasion a river flooded from its dry bed; always there was a spring, and greenery.

A city rose nearby, and immensely thick walls were erected to protect it from the marauders of the north. In those days the Great Silk Road ran through Tunhwang, rather than Ansi, which was closer to the lands of the Mongol tribes, and weaker in its fortifications.

At Tunhwang the Silk Road divided. One branch ran west to Hami, and thence to Persia. Another fell off to the south, traversed the cruel Lop Nor Desert, and scaled the towering mountain passes into India. The traders carried silk, jewels, and lacquered chests of tea westward through Tunhwang. They returned with gold and silver from the Middle East and India—and new faiths and religions, including Nestorian Christianity, Mohammedanism, and Buddhism.

By the fourth century after Christ, Buddhism was firmly entrenched in China, and was the principal religion of the merchants whose hazardous routes ran all the way from the China Sea to the Mediterranean. Near the city of Tunhwang, in a great cave hollowed in the gorge of the River Shara, Buddhist monks established a temple. There the traders prayed for a safe journey on their way out and gave thanks upon their successful return. This temple rises ten stories high against the sheer cliff. Only one face can be seen from the outside. All the rest is contained within the cave. In the vaulting center chamber incense never ceases to smolder, and it resounds with the vibration of brass gongs beaten for prayer. Within the space of a mile, more than five hundred other caves and grottoes honeycomb the cliff. In these are found the Thousand Buddhas—and countless more.

This shrine began to blossom during the fourth century, when a merchant commissioned an artist, probably a monk, to dedicate one of the smaller caves to the success of his expedition and his safe return. A smiling and benevolent Buddha was erected, and the cave was decorated and painted. Apparently the expedition of this merchant was unusually prosperous, for others quickly followed his example. For more than a thousand years, during the rise and fall of eight Chinese dynasties, the finest Chinese artists were commissioned to raise Buddhas, and cover the walls of the caves with frescoes. Word of the caves spread across China, and it is recorded that in a single month 50,000 pilgrims came to Tunhwang to pray and to view the wonders of the caves.

As other avenues of travel opened China to the world, the Silk Road dwindled in importance during the seventeenth century, and the city of Tunhwang shriveled. Whole districts fell into decay, and the caves were looted and neglected. Foreign archeologists and explorers stripped the caves of manuscripts and *objets d'art* during those centuries. Chinese looted them of metal. White Russians, fleeing the Bolshevik revolution, somehow found their way to Tunhwang, and made their homes in the caves, blackening the walls with the smoke of their cooking fires. Still, the caves remain one of the largest repositories of Chinese religious art in the world today.

At Urumchi we had been told that only a few foreigners had visited Tunhwang. The caves were something that Marco Polo *hadn't* described, although he had passed nearby. While Tunhwang was only seventy miles from Ansi, the road was but a rutted path across rock and desert. Nor was there regular transportation to Tunhwang. Its surviving 20,000 inhabitants lived in almost complete isolation, sustaining themselves as farmers, and trading with the nomad Mongol and Kazak herdsmen.

I had developed a severe earache on the long cold ride to Ansi and Franc heated rocks and baked potatoes, pressing them against my ears, and finally poured hot soybean oil into the ear channels. Despite my discomfort, we hitchhiked a ride to Tunhwang the next day on an army truck carrying a load of felt *yurts* for the garrison there.

That drive, which started at seven in the evening, was sheer horror. Since Kazak bandits had been raiding in the area, and the truck carried no armed guard, the driver asked Franc to ride on top of the cab, keeping his gun ready. Despite long johns, GI shirt and trousers, three pairs of socks, and a flight jacket with fur collar, I froze. Sometimes my ears hurt so that I cried. But I was riding over the rear wheels, so fortunately Franc couldn't hear me.

After eight hours of bumping and lurching, of flat tires and burned-out fuses and choked gas lines, we came to within two miles of Tunhwang—and ran out of gas. The mechanic walked back to the last camel stop and returned with all the gas available there, one quart. The truck ran another half mile, gasped, shuddered, and stopped. We walked from there, stumbling in the darkness, carrying our luggage. At five in the morning we staggered into the army barracks. I collapsed into sleep on the orderly room floor, too exhausted to unbutton my coat.

In the morning our luck changed. Colonel Chou, in charge of the garrison, insisted that we be his guests and we didn't play too hard to get. Servants whisked our bags to his house, and we met the colonel's charming wife who loaned me her porcelain hot-water bottle, used by Chinese women to keep their hands warm during a winter journey. I used it for my ears and soon felt better. Meanwhile Franc and Colonel Chou rode horseback across the dunes to Crescent Lake and its abandoned temple, from which they returned jubilant, having shot two large bustards, a bird somewhat like a crane though larger, which, diced and sautéed with noodles and cabbage, tasted exactly like beef. But like all fowl served in China, there seemed to be a bit of shattered bone in each bite. A Chinese cook is helpless without his cleaver.

At dawn the next day we rode to the face of the cliff. Much of the cliff itself, where outside walls had crumbled, was covered with murals and frescoes that came to life as they were touched by the rays of the sun. Picturesque wooden balconies marked the entrances to the grottoes. Even narrow niches in the rock contained small statues.

Dwan Li-sen, an artist working on the restoration of some of the caves, escorted us through the Temple of the Great Buddha. We entered through an archway exquisitely carved, and painted with deep reds and golds, pigments that had withstood the passage of centuries. We passed down a hallway the walls of which were covered with Sung Dynasty murals of the temple guardians —monsters and dragons. As our eyes became accustomed to the gloom, an enormous figure loomed above us. It was the Great Buddha, which we estimated to be 180 feet high from his crossed feet to the top of his head. Scores of artists, working for many years, had carved this Buddha, comparable in size to the Sphinx

of Egypt, from the virgin rock of the cliff itself. Then the statue
was coated with plaster and paint. But the Great Buddha, Dwan
told us, was comparatively modern. That is, work on him ended
about the time of the American Revolution. For real beauty, he
said, we should see the smaller grottoes, and the ancient statues
at the south end of the cliff.

We visited twenty-two caves constructed during the Northern
Wei Dynasty from the years A.D. 386 to 534. The fresco Buddhas
looked as if they had been freshly executed, for the dark, dry
interiors of the caves perfectly preserved this ancient art. The
colors remained rich and deep, with striking black accents, and
the graceful figures, with flowing garments, riding tiny clouds
to paradise, conveyed a powerful sense of movement.

For three days we climbed and walked, probed and photographed the sacred cliff, absorbing its lore and marveling at the
exquisite artistry and colors. Many of the caves were linked by
natural galleries, and corridors had been cut into secluded sections, making it possible to walk a mile or so on each level without seeing the sky. Nature, and the devotion of Buddhist traders,
had created galleries larger than those in the Vatican.

Especially fascinating were the paintings of the Sui and Tang
dynasties, the golden era of Chinese art. These pictures date from
A.D. 589 to 907 and cover the walls of 264 caves. The Sui and
Tang caves reflect the strong Grecian influence which came to
China via India and its Gandhara school. Here I developed a
strong preference for the Buddhist conception of paradise. Those
who have achieved heaven recline in elaborate pavilions around
lotus-covered lakes. Celestial beings, called Fu, sing and dance for
them, and scatter over their heads a soft rain of delicate blossoms. These paintings seemed "Japanesy" to me, and Franc remarked that it was little wonder, as early Japanese artists had
patterned their style on the Tang dynasty masterpieces.

A scattering of devout Buddhists still visited the caves. Some
were Outer Mongolian herdsmen, weighted with dirty sheepskins, their hair and bodies coated with grease. At the beginning
of winter the Mongols lard their bodies against the cold, and

during the rest of the year do not bother to bathe. As Mongols associate mostly with other Mongols, they are not aware of this powerful aroma. I wished for a clothespin.

We stayed in Tunhwang until we ran out of color film, partly on the hunch that this might be the last chance for a Westerner to see and photograph the caves. They are now in the hands of the Chinese Communists, who recently issued a stamp with a Tunhwang motif.

ALTOGETHER, it took the truck twenty-four hours and eighteen blowouts to make the seventy miles back to Ansi, but the trip was lightened by a memorable bit of Chinese comedy. We stopped to repair a flat at the Inn of the Fresh Water Spring, once the midway oasis on the road, but now fallen into disuse, and inhabited only by an aged farmer and his wife. We had been on the road all day and were starved.

The old couple could not feed us, having barely enough for their own scanty supper. One of our "yellow fish," however, was a sharp city boy, wearing the Gobi version of a zoot suit, tight-fitting Western trousers, a gaudy sports shirt and tie, and a leather jacket under a sheepskin coat that trailed the ground. He drew the farmer aside, paying no attention to Franc, who he assumed did not speak Chinese.

"Old one," the zoot-suiter said, "here is your chance to make some money. While your wife is talking, steal her supper and bring it to me. I'll pay you well."

The farmer protested at first, but the city boy kept raising the price until the farmer agreed to the deal.

Franc took an immediate dislike to what he called "this Shanghai type," and went to warn the old man's wife that she was about to lose her dinner. He found the wife in the kitchen of the inn, sitting with another of our fellow passengers, both bolting bowls of noodles. "Hurry!" Franc heard her warn the traveler. "Finish the bowl and leave me. If my husband finds I have sold his dinner, I shall surely be beaten. As soon as you

have gone I'll cry out, and say someone has stolen our food."
Seeing clearly that she was hardly in need of his protection, Franc
quelled his chivalrous impulse and retreated to let events take
their natural course.


FROM ANSI to Wuwei to Lanchow we rode on postal trucks, slept
with our boots on, and feasted on such exotic fare as dried sea
slugs. At Yumen we passed through the famous Jade Gate, built
to mark the farther border of ancient China, and from there on
were flanked by the Great Wall. For miles and miles we could see
it snaking over the hills, sometimes coiling to enclose an oasis
town, sometimes sliding away and vanishing in the harsh waste-
lands. Where stone was scarce, the Wall was built of packed earth
and now was badly eroded. From our truck-top seats we admired
its incredible length. If you watched it long enough, it developed
a hypnotic effect upon your senses, like watching the wake of a
ship, or the rails slip away from the end of a train.

Our fellow passengers on board these trucks were invariably
friendly. We shared our food with young soldiers, aging peasant
farmers, and merchants bound for Lanchow to buy fabrics and
pots and pans. At Kiuchuan and Kanchow, Shantan and Wuwei,
our hosts at the *lui-gwans* were kind, and the food delicious. The
mud *kangs* were hardly soft and yet we slept well. Our fellow
passengers never failed to split a melon with us. You can have a
miserable few days traveling first class on the *Queen Elizabeth,* or
the *United States,* or a wonderful time riding a truck over the
roughest road of the Gobi Desert. It depends on who's in the
next stateroom, or on the adjoining *kang.*

When we came at last to a smooth highway following the
course of the rushing Yellow River, the Gobi was behind us. The
countryside changed into an Oriental Netherlands, with water-
wheels a hundred feet tall lifting water into irrigation ditches.
Then ahead we saw the walls of Lanchow, and we passed through
its massive gates. We were in a city again, we had returned to
civilization—back to electric lights and running water, beds with
springs, knives and forks. We went to the Northwest House,

In Hami (Sinkiang), Franc roman-rides two perplexed camels in the compound of our lui-gwan. Caravan camels are used to shuffling along in single file, and the idea of walking side by side didn't appeal to these two. They humored Franc for a while, and then abruptly parted company, leaving a nice space between themselves for Franc to fall into

Captain Hwang of the Chinese army shares a melon with me in the Gobi. This gravel-strewn, treeless, arid terrain extends for hundreds of miles.

Somewhere between Hami and Ansi, on the edge of the Gobi, our overloaded truck blew out two tires at once. Bags of wool, rolls of hides, oil drums, crates, gasoline cans, and about twenty passengers made up the overload.

The Caves of the Thousand Buddhas, Tunhwang. Bells hang from the upcurled roof points of the structure which protects the Great Buddha. Whitewashed entrances lead into cave shrines, four levels of which are visible.

Lanchow's only modern hotel. and asked for a room with the big-gest bathtub. It was very impressive, but so were the rings we left in it.

We planned to remain in Lanchow until we located, and vis-ited, the grave of Genghis Khan. In the *China Year Book of 1947* I had read a cryptic, matter-of-fact item—"The remains of Gen-ghis Khan, guarded by the Ikhchao League, were removed to Kansu Province in June, 1939." An American military attaché had told us, somewhat uncertainly, that he thought the grave was near Lanchow. None of our Chinese friends had ever seen the grave, or knew anyone who had seen it, yet the story, so far as we could ascertain, could be true.

For seven centuries the remains of Genghis Khan lay in a secret place after his death in 1227 at Liu Pan Shan, on the Suiyuan-Shensi border. Always this place was guarded by a Mongol band, the Alashan, now part of the Ikhchao League. They had been assigned this honor when the Khan of Khans died in his *yurt* at sixty-five, of a long-lasting disease perhaps occasioned by old wounds. In 1939, when the Japanese were sweeping province after province in China, the Ikhchao League, faithful to its trust, peti-tioned the Chinese government for permission to remove the casket to a safer place. This granted, the remains were brought to central Kansu, of which Lanchow was the capital, on the fringe of Genghis' native Gobi.

In the Gobi, and indeed in all Central Asia, there was a belief that whoever possessed the bones of Genghis Khan would one day rule the world. It was partly because of this tradition that Chiang Kai-shek made sure the casket would not fall into the hands of the Japanese.

For me the ringing name of Genghis Khan had always pos-sessed a special fascination, although much of his philosophy, and his deeds, made me shudder. "A man's greatest joy in life," Genghis Khan had said, "is to break his enemies, and to take from them all the things that have been theirs, and to hold in his arms the most desirable of their women."

A cycle of searing summers and frightful winters forced the Mongols to seek *lebensraum* beyond the boundaries of the Gobi, and Genghis Khan, "The Scourge of God," led them to conquest, the first time in 1211 against North China. In one expedition, he laid waste ninety Chinese cities, slaughtering the inhabitants and leveling the ruins until a horseman, riding at night, would not stumble when passing over the sites, or know a single hut had been there.

It is said that Genghis Khan, when born in 1162, had the birthmark of a clot of blood in the palm of his hand. To those of his father's tribe, this meant that he would be a great killer and warrior. He didn't disappoint them. He killed his first man as a stripling of thirteen, and thereafter terror became his weapon. He had his enemies nailed to wooden horses, or boiled in huge pots, or skinned alive. He conquered all of China with 250,000 soldiers. His secret was stealth, speed, and mobility. His was an army of cavalrymen. The Mongol warrior was tough as his saddle, mounted on a hardy pony that could outlast any blooded horse of Europe. He carried a powerful bow, a cutlass, and a dagger.

After Genghis Khan united the Mongols, he gave them a code of laws, and laid the foundations for efficient administration of his empire. He opened communications and trade routes that stretched across more than half the then known world. Oddly enough, religious tolerance existed under his rule. The first of the laws, called the Yassa, was like the first of our Ten Commandments. "It is ordered to believe that there is only one God, creator of Heaven and earth, who alone gives life and death, riches and poverty as it pleases Him, and who has over everything an absolute power."

Under this law, Nestorian Christians, Buddhists, and Moslems worshiped in peace. It was possible, under this rule of Genghis Khan and his descendants, to travel the length and breadth of the empire without fear of molestation. The most fearsome marauder of all time outlawed banditry. While pillage was the right of the warrior, stealing in time of peace was punishable by death.

Though the empire of Alexander the Great withered soon after his death, Genghis Khan proved a wiser administrator. His sons and grandsons continued his rule and expanded his conquests. His son, Ogotai, swept the regions west of the Caspian. A grandson, Batu, advanced to the Adriatic and into Austria and Poland. Other armies of the khans fought in Korea and Persia. The Mongols rolled north and west as far as Finland. Another grandson, Hulagu, humbled Bagdad and Damascus, advancing almost within bowshot of the quaking gates of Jerusalem.

Kublai Khan, the greatest of Genghis Khan's grandsons, consolidated his hold on all China, sent forth a flotilla to invade Japan, and expanded his kingdom south to Bengal and the Malay States. After the death of Kublai, the Mongol empire gradually dissolved, but like its tough founders, it died hard. The Mongols kept China in thrall until 1368, and not until 1555 did Ivan the Terrible defeat them, weakening their grasp on large parts of Russia. Only in the middle of the eighteenth century did their descendants in India, the Moguls, surrender to the British. For six hundred years their power extended beyond their own lands.

From two unlikely sources we picked up valuable clues. From Bill Hassig, a jaunty pilot for the Chinese National Airline and a veteran of the Hump, and from Claude Appel of the Seventh Day Adventist Mission ("These Adventists know everything," explained Bill, "they've been here forever.") we learned that Genghis Khan's grave was somewhere near the village of Yu Chung, fifty miles southeast of Lanchow.

The isolated Adventist missionaries in Lanchow operated a hospital outstanding in China, in that it was clean, modern, and welcomed rich and poor alike. A wounded coolie received equal attention with the governor's son, and the people of the province accorded these Americans a respect that was almost reverence.

Appel, the young director of the hospital, invited us to a vegetarian lunch, after which we all set out for the country, but not before our Adventist host asked a blessing on the hospital's one jeep. The road led us through loess country, earth so soft and porous that cart tracks dig into it like plows. In time the roads become one large rut, almost a ditch, and driving through it, our heads were barely even with the fields on either side. We literally saw the farmland at grass-roots level.

Near the tiny village of Yu Chung, in the green and wooded

valley of Tasurka Shan, three ancient Buddhist temples sat high
on a bluff. Two of the temples were typical of countless others in
China—loose tiles, cluttered courtyards choked with weeds, listless monks, and an air of decay and neglect. The third temple
was different.

Neat and well swept, its door was barred and chained. Two
stocky, powerful Alashan Mongols guarded the entrance, immobile and silent and leathery as wax exhibits in a museum.
Claude Appel addressed them, but they replied noncommittally
in monosyllables. He had to search out the tribal leader, a huge
bear of a man, wearing a chain of heavy keys around his neck,
who unlocked the temple door.

Inside, in the center toward the rear, loomed the bulk of a
coffin. At first sight, in the dim light, the casket and walls seemed
black and shapeless. Then color and details began to emerge from
the gloom. The ceiling and walls were completely draped with
heavy cloth-of-gold, so that the room was not a room at all, but
the replica of a Mongol chieftain's tent. The floor was covered
with rich Persian carpets. Heavy, carved chests and low tables
were arrayed along the walls. The casket was covered with layer
after layer of heavy silk. Reverently, the guard lifted them off,
and we saw a massive block of silver, squarish in shape rather
than oblong.

In the shadows to the right stood another, though smaller,
casket, containing, we were told, the remains of Genghis Khan's
second wife, unnamed and unknown. This casket was also of silver but less ornate. What happened, I wondered, to the bones of
the first wife, Bourtai, whom history says he deeply loved?

To the left stood the yak-tail standard, symbol of the Mongol
leader. Leaning against the wall was a heavy top for a tent pole,
five feet long and tapering to a gold-covered knob. This orna-
ment decorated Genghis Khan's *yurt,* always pitched on the highest ground of the Mongol encampment. When the warriors could
see the gold knob glinting in the sun, they knew their leader was
in residence.

On either side of the tent were two cavernous silver urns, resting in wooden pedestals, containing the carcasses of sacrificial

sheep. On special Mongol holidays, the guards told us, they killed a hundred sheep. Small bowls, containing offerings of red peppers, rice, or dates, were arranged beside the casket. Wine in brass cups, offerings from pilgrim Mongols, flanked the food. Incense burned in bronze bowls, and streamers of pungent smoke floated in an eerie haze over the casket.

In the rear of the temple hung an oil painting, said to be a likeness of the Great Khan, sent in tribute by a Russian czar centuries ago. It fitted the general description left by historians, one of whom wrote: "The Khan was distinguished by his strong features, catlike eyes, wide forehead, long beard and great size."

Buried with the Khan, supposedly, is his sword and some of his giant pearls. Nobody knows for sure, for within the memory of modern man the coffin has not been opened. All this was explained by the deep-voiced tribal leader and interpreted by Appel. The casket of Genghis Khan was a sight I had never even hoped to see, and indeed could hardly believe existed. I tarried over it as long as I could.

Yet, on the road back to the mission I was troubled with doubts as to the authenticity of what I had seen. Marco Polo, come to Cathay to seek Kublai Khan, grandson of Genghis, was certainly closer to the events of that day. Furthermore, he was a good reporter. And Marco Polo had written:

"It has been an invariable custom that all the grand khans should be carried for interment to a certain mountain named Altai, and in whatever place they may happen to die, although it should be a distance of a hundred days' journey, they are nevertheless conveyed thither." The Altai range is in the western part of Outer Mongolia, many hundred miles west of the spot where Genghis Khan died, and hundreds of miles from the village of Yu Chung.

Claude Appel pointed out, however, that Marco Polo may have been referring to the sons and grandsons of Genghis Khan, for he did not mention Genghis specifically. Furthermore, the Alashan Mongols have always lived in Suiyuan Province, where Genghis undoubtedly died in 1227. Whether the bones of Genghis are in the casket or not, all the Mongols believe it, and they believe that power and might and mastery of the world rests in that land which numbers the bones and the yak-tail standard among its treasures. The Communists have the temple now.


WE FLEW FROM LANCHOW to Peiping, the beautiful city that was old before Genghis Khan was born, and that he destroyed after "a glorious slaughter," and that Kublai Khan rebuilt, calling it Khanbalig, or Great Capital.

Marco Polo reached Peiping at the height of its magnificence, when it was undoubtedly the largest city in the world, surrounded by immense earthen ramparts forty feet high, sixty feet wide at the base, and twenty miles in circumference. Peiping's population, even then, was two million, several times larger than London of that day.

For me, the Forbidden City, the Tartar walls, and Drum Hill, paled in interest before the Marco Polo Bridge, seven miles from the inner city, beyond the Gate of Prolonged Righteousness. Marco Polo crossed this seemingly ageless and indestructible bridge, spanning the Yung Ting River, in 1275, and there first glimpsed the walls of Khanbalig, which he called Kanbalu. Franc, too, wanted to see the bridge, but as a contemporary historic monument. On July 6, 1937, Japanese and Chinese soldiers had clashed on it, and many years of war in Asia followed.

As I leaned over the stone rail of the center span, I timidly broached a subject that had been in my mind for weeks. "Franc, do you realize that when he crossed this bridge, Marco Polo had reached the court of Kublai Khan and finished his journey?"

Franc eyed me suspiciously. "If Polo were alive today, I could use him as a correspondent in a divorce suit."

"Not only that," I rushed on, my pet cat almost out of the bag, "but do you realize that we've followed his trail all the way from Hami across the Gobi and central China?"

"Or I could sue him for alienation of historical affection . . ."

"So why don't we do the rest of it? Why don't we retrace all Marco Polo's trip—from Venice east?"

Franc laughed and looked at me as if I were slightly mad. "I still ache from the Gobi. All I want to do is get back to our house

in Shanghai, stretch out on my poor back, and have Ah Tsung
mix me a barrel of martinis."

I didn't press him, immediately. At least his answer was not a
flat and candid no. But all during the rest of our stay in Peiping
we looked at the city through the eyes of Marco Polo. I quoted
my Venetian friend about the manner in which Kublai Khan
lived, with four wives and innumerable concubines, and a hundred fresh maidens brought from the provinces each year. Of
these, according to Polo, he took his pick, and distributed the
residue to his nobles. The home life of the khans seemed to interest Franc, if the arduous journeys of Marco Polo, at that
moment, appalled him.

The next week we flew back home to an uneasy Shanghai.
There was no denying the city's ominous atmosphere. Up in the
north and west the fighting was going against the Nationalists,
and each day the Communists moved closer. Even the foreigners
in Shanghai, usually so busy making money and throwing parties,
began to worry and consult their steamship and air-line agents.
Their judgment, casually spoken over drinks at the clubs, was:
"There's always fighting in the north, you know, but this time
it seems different." Everyone felt the change, a cold wind stirring
out of the steppes. Many had been prisoners of the Japanese,
none wanted to be prisoners of the Communists. Having experienced a brief sample, neither did I.

We had planned to make our home and headquarters in
Shanghai for many years, but now we decided it was time to
leave. Temporarily, we hoped. We rented our house, and found
positions for our servants. What we could not easily ship home
in foot lockers, we stored in the Broadway Mansions, headquarters of the American Military Mission, and in the Foreign Correspondents Club.

In our years in the Far East we had accumulated possessions
that we prized highly, and hoped would be part of our home always, wherever it might be—the finest lacquer screens, antique
Oriental furniture, Chi'en Lung vases, delicate porcelain and old
silver, Han bronzes, hand-embroidered linens. We never saw any
of it again.

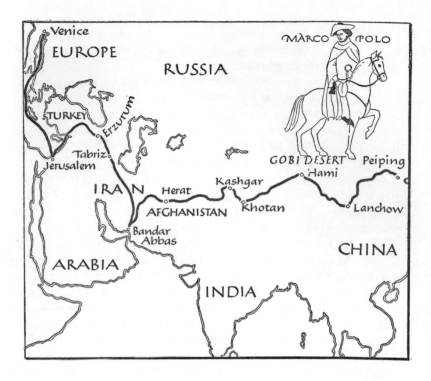

# 3

# THE TRAIL OF MARCO POLO

EVEN BEFORE we left Shanghai our future course was set. Franc, too, had begun talking about Marco Polo, tracing his route on old maps, muttering about Afghanistan and mountain ranges with queer names, reading up on the Shah of Persia. At last, and of a sudden, he had said it: "If you want to do this Marco Polo trip, then I suppose you must," as if the idea wasn't pulsing in his own head too. We would follow Polo's footsteps from Venice east to China. Franc had ten thousand dollars saved which we could devote to this whim of mine. He wrote it off under the heading: "Extended honeymoon, education, and peace in our house."

A quick flight across the Pacific from Shanghai dropped us into San Francisco, and the shock of returning to one's own land after years in the Orient was like immersion in clean, cold water. Of a sudden we were carrying our own bags, the officials were all efficient, "face" was of no importance, "squeeze" was unknown, and everybody spoke the same language, rapidly.

We went to Texas and Kansas to meet all our respective and numerous in-laws. They listened patiently to tall tales of the Gobi Desert, and then incredulously to our plans for following Marco Polo's trail. "You're not going all the way around the world to go *back* there, are you? But why?" There simply was no logical answer. It wasn't enough to say that our eyes were on the horizon. An uncle of mine had the last word—"That Polo fellow died a few hundred years ago, didn't he? That's what coyote hunters would call a pretty cold trail."

It is generally believed that your first act, when planning so ambitious a journey, is to lunch at the Explorer's Club, and then beat your way down Fifth Avenue, through dense crowds of overdressed natives, to Abercrombie & Fitch. There you are outfitted with butterfly nets, snake serum, elephant guns, pith helmets, and beads for the savages.

Actually the first thing to do is to get "shots," collect visas and maps, and inquire about the type of officialdom, customs, and currency regulations you are likely to encounter in the countries you intend to visit. If these onerous chores are not carefully done, you are likely to find yourself minus cameras and film in a stinking jail five hundred miles from the nearest American consul, and just as far from a workable telephone. As a matter of fact, no matter how carefully plans are laid or how many credentials, passports, exit permits, letters of credit and introduction, and police identification cards are secured, travelers in far places are likely to find themselves in jail anyway. We did.

Fortunately, one of the first people we met in New York was Evert Barger, our urbane and learned British friend of Shanghai. Barger had led an expedition through Afghanistan for Britain's

Victoria and Albert Museum. He knew a great deal about northern Afghanistan and the forbidden and forbidding Wakhan area. In all probability he knew more about the Wakhan than most Afghans. Over coffee in our hotel, he listened carefully to our plans, and then he said one word, politely—"Impossible!"

We were stunned.

"I do not speak solely of the physical difficulties," Evert continued. "You can imagine what they will be. I simply point out that to follow Marco Polo from Afghanistan to China you must traverse the Wakhan corridor. No Westerners have been permitted even to enter it for a hundred and ten years, and many have asked." Then he looked at me and smiled graciously. "No woman has *ever* attempted it. It is a high and dangerous region. Rough country. No place for a lady."

"Jean has just crossed the Gobi," Franc ventured hopefully.

Evert hastened to say that we must not misunderstand him. "There are many things that women can do as well as men, or better. But going through the Wakhan is not one of them."

Franc amazed me. "I'm beginning to believe she can go any place I can."

I silently cheered.

Evert examined me with critical eyes, as if I were a fast filly that might fade in the stretch, or a new car with too little horsepower. "Well, that's that," he shrugged. "Now let's discuss the political obstacles. You won't have much trouble in Turkey, although Marco Polo traveled through what is now a restricted military zone near Mt. Ararat, on the Russian frontier. You are liable to have a great deal of trouble in Iran, for Polo crossed Azerbaijan, near the Russian border. Foreigners are never welcome there. But your real obstacle will be Afghanistan. You may not even be able to get a visa, in the first place, and if you do get a visa it would be a miracle if the Afghans permitted you to traverse the Wakhan."

Evert explained that our trail would follow the upper reaches of the Oxus River, the border between the Soviet Union and Afghanistan. The Afghans were anxious not to antagonize their powerful neighbor, and few things antagonize the Russians more than a pair of Americans wandering about their frontiers.

"But if you do get a visa to Afghanistan," Barger continued, "go first to the capital, Kabul. Only the King himself can give you permission to penetrate the Wakhan. He is the only one who dares say yes. His ministers and provincial governors can only say no."

Barger gave us much other sound advice. We could procure the best map of the Wakhan at Stanford's, in London. We were not to be disturbed that they were twenty or thirty years old or that great sections were marked "unsurveyed." They were as accurate and detailed as could be found.

Few other persons remained who might be helpful. Sir Aurel Stein, the German Le Coq, and Sir Eric Teichman, noted explorers of Central Asia and Afghanistan, had been killed, or had met a natural death, during the war.

Before we sailed we received a letter from Evert, along with valuable letters of introduction. "My thoughts go with you in your great enterprise," he said, "and you can be sure that some day, before I lose control of my legs, I shall follow in your tracks." His phrase gave me a lift. I hadn't thought of the trip as a "great enterprise," but it was pleasant and flattering to find that someone else, a highly regarded explorer and geographer, considered it so.

We replenished our camera equipment in New York, investing a staggering amount in color film and flash bulbs, and we bought a Polaroid camera. We were to discover that a Polaroid is not only a lot of fun for the person who owns it, but that it can open palace doors and border barricades. As baksheesh, a photograph is better than money. Nothing so pleases and inflates a petty official as to have his picture taken and handed to him on the spot.

It was possible to collect most of our permits in New York, but for visas to Afghanistan and Iran we went to Washington. While packing, I came across the color pictures we had made at the Caves of the Thousand Buddhas. In New York, in a hotel room high above Fifth Avenue, the dying city of Tunhwang and its ancient caves seemed unreal as a dream, yet a fascinating dream.

"Franc," I suggested, "let's take these pictures to Washington and see if *The National Geographic Magazine* will buy them."

"Nonsense," Franc said. "Those pictures aren't *Geographic* caliber. I have a small reputation as a writer of articles, and I don't intend to louse it up now by submitting amateur photographs."

For the moment I played the obedient wife. "Yes, dear."

As soon as we reached Washington I went to the imposing stone building that houses the National Geographic Society. I had practically teethed on its magazine. For years my grandfather and father had every volume bound. I was received courteously, as befitted an old subscriber. The editors would look at our pictures and let me know.

Three days later a letter came to our hotel. *The Geographic* was interested. Would we visit them and discuss an article? "Franc," I said, hoping I wasn't lighting a fuse to a powder keg, "I have just received a letter from *The National Geographic*—"

"Tell them we're already members."

"It isn't that," I said. "It's—"

"Well, send them a check."

"Franc," I said, "it's about the Tunhwang pictures."

He stood up straight, looking formidable. "So you did it!"

"Yes."

"I now have a volunteer literary agent."

"Franc, they're interested. They want to see us. They want to talk about an article!"

"That doesn't mean a thing," Franc said. "They're just being polite. Don't get carried away."

At *The Geographic,* an editor escorted us to a projection room. There our photographs were enormously enlarged, every defect glaring from the screen. I was sure they were worthless. The chief of the illustrations division and his assistant fired questions at us as picture after picture was projected. At the end of an agonizing hour he leaned back, rubbed his chin, and said,

"I think we have enough good slides for sixteen pages of color. Now the editors will talk to you about the text."

I've never felt so relieved in my life—or so delighted.

When we told them about our Marco Polo plans, the editors were particularly interested "in the remote possibility" of our passing through the Wakhan, one of the least known regions of the earth. Would we keep in touch with them? Thus began an association that has lasted ever since. Now our full-time job is writing stories and taking photographs for *The National Geographic*. We travel the world as a profession as well as for pleasure.

We were not so fortunate with our visas. After eight forms, six photographs, and seven days, the Iranian embassy gave us a visa to enter their country, but it was valid for only three months. We would have to hurry if it would still be in effect by the time we reached Persia.

The Afghan embassy could not help us. The embassy in Washington was not permitted, the first secretary explained, to issue visas except upon specific authorization from the foreign office in Kabul. He doubted that the foreign office would give such authorization.

"If we make a request," I asked, "how long would it take to receive an answer?"

"Perhaps three months," the first secretary said, "perhaps longer. Communications in my country aren't of the best, and there would be a thorough investigation of you and your intentions, before you were permitted to enter."

It didn't sound too encouraging.

"By the way," he asked, "what *are* your intentions?"

We explained our desire to follow Marco Polo's trail across Asia. A friendly gleam lighted his eyes. "Wonderful idea! Impossible, but wonderful," he said. "I'll help you if I can."

We left identification photos, letters of recommendation, the many completed questionnaires and applications (you would have thought we were applying for a job, not a visa) and laid all our hopes in his hands as we said good-by that afternoon in early

March. He would forward this mass of material to Kabul. If a visa was granted, he said, we could pick it up at the Afghan embassy at some capital along the route. Perhaps Paris or Ankara, perhaps farther east. If not—he was very sorry.

We understood what a gamble this was. We might travel across half the world, and then be turned back. But it was a gamble we had to take, if we were to beat the snows to the High Pamirs.

ON BOARD the *American Traveler* bound for Plymouth, Franc used the ten days to write the article about the Tunhwang caves for *The Geographic*. We remained in London only long enough to buy our maps and arrange for our photographic equipment to be transshipped to Venice. At the office of a famous British travel agency, the girl at the counter suggested that we send the big aluminum case by sea to Rome, and have the agency's Rome office handle the transfer by rail to Venice. Franc agreed, and then asked, "What counter do I go to to insure this shipment?"

"Are you going to insure with *us?*" the girl asked, horrified.

"Certainly. For about two thousand dollars."

"Well, in *that* case," the clerk said, almost indignantly, "we *certainly* won't send them through Rome. Our Rome office steals *everything!*"

Paris nearly wrecked our itinerary. We had planned to spend three days there, but it was April, the chestnut trees were in bloom, and the boulevards were glorious with color. A few months of marriage had taught me that Franc is something of a gourmet. In certain cities he has trouble with his waistline. Travel, I had discovered, gave him an excellent excuse to over-indulge at the table.

"After we leave here," he said solemnly, "we won't get any-thing good to eat. We'll lose a lot of weight on that long hike over the Pamirs. We're liable to cross deserts where food is scarce. We may see famine areas. Better store up a little reserve."

I'm wise to that "after we leave here" routine now, but it was a fresh experience then. He says it in New York before we leave for Paris, and in Paris before Rome, and in Rome before Cairo. The grass is always dead on the other side of the street. For Franc's tombstone I plan the simple epitaph:

AFTER WE LEAVE HERE
WE WON'T GET ANYTHING
GOOD TO EAT

But in those days I was gullible. Every day we "stored up a little reserve" in Laperouse and Maxim's and the Ritz and the Tour d'Argent. The three days became three weeks before Franc casually remarked one morning that the snows come early in the Pamirs. Wouldn't it be wise to postpone Marco Polo until next year?

That did it. My cherished project was being threatened by a cabal of chefs. I waited until a particularly fine lunch had put Franc in a mellow mood, and then I steered him into a travel agency, where we booked passage on the Orient Express, leaving for Venice the next night.

The next evening, after a private farewell banquet of Homeric proportions at the Ritz, calculated to keep Franc in calories for at least a month, I resolutely and hastily towed my recalcitrant husband to the station. We got the bags from the check room, rounded up our three porters, and scrambled aboard just as the Orient Express began to move. I had hired the porters myself, in advance, two of them to carry the luggage and the third to push Franc. As I boarded the train my last thought was that the critical visa for Afghanistan hadn't arrived at the embassy in Paris. Somehow, somewhere, we would just have to get it.


FROM THE STATION in Mestre a gondola ferried us to a *pensione* in Venice—the same inn where I had stayed after the German surrender. The room which then had seemed so airy and comfortable now seemed too small, and I wondered why until I saw a large husband barging around in it. But the atmosphere was still delightful as a Verdi opera. Old men were fishing in the canals. Women were shouting across their back balconies. Groups of young people strolled along the canal banks under our window, singing.

Our first mail in Venice contained a letter from *The National Geographic* with praise for our story on the Caves of the Thousand Buddhas, and a fat check. We sat in the warm Italian sun and passed that check back and forth, admiring it. We had found a way to live, forever.

Time was running out on us if we were to cross the Pamirs before the snow blocked the passes, and reach Urumchi ahead of the Communists who were at that moment sweeping south and west. We had two goals in Venice. We had to visit the library and learn all we could of Marco Polo and his travels from the priceless original records housed there. And we wanted to see and photograph his home and place of burial.

That afternoon we went to the Customs Bureau to pick up our cameras and film, and ran into a comical impasse. Instead of billing the suitcase as "personal effects only," the British had meticulously listed it as "new camera equipment." The Italians suspected we were not simply passing through their country, but that we had brought in cameras and film to sell on the black market.

We pleaded and argued to no avail. Then Franc, who was carrying our Polaroid camera, invited the chief of the customs office to step outside for a portrait. "Ah, no," said the chief. "Who would want to take a picture of me?"

"Your uniform is magnificent," I said, "and besides, you are very photogenic."

"Oh, not really," he said, smiling broadly toward the camera.

Franc snapped the picture and presented him with the print. "Madame," said the delighted inspector, "open the package, and if in truth it holds *any* personal effects, we will allow the entrance of this equipment."

The aluminum case was placed on the table and the seals cut. I reached inside and brought out a black satin, oblong-shaped changing bag, at the top of which were two short sleeves with elastic cuffs. It is actually a portable darkroom. When a camera becomes jammed, or if film must be rewound, the camera is

placed inside the sack, zipped light-tight, and then one's hands
are inserted through the sleeves where they can work in protec-
tive darkness.

I held the bag up by the sleeves. It looked exactly like a child's
windbreaker. "Ah," he said. "Personal effects. You have a little
one. You are free to take the baggage, madam, although I consider this whole matter of Marco Polo very mysterious." Had he
examined the "windbreaker," he would have considered that
mysterious too. There was no opening at the top for a head.

We hired a young Italian, Luigi Di Lozzi, to help us with
research in the library. Luigi was not averse to publicity, and a
few days later there appeared an item in the *Venice Gazette*.
"Mr. and Mrs. Franc Shor," it read, "the distinguished American journalists and geographers, have arrived in Venice to pre-
pare for a trip in the footsteps of Marco Polo. While conducting
their research they are being assisted by the Italian journalist
and scholar, Luigi Di Lozzi."

The next day the manager of the Luna Hotel called upon us.
Would we, he asked, honor the Luna by staying at his hotel?
Without charge, of course. He explained that if "such distinguished Americans" as we stayed at the Luna, it would attract
other guests. This we doubted, but not out loud. We accepted
his invitation and for the first time since our marriage luxuriated
in a swank bridal suite, thanks to the volunteer press agentry
of our "Italian journalist and scholar."

The Venetian Library, called Marciana, was founded in 1305
by Petrarch, the great poet, scientist, and philosopher, and
housed in a palace opposite that of the Doge. Piatro Zorzaenello,
the director, escorted us to the room where the Polo mementoes
were kept. These included fifty-seven versions of the *Travels,* the
first dated 1496, Marco Polo's will, and legal documents of the
time concerning his property.

A young assistant tossed these historic documents on the table
as casually as if they were yesterday's newspapers. We were flab-
bergasted. In the United States such relics would be preserved
in helium, under glass, and nobody would be allowed to touch
them, much less play catch with them.

Near the center of the room, illuminated by soft light from a leaded-glass bay window, stood an enormous globe, very old. The continents were misshapen and out of place, and there were seas where no seas should be. But when Marco Polo set out for the East, there was not even such a globe as this, for the earth had not been proved to be round.

Marco Polo was born in Venice in 1254, of a noble family engaged in trade with Constantinople. His father, Niccolo, and uncle, Maffeo, traveled to the East before him, yet of this earlier journey little is known, for the elder Polos were merchants, not scribblers. Niccolo and Maffeo found the route to the court of Kublai Khan through an accident of war. They had set out on a trading expedition across the Black Sea from their base in Constantinople. When they reached the Crimea they found their return cut off by a Mongol war. There was nothing for them to do except travel eastward.

In Bokhara they found profitable business, and tarried there three years, meeting in the course of their trade the envoys of Kublai Khan. These emissaries persuaded the elder Polos to accompany them to Cathay. There they were hospitably received by the Great Khan, who was astonished at their tales of the Western world, and particularly impressed by their account of the philosophy of Christianity. Kublai Khan, a wise and farseeing ruler, decided that what Cathay needed was a spiritual renaissance. He dispatched the Polos back to Europe as his ambassadors to the Pope, with the request that the Church send two hundred missionaries to introduce Christianity to China.

Had this enterprise succeeded, history might have been changed. How different might be the relations of a Christian China with the rest of the world today! But when the Polos reached Acre, in Palestine, they learned that the Pope was dead. They returned to Venice to await the election of a new pope. After two years the election still had not taken place, but the Polos felt duty bound to return to Kublai and explain the delay. They took ship from Venice in 1271. This time Marco, then seventeen years old, accompanied them.

As they journeyed through the Levant they learned that the

Legate of Syria finally had been elected Pope. They visited him in Jerusalem, but the Pope, like many others in succeeding centuries, discounted the Polos' stories. Instead of the requested two hundred missionaries he sent only two preaching friars. When the Polo party reached Armenia, the friars, alarmed at news of wars ahead, returned to Jerusalem.

In Shangtu, near Peiping, the Polos were welcomed back by Kublai Khan, who was particularly taken by Marco. This bright young man quickly learned the language and customs of Cathay, first as a protégé of the Khan and soon as a trusted adviser. On the Khan's business he traveled as a roving ambassador through isolated provinces and subject lands, even as far as India.

After seventeen years at the court of Cathay, Marco's father and uncle longed to return home. They were growing old and they wished to die in Venice. The Khan was reluctant to let them go. But at that moment a squadron was being prepared to escort a Mongol princess to Persia, where she was to marry the king. The Persian envoys insisted, perhaps at the secret urging of the Polos, that the three Venetians accompany the party, for they were expert navigators and had knowledge of the Western secret of sailing by the stars.

They sailed from China in 1292, and it took them more than two years to reach Persia. Six hundred men died aboard their ships, not unusual in an age when even the shortest journey was toothed with danger. While traveling overland across Persia they learned that the Great Khan had died. Saddened, they reached Venice in 1295.

Strange accounts, perhaps apocryphal, tell of their homecoming after an absence of twenty-four years. When they appeared at their home in Venice they were in rags, and unrecognized. But hidden under the rags were sacks of jewels, an immense fortune that sustained the Polos as leading citizens of Venice for generations.

A year after their return, Venice warred with Genoa, its sister city-state and rival for command of the seas. Marco commanded a galley which his family had equipped and sailed in the fleet of Andrea Dandolo. In the Venetian defeat, Marco was taken prisoner and carried off to Genoa. During his three years' imprisonment he dictated his account of the *Travels* to a cell mate from Pisa.

Released and returned to Venice in 1299, he married, and built a minor Venetian palace. He acquired the nickname "Il Milione"—he of the million lies—because of his fabulous stories of China. Not during his lifetime was his story wholly believed, and the map of Asia was not redrawn until fifty years after his death. Some few had journeyed to the East before him, but it was Marco Polo who sang of its splendor, explained its customs and culture, and placed Asia, the largest continent, with some accuracy on the map of the world.

Now Franc and I sought out the home where he had lived, and the place of his burial. The original house, one of the oldest and most beautiful in Venice, was burned in 1597, and the Malabran Theater was erected on the site. Yet the area is still called Corte Milione, and we walked through the archway which once led to the house. We had no luck in locating the Polo grave, said to have been in the courtyard of the Church of San Lorenzo. What remains of the church is now a dismal municipal warehouse. The grave was moved in 1502 when the church was remodeled, the caretaker told us, but now no one is sure which weathered stone block stands over Marco's bones. But Marco Polo's memory is housed in something more substantial than granite. His was the genius of a teller of tales. The *Travels* is his monument. That one slender volume has captured, for kindred spirits through the ages, the lure of unknown lands. His was the grand tour of all times.

So we prepared to follow him. The first leg of our journey, as with Polo, was to be by ship to Israel—Palestine in his time.

But first we had a farewell interview with the mayor of Venice, Signor Giovanni Batista Cianquinto, arranged by the clever Luigi. We were a bit surprised, just before being ushered into his rococo office, to learn that the mayor was a Communist. He greeted us with enthusiasm, and asked a favor. "When Marco Polo left on his great voyage, he carried letters from the Doge to Kublai Khan. So I have written a letter to the mayor of Peiping. Will you deliver it, with my compliments?"

We said yes, with certain mental reservations. News had just come of Peiping's fall to the Reds, and the thought of carrying a document from one Communist leader to another was disquieting. (Dear FBI: We didn't deliver the letter!)

We left almost all our "city" clothes in Venice, for nine-tenths of our travel would be strictly backwoods. I took one black evening dress, hopefully, in case we were asked to some formal function in a far capital. But most of our clothes were strictly GI, for surplus army clothing is more durable than what you can buy in sporting-goods stores, and much cheaper. Our luggage consisted of two barracks bags, one kit bag, two musette bags, the aluminum box containing several hundred rolls of film, eight cases of flash bulbs, three cameras, a tarpaulin, two sleeping bags, and a portable typewriter—a veritable mountain of equipment destined to be lugged by horse, yak, and hand across deserts and over high mountain passes.

There lay ahead, we knew, long and lonely evenings to be passed we knew not where. Every pound of baggage was something to be considered carefully, but space had to be made for a few treasured books. With us went *Alice in Wonderland* (Jean), the poems of A. E. Housman (Franc), an anthology of British verse (Franc) and two volumes of *Marco Polo*—the Everyman pocket version, and a richly bound Frampton edition containing what we believed to be the best study ever made of our predecessor's exact route. In case we should encounter people interested in America, we added a half-dozen issues of *The National Geographic Magazine* containing stories and photographs about our own country. What we didn't know was that we would find people who had never *heard* of America.

# 4

# VENICE TO TABRIZ

THE ABAZZIA, on which we sailed to Tel Aviv, was a pleasant
ship, and her passenger list was primarily composed of Jewish
refugees en route to their new land. Because few of the immigrants could afford to travel first class, and as they were the
people we wanted to know, I shared a second-class cabin with an
aging Polish woman whose arm still bore a tattooed identification number from the Dachau concentration camp. She frequently screamed in her sleep as the horrors of those years possessed her dreams. Franc traveled steerage, sharing a cabin, lined
with triple-tiered bunks, with a young Canadian, two sturdy

Swiss, a French priest, an Austrian merchant, and a London rabbi with an extensive beard and a large tin box in which he carried enough kosher food for the voyage. We were a floating microcosm of the United Nations.

They came from everywhere and every level of society, with nothing in common except their religion, but that seemed enough. The German tailor, the Czech electrician, the pampered White Russian beauty from Shanghai, and the law scholar from Poland sat together on hatch covers, studying maps of Israel, or played deck games in which the scores were shouted in half a dozen languages. At night they organized group entertainment, and danced strange figures, the folk dances of many nations, and listened with tears in their eyes while the oldsters told tragic tales of the hells of Buchenwald and Belsen. Some were eager and some cynical, some desperate and some already disillusioned. They had come together from the four corners of the earth, the hunted and the hopeful, but now, on the deck of the ship, together they reveled in the sense of belonging.

There were two persons on that voyage whom I shall never forget. Both were British by nationality, Jewish by faith. Both were immigrants. There the resemblance ended.

Mrs. Elko Landsberg, in her mid-forties, had operated a beauty parlor in one of those villages in Wales which only a Welshman can pronounce and only a geographer spell. Her two teen-age daughters and her tall son were lean and brown, ready and eager for the hard life they expected to face.

"I have been happy in Wales," she told me, as we sat together on the moonlit deck one quiet night, "but always I have had Israel in my heart. When my husband died I supported the children with the beauty shop. I sent them to school, but every summer they worked with the Land army. In Israel they will have to go into a *kibutz*, so it is good for them that they know about farming. They are prepared.

"I got a good price for my beauty shop. With the money I'll buy new equipment and open a shop of my own in Haifa. My children and I will be separated and that will be hard, but we will be together in our own land. That will make up for hardships."

The other was a former colonel in the British army, with moody dark eyes, distinguished, reserved, traveling first class. He seemed to feel it necessary to explain what he was doing on this ship. "I had a good job with the Middle East branch of a British company when war came in 1939," he told us. "I joined up early, and promotions came quickly, and for the last two years of the war I was a full colonel. I had a lot of men under my command. And responsibility. I suppose I grew during those years. A man couldn't help it.

"When I was demobbed the company asked me to come back to the old job, at the old salary. I just couldn't go back to that level. So I quit, and returned to England to look around. Couldn't seem to find anything that satisfied me.

"Well, my mother was Jewish, and I knew the Middle East. I decided to make the break and come out here. I learned Hebrew, studied the history of Israel. Now here I am, an immigrant." He folded his arms on the rail and looked down at the noisy, uninhibited humanity crowding the steerage deck below. "My trouble," he said, his eyes clouding, "is that I still think of *them*"— he nodded at the mass below—"as *they*."

We had been more than a week at sea when we docked at Tel Aviv. The Israeli consulate in New York had given us a letter to government officials, and we asked them for help in finding an interpreter. They loaned us Arnold Appelbaum, fair, slender, and handsome, and with Arnold came Sylvia. "I hope you don't mind if we both come," explained Arnold, "but I got out of the army only yesterday, and before I return to my law practice we had promised ourselves a belated honeymoon, starting today."

Arnold and Sylvia were Sabras, almost a people within a people. The original Sabra is a cactus plant, tough and dangerous and native to Israel. So are its namesakes. They were born in this land, and perhaps more than anyone else they are responsible for its survival. They formed the hard core of the Israeli Army, and they held the line against the Arabs while the Jews of the world gathered reinforcements. Present-day Israel owes a tremendous debt to them, and Franc said as much to Arnold.

"Maybe so," he smiled. "If we hadn't been here the immigrants wouldn't have had a country to come to. But if it weren't for the immigrants, we wouldn't have a country to look forward to. It works both ways. We need each other."

They took us to Acre, where Marco Polo had spent long months awaiting the election of a new pope, and we walked through the same iron-studded gates that had swung open to welcome the Polo party. We drove through the rocky hills to Jerusalem, and found a city battle-scarred and trigger-happy with tension, divided by the insecure peace between Jew and Arab. I had never visualized the Holy City as a battleground. The debris of war was everywhere. We walked past shell-pocked buildings, sand-bagged pillboxes, and rubble-filled alleys. We were not permitted to cross the cease-fire line. Across a barbed-wire barricade, we gazed at the ruined buildings on the Arab side. They were, we knew, manned by well-concealed fighters of the famous Arab Legion. We were anxious to get a picture of these soldiers.

"The old rabbit-hunting trick might work," Franc thought aloud, while setting up a tripod and mounting a camera. Carefully he focused on the top of a blasted building. Then he readied the cable release in his fingers, threw back his head, and unloosed an unearthly Indian war whoop.

Three turbaned heads instantly popped up on the roof line. I heard the shutter snap. The heads disappeared. We had our picture.

At the cease-fire line on the other side of the city, Franc yielded to the inner hunger of every photographer for "just one more." But this time when he let go with a war whoop, no head appeared. Instead, a rifle cracked and a bullet flattened on the stone wall five feet above our heads. Franc didn't bother to separate camera and tripod. He just picked up the entire assembly and started rapidly toward our car. "Wrong kind of rabbits," he muttered.

At Jerusalem's once luxurious King David Hotel, now bombed and bullet-scarred, we met an old friend from Shanghai, Dr. Jerome Peterson, who had served with UNRRA in China and now worked with a UN emergency relief team among the Arab refugees in Gaza. He spoke glowingly of the Arab people. One anecdote in particular I won't soon forget.

"These Arabs," he said, "they've lost everything—homes, fields, and savings, and they live in squalor in the refugee camps. But they've kept their sense of humor.

"Last week I was watching them make application for special ration cards. Nursing mothers get an extra allotment of milk and fruit, and the tent was crowded with women, most of them carrying the yelling and kicking evidence of their motherhood. But one slender young woman came to the examiner's desk without her baby. The child was ill, she explained.

"In charge was a pompous British doctor. He told her he couldn't issue extra rations without evidence that she was a nursing mother. Didn't faze her a bit. She just unfastened her dress, lifted a plump breast, and squirted a stream of milk straight into the doctor's face. She got the card."

WE EMBARKED for Mersin, the port where Marco Polo first landed in Turkey, in the rusty little Turkish freighter *Neçat*. Neçat means "good luck" in Turkish, and one look at the dilapidated vessel suggested that we might need it. But the purser assured us that the *Neçat* was indeed a lucky ship. "She has sunk twice in the past ten years," he explained, "but both times she was fortunately raised. But don't worry. This is her last voyage. After this trip she's to be broken up for scrap."

Thus reassured, we made our way to our tiny cabin. We had hardly put down our bags when the door burst open, a worried-looking Moorish steward rushed in, lifted the pillow from a bunk, picked up a handful of tiny packages, and rushed out the door. A moment later he dashed back in, stripped back the mattress from the other bunk, extracted a long string of pearls from the springs, and raced out. Ah, the Mysterious East!

We dined in a small saloon on the upper deck with a dozen other passengers, all Turks. We had just seated ourselves when a large gentleman, wearing a rumpled white jacket and blue trousers, entered, walked to our table, and bowed. "Afyet Olsun," he said.

Franc and I looked at each other blankly. My quick-witted spouse decided that Afyet Olsun must be a Turkish dish and the man a steward. "Yes," Franc said, "I think we'll have some."

The newcomer looked confused, and shook his head. "No, no," he said. He put his hand to his breast and bowed slightly. "Afyet Olsun," he repeated.

Franc stood up. "Sorry, should have realized," he murmured to me. "Lots of these ships have Scandinavian captains." Franc stretched out his hand. "Franc Shor," he said. "Glad to meet you, Captain Olsun."

The man's look of confusion deteriorated into consternation. "No!" he said louder. "No! Afyet Olsun!"

By then everyone was listening. A pleasant Turk at the next table rose and came to our rescue. "Excuse me, but I speak English. Permit me to help you. This gentleman is the captain of the *Neçat*. He is wishing you 'Afyet Olsun.' That is Turkish for *bon appétit*."

Our fellow passengers started teaching us Turkish after that, and we taught them the English names of the dishes we could recognize. Only "Captain Olsun" failed to join in the camaraderie. He kept busy listening to the ship's engines, as apprehensive as a physician applying a stethoscope to a damaged heart. Every few minutes the cacophony of the engines would be interrupted by a horrid clashing of gears and clinking of metal. At each crash the captain would leap to his feet and stick his head out of the saloon window. It was not a reassuring performance.

Nor was our concern about the security of the *Neçat* lessened when we docked at Iskenderon, once known as Alexandretta, our first port of call in Turkey. Franc was peering through the porthole when he suddenly shouted at me, "Good lord, look at this!"

I crowded him out of the porthole. The ropes by which we were made fast to the wharf were highways for rats, and they were all moving in one direction. They were leaving the ship.

But the rats were prematurely apprehensive. We did reach

Mersin, a harbor so shallow that it could not even accommodate
a ship of the *Neçat's* modest draft. A launch came alongside,
deep-laden with boxes, bails, baskets, potted plants, plows,
kitchenware, picture frames, and sixty deck passengers ready
to scramble on board. On the other side of the ship a lighter
was unloading freight. Stevedores were streaming aboard to load
bales of cotton and sacks of wheat from other lighters. Whistles
were tooting and men were swearing in Turkish, and we were
caught in this maelstrom of incredible confusion.

As our pearl-smuggling steward had vanished, Franc resorted
to the only infallible international means of communication. He
took a stevedore by one arm and pointed to our luggage. In the
fingers of the outstretched hand was a five-lira note, worth about
two dollars. Almost immediately our luggage was placed in a
rope sling, fragile flash bulbs on the bottom and heavy suitcases
on top, and plummeted into a launch.

It is difficult for a waterfront town to be entirely unattractive,
but Mersin managed it. It was not even picturesque, except to
the nostrils. The streets were dirty and narrow, and the moment
our luggage hit the dock a crowd of ragged porters swarmed
over it, each determined to get one piece, preferably the lightest.
They fought among themselves like jackals, two of them grab-
bing a single bag and trying hard to pull it apart. Franc tried to
stop the brawl, but nobody paid him any attention. We were
saved by the Mersin customs officials. They beat off the struggling porters, spread the contents of all eight bags on the dock
and examined everything as carefully as if they expected to find
diamonds. Satisfied at last, they accepted cigarettes, affixed a
few tags and seals to the empty luggage, and left us to repack
while the shouting porters were attempting to snatch the bags
and suitcases from under our hands.

At dusk we got everything loaded into a donkey cart, ourselves wearily balanced atop the load. Fourteen porters held
out eager hands, each insisting he had carried all eight bags.
Franc handed a five-lira note to the largest and toughest-looking
porter, made a sweeping motion to indicate it was for everyone,
and shouted to the driver to take off in a hurry. As we left, the

porters were in a snarling heap. Underneath was the large man
with the money.

The donkey cart stopped at the Taurus Hotel. The sign said
"*Oteli*," but it was more like a barracks, with five iron beds to
a room. We were too exhausted to look for something better, but
before we could get settled three policemen appeared and politely
indicated that we were to accompany them. In sign language, we
asked where we were going. "*Oteli*," said the ranking policeman.

"But this is an *oteli*," I protested.

The officer clasped his nose between thumb and forefinger in
a standard international gesture. We agreed, and followed to
the Istanbul Palas, apparently the rendezvous of Turkish traveling salesmen and a considerable improvement over the Taurus.
But more important, there we met our benefactor and guide, the
omnipresent and inimitable Yanko Dabanovic.

Yanko was large, plump, and balding, with the pink face of
a forty-five-year-old baby. He appeared at the hotel desk while
we were signing the complicated registration forms, and introduced himself in excellent if somewhat stilted English. He was
a Turk of Yugoslav ancestry, a businessman of Mersin, and he
alone in town spoke English. He was, he said, at our service.
It turned out that he meant just that.

He began by getting us the best room in the hotel. It was bare
and drab and dimly lighted by one dangling, fly-specked bulb,
but it had toilet facilities at a reasonable distance, down a flight
of stairs and at the end of a long hall, and it had only three
beds. It was midnight when we said good night to Yanko and
settled down for needed sleep. I settled down, that is. The bedbugs ambushed Franc. There is something about my husband,
particularly during his well-fed periods, that appeals to everything
that crawls or flies or bites. On the other hand, insects and rodents
rarely nibble on me, and there are times when this situation causes
strain on the marital bond. Franc seems to think that I am in
league with the insect world. That night the bugs chased him
from bed to bed, and sought him out when he tried to trick
them by sleeping inconspicuously on the floor. They completely

ignored me, but Franc didn't. He kept waking me up to inquire how many times I had been bitten. When I said none at all, he would regale me with the number and severity of his wounds. I don't know which of us suffers most on these occasions.

Yanko Dabanovic came to our door early the next morning. Breakfast, he said, was ready in his room. Would we please join him? We were reluctant, fearing to impose, but he insisted. A feast was laid out on a scrubbed wooden table in his bedroom, so different from our conventional bacon and eggs that I jotted down the menu in my diary: cucumbers, goat cheese, dried ripe olives, tomatoes, boiled eggs, yogurt, delicious flat bread, preserves which Yanko proudly stated had been sent by his mother from Istanbul, and tea. While we ate, Yanko discreetly asked what we were doing in Mersin.

Our plan, we explained, was to follow Marco Polo's trail across eastern Turkey, through Erzinjan and Erzurum and past Mt. Ararat, and get into Persia before our visas expired.

Yanko pointed out that such a route was impossible without permission from Ankara, the capital. Ararat, one slope of which lies in Russia, was in a restricted military zone, and barred to foreigners. "To reach Ankara," he said, "you must first go by train from here to Adana. There you will catch the Baghdad-Istanbul Express. You can leave here tomorrow night. I'll attend to the reservations. Just leave everything to me."

We protested, but Yanko had adopted us. He assured us, beaming all the while, that his business—importing and exporting grain—wouldn't suffer if he took a day or two off. For the remainder of the day he insisted on acting as our guide, showing us through the bazaar, accompanying us to lunch and then on a carriage ride through the countryside in the afternoon, even playing host at dinner at his club that night. And always he talked of America and American authors, as he knew them from afar.

"I have learned my English from books," he said. "I do not read novels, but only the works of your great American philosophers, like Dr. Frank Crane and Harry Emerson Fosdick. I have a complete set of the works of Dr. Crane, and I have read every word dozens of times. I try to pattern my life on his teachings."

Neither Franc nor I was familiar with the writings and the philosophy of Dr. Crane, so we maintained a discreet silence and looked impressed. But the following day, when Yanko again insisted that we breakfast in his room, we began to suspect that his interest in us was more than philosophical. That evening, when Yanko drove us to the station in a horse cart, and then insisted on accompanying us to Adana, his attentions began to seem sinister. "I've been worrying about you making your connection in Adana," he explained. "No one in the station there will speak English, and you might have trouble. I'll just ride with you to Adana and be sure you're safely off to Ankara."

That was too much for Franc. I could see him back away, his eyes glinting with doubts. When we had a moment alone—such a moment was hard to find with Yanko around—Franc voiced his suspicions. "No one in the world is this good-hearted," he said. "There is only one explanation, and that we should have guessed long ago. Yanko is with the Turkish Secret Police. His job is to keep track of our movements. And he's certainly doing his job."

I didn't want to believe it. I had become quite fond of big Yanko, with his soft voice and his baby face and his quotations from Dr. Crane. But I had to admit it was the only plausible explanation.

Something of our suspicions seemed to communicate itself to Yanko, and our conversation was awkward and halting during the ride to Adana. He helped us make a reservation for the Baghdad Express, which wasn't to leave until evening, and then Yanko said, "Let's go to a restaurant and have a cup of coffee. Then I shall be delighted to show you Adana."

As we sipped our coffee Franc decided to speak honestly. "Yanko," he said, "you've treated us wonderfully. We'll always be grateful to you, but I'm sorry you've kept up the pretense so long. I'm not a child. I know you're with the Secret Police, and that your job is to keep track of our movements. We don't mind, since we have nothing to hide. But why don't you be open and aboveboard about it?"

I've never seen such a look of absolute hurt as spread over Yanko's round face. His chin quivered. Tears filled his china-blue eyes and one or two rolled down his pink cheeks. How could we have so misjudged him, he asked, his voice breaking. "The philosophy of Dr. Frank Crane teaches Service," he protested, pronouncing the word like a prayer. "Service to others, Service above self. For years I have been hoping that I would meet some Americans so that I could show them that I too understand Dr. Crane, and put Service above self. And you think me only a police spy!"

We were ashamed and embarrassed by our cynicism, and we apologized. Yanko wiped his eyes and patted our shoulders and told us to forget it. Then, having fully recovered his garrulous high spirits, he showed us Adana, which for centuries had been a crossroads for travel between Constantinople and the Syrian coast, and through which camel caravans still pass on occasion. During World War II it was a secret American air base, and its strategic importance has not dwindled. The air base at Adana now supports the port of Iskenderun, and the seaway to the British stronghold of Cyprus. If war came, Adana, known to but few Americans, would be of great use to the Western cause.

It is difficult to think of anything more modern than a cross-bow when you see Adana. *Shish-kebab* and yogurt were hawked on the streets, like Good Humors at home. Licorice water was sold from mobile brass casks, and men sipped *arrak* in shady cafés. Yanko took us through a cool city park where cement Venuses, elks and cherubs, all badly done, lined the walks. But nearby, in a small museum, were magnificent examples of Greek sarcophagi, weathered by two thousand years, that would be coveted by New York's Metropolitan Museum.

Yanko showed us a bridge of many arches, spanning the wide Yenice River. "It is believed," he said, "that after Marco Polo landed in Mersin he came this way and passed across this bridge. I believe this too, because Adana was the natural route to the East. If he came this way he must have crossed here."

I recalled Marco Polo's first impressions of the Turkomans.

Franc stands against a western section of the Great Wall in the vicinity of Yumen. Eroded sections stretch for miles beside the road to Lanchow. Walls were constructed by ramming mud and clay into wooden forms and packing it down.

In Lanchow, we saw this bottom-side view of a Yellow River raft made of inflated pigskins, topped with a light bamboo frame. The rafts are very light and easily carried back upriver.

Here I am examining the will of Marco Polo in the Marciana Library in Venice. Numerous early editions of the *Travels* are piled on the table.

We test the mineral spring in Erzinjan, Turkey, mentioned by Marco Polo. This little-used spring is several miles outside the present town of Erzinjan, and the sulfurous waters are not enticing.

"A rude people," he wrote, "and dull of intellect." Poor Marco, he had no Yanko following the teachings of Dr. Frank Crane for a friend and guide.


THE BAGHDAD EXPRESS to Ankara was well appointed, if you like green plush, and fast as any train in France. At the station in Ankara I pushed my way through a door marked *Kudinlara,* which is Turkish for "ladies," and came out again in a flustered hurry. The "ladies" I found inside were Kurds from the hills, and it was obvious that they had never seen toilet facilities before and had no idea of the purpose of the fixtures. It was a noisome shambles.

Ankara, like Canberra in Australia and even our Washington, is an artificial capital, constructed purposely as a capital city. It is the personal creation of Mustafa Kemal Ataturk, the late "father of the Turks," one of the great dynamic leaders of our time. It is a modern city of wide boulevards and stone buildings. Its hotels serve fine food and its night clubs are as gay as any in Europe. The farther east we traveled, the more we marveled in retrospect at modern Ankara.

Ataturk set Ankara alongside the ancient city of Angora, almost in the center of the Anatolian Plateau, for two reasons. The ancient capital Constantinople, now Istanbul, he considered a "foreign" city, for it was crowded with Armenians, Greeks, and Europeans. Secondly, he wanted a capital defended by space. For many years no motor roads ran into Ankara. Ataturk wanted to make it difficult for a potential enemy—meaning Russia—to reach the capital.

It was Ataturk who emancipated Turkish women, made it unlawful for them to veil their faces and for men to wear the fez. He abolished the harem, and decreed equal civil rights. Today many women hold government positions, teach in the universities, and are lawyers and doctors. A Turkish woman was head of the Associated Press bureau in Istanbul. How amazing it is to realize that many of the middle-aged women who have attained eminence were born in harems! In one generation, Ataturk's dynamic will completely changed a nation. Although Ataturk was an all-powerful and often ruthless dictator, he ordered that at the end of a growing-up period there should be free elections, which have taken place.

I remember Ankara's Park Oteli chiefly for the touring English ballet troupe staying there. Slender girls and lithe young men filled the bar where we repaired each evening for a screwdriver—a noxious combination of orange juice and vodka which was born in Ankara and has since migrated to America.

A group of the dancers occupied a table next to ours each night, and Franc spent entirely too much time regarding a youthful strawberry blonde. I thought her a spindly creature with a definitely sallow complexion.

"I can't understand," I told him one evening, "how such an unattractive girl could have the nerve to try to make a living as an entertainer."

The hotel clerk told us that the troupe was performing at the Ankara Opera House the following evening. We both love ballet, but we hesitated, fearing that the type of company which would be touring the Middle East might be something less than brilliant.

Franc, after a couple of screwdrivers, decided to face the problem squarely. He approached his strawberry blonde, with whom we had developed a smiling acquaintance, and introduced himself.

"Forgive a frank question," he ventured, "but will your performance here be classic ballet or simply—uh—folk and tap dancing?"

The blonde smiled graciously. "I think you'll find it fair enough ballet," she said. "Some of our people are quite good. This"—she introduced a dark and handsome young man—"is Michael Soames. This is Alexander Grant. My name is Moira Shearer."

Tongue-tied with embarrassment, we met the rest of the Sadler's Wells company.

At the ballet I learned that what we consider the typical

Turkish harem dress—little boleros and transparent baggy
trousers fastened at the ankles—isn't originally Turkish at all
but was imported from the Parisian stage. In the nineteenth
century a Turkish sultan, visiting Paris, attended a musical
show. The chorus wore this costume in one number, and the
girls were so fetching to the sultan's eyes that he offered to buy
the entire chorus line for his harem. No sale. So he bought the
costumes instead, and brought them back to Constantinople
for his own girls.

In ANKARA the government quickly granted our request to pass
through the restricted zone near Mt. Ararat. Further, we received
the help accorded all foreign correspondents in Turkey, including, for $3.50 a month, a pass good on every railroad in Turkey
and lowered rates for air travel.

From Ankara, we rode a train for three days on a winding
route eastward. Our sleeping car was of 1900 vintage, but the
car steward compensated by keeping a pot of tea on boil for us,
and explaining in halting English the rugged land through which
we chugged. Steadily the terrain rose, the mountains on either
side grew taller and steeper, and the engine puffed and labored
up the grades, slower and slower. The Turkish engines have
a wonderful whistle that cries *whoopee, whoopee,* in sheer delight,
and the engineers apparently enjoyed the sound too. They pulled
the cord for every cow and curve.

There was no dining car. On station platforms in hill towns
with unpronounceable names, we ate *kebab* and *pilaf* and
yogurt, flat bread, and meat patties with chopped green onion.

We were headed for Erzurum, heart of the military zone
where Turkey faces the Soviet Union across a border that is a
no-man's land, brooding and dangerous. Erzurum was the end
of the line. There the steel tie with European civilization ended.
Indeed, when I think back on it, after we left Ankara, each
thousand miles through Turkey, Iran and Afghanistan seemed
to carry us backward in time a hundred years.

On the way to Erzurum, we made the mistake of stopping at

Erzinjan, in Turkish Armenia. Marco Polo had written of this town: "It possesses the handsomest and most excellent baths of warm water, issuing from the earth, that are anywhere to be found." This sounded irresistible to such as we, grimy with cinders and smoke. Besides, if we didn't bathe in Marco Polo's warm springs, we might not have a chance again for hundreds of miles. But Erzinjan, we discovered, had changed.

At three A.M., three sleepy, grumbling porters stumbled down the tracks with our bags through the darkened, silent town. At the third *oteli* we tried, a tubercular night clerk agreed to let us sleep in the restaurant. Franc spread his sleeping bag on the floor and I made myself reasonably comfortable on three straight chairs lined together. We had just fallen asleep when the clerk shook Franc awake and announced that a room had been vacated for us. We were shocked to see a cowed and sleepy Turkish family being herded out the door. We protested that we were delightfully comfortable where we were but the clerk wouldn't listen. He had cleared a room for us and in it we would sleep. All our conversation was conducted in sign language, charades to an unresponsive audience. To end further argument, the clerk hammered the hotel door shut with a long nail. No one else could get in, and we couldn't get out. In our littered and filthy room, the beds smelled so strongly of feet and garlic that we slept on the floor fully dressed.

At nine the next morning we were having tea in the restaurant when the police arrived. No stranger enters a Turkish town without coming under surveillance. An officer in wrinkled uniform and a detective in a straw hat examined our passports, pretending to read them, and seemed impressed by our credentials from Ankara. We filled out the usual forms, and the detective, to whom we referred as Straw Hat Bey (Bey being the title for Mr. in Turkish), adhered himself to us and never let us out of his sight.

Our first encounters with the Secret Police were annoying to a couple of people brought up in a land where such things didn't occur, but eventually we learned to take advantage of their curiosity. We would leave the train or bus, pile our luggage in a neat mound in the center of the station platform, and stand beside it looking as if we didn't care if we ever left. Within a few minutes the intelligence agents would tire of waiting for us to make the first move, and take matters into their own hands. They would approach, examine our passports and permits, and load our luggage into a droshky. We had trouble getting hotel rooms, but they never did. Invariably they would escort us to the best hostelry in town, fill out the endless registration forms, wait to assure themselves that we stayed where we had been put, and arrange for us to be awakened in time to catch eastbound transportation. It was an arrangement which pleased everyone; they knew exactly where we were at all times, and we were always sure of a place to stay. It was like being met by a Thomas Cook man at every stop. All they lacked were caps lettered "Secret Police."

I asked Straw Hat Bey whether there was anybody in town who spoke English, at which point he suddenly remembered something. He took a note for us from his pocket. "Dear Friend," it read, "this hotel is bad. There is a fine hotel. We better go there, please." At the "fine hotel," which was new and clean, we met the only man in town who spoke English, the author of the note, the town doctor. Apparently he was attending to our health by guiding us to a cleaner bed and board.

Many of the women of Erzinjan wore veils, despite that edict of Ataturk's which prohibited them from covering their faces. In the remote hill villages this edict was impossible to enforce; these were tribal women come to this city of eleven thousand to sell produce on bazaar day. I also noticed that most of the children were chewing bubble gum.

We asked Straw Hat Bey about Marco Polo's hot springs and he inquired of others, but nobody understood. I made motions like a spring gushing from the earth, and that worked. There was such a spring, but it was ten kilometers from town and no one bothered to go there any more.

We took Erzinjan's lone taxi over a frightful path, often blocked by herds of sheep, mules and cattle. Inside a dilapidated mud building was a twenty-by-twenty-foot pool filled with bubbling warm water. Dutifully and dubiously we dipped our feet in the murky, sulfurous water. Either Marco Polo had very little bathing experience, or the years had dealt harshly with his "handsome baths."

The region north of Erzurum was important to us for there Marco Polo recorded for the first time the use of petroleum for fuel. "To the north lies Zorzonia" (now the Soviet Republic of Georgia), he wrote, "near the confines of which there is a fountain of oil which discharges so great a quantity as to provide loading for many camels. The use made of it is not for the purpose of food, but as an unguent for the cure of cutaneous distempers in men and cattle, as well as other complaints; and it is also good for burning. In the neighboring country (now Iran) no other is used in their lamps, and people come from distant parts to procure it." They still do.

Probably this fountain of oil bubbled from the earth near what is now the great Soviet oil port of Baku, on the Caspian in Soviet Azerbaijan. It is doubtful that Polo saw this sight personally, for his travels led him east instead of north, and he circled south of Mt. Ararat on the identical route we were to take.

At Erzurum a successor to Straw Hat Bey met us at the station, notified in advance of our coming. This Secret Police officer, whose headgear won him the title of Straw Hat Bey II, was wonderfully helpful, racing back and forth with the papers and credentials that would allow us to stay the night in his city, and booking our passage on the bus to the Iranian frontier.

Unfortunately the bus company would not accept either dollars or traveler's checks but demanded Turkish lira. After much abortive sign language, the bus company produced a young man who spoke English, one Erol Osman, returning to Istanbul with his father, a Turkish veterinarian, from six years in Afghanistan. He not only cashed our checks but gave us some disturbing information about the difficulties of getting to Tabriz, in Iran. There wasn't any regular bus service from the border to Tabriz, 350 kilometers inside the Persian province of Azerbaijan, and he seemed dubious about our getting there at all. When we told him we had no visa for Afghanistan but expected to pick one up in Tehran, he was both astonished and pessimistic.

The bus didn't leave until nine A.M., but there was a loud knocking on our door at seven. It was Honest Erol. He feared that he had not given us the proper exchange for our checks, and pressed more money on us. "Also I wish you the good luck," he said. "Of it you will need."

Our bus was an old-fashioned, square-cut jalopy of uncertain make, and twenty-two of us were packed inside, including those who sat on stools in the aisles. Our fellow passengers included a Turkish colonel traveling with his wife, a self-conscious beauty with eyelashes an inch long, eyes shadowed with kohl, and a high pompadour hair-do. She couldn't keep her fingers off her elaborate curls, and when the bus started and the wind ruffled her precious hair-do, she ordered all the windows closed. Thereafter, we stifled.

A Turkish major sitting nearby kept smiling at us, and at length he spoke, in perfectly accented English. "How do you do," he said. "You are welcome. Please sit down."

We were already sitting down, but I overlooked this. "It's wonderful to meet someone who speaks English," I said. "Do you know how long it takes to reach the border?"

"It is a very nice day," he replied. "I hope you are comfortable."

"Quite comfortable," I said. "But how long does it take to reach the border?"

"I hope you will stay for dinner," he replied brightly. "We are having roast beef and potatoes."

"We'd be delighted," I said, realizing that the conversation had somehow gotten out of hand. "I haven't had roast beef in a long time. But, by the way, when do we get to the border?"

There was a long, embarrassing silence. Then, in awkward, broken English the major said: "My English no more. I study on linguaphone. First lesson called Mr. Brown at home. Have used all first lesson words. Good-by, please."

As we had exhausted the communications facilities on that bus, we would have to depend on our eyes alone to absorb the land east of Erzurum. Roman towers squatted on the hills, for this junction of Russia, Turkey, and Persia has long been of strategic importance. The Caesars had defended it against barbarians from the north, and Alexander's legions had swept across it on their drive to India. And now, the United States was committed to its defense against the Soviet Union. Every few miles we passed Turkish army camps where we caught glimpses of American officers of the Military Advisory Group, and waved to them happily. For some reason they didn't recognize the dusty couple on the back seat of that provincial bus as fellow countrymen. We saw tanks and artillery, obstacle courses for infantry training, and soccer fields, for soccer is the baseball of Turkey.

Spring was the perfect time to cross high Anatolia. Patches of snow still clung to the highest peaks and the rolling upland pastures were an almost electric green. The valleys were carpeted with flowers, and farmers were plowing with teams of twelve animals, usually ten cows and two buffaloes. Occasionally, we saw a horse and a scrawny camel hitched together in an unlikely team.

In small villages, we were served tasty hot meals in the local restaurants. Since we could never understand what the waiter said was on the *plat du jour,* he'd invariably lead me by the hand into the kitchen, lift the lids off the bubbling pots, and allow me to taste the dish, or sniff. Then I'd point out what appealed to me. One day, when I had acquired a few words, I said I wanted only "vegetables." The waiter brought me a steaming bowl containing boiled potatoes, plums, apricots, green beans, and whole garlic. After that I reverted to my custom of going into the kitchen. Usually there were lamb stews, eggplant in oil, and yogurt topped almost every dish. Piles of fresh lettuce were served for dessert, and always there was coffee, thick as mud and heavily sweetened.

One noon we came to the village and castle of Pasinter, which Marco Polo called Paipurth and mentioned because of its rich silver mine. But Pasinter today is a village in ruins, the mine long since exhausted. At lunch, after Franc paid the bill, an old man in rags, who had been watching us, came to our table and held out a clawlike hand. He was not begging. In the hand was a small, perfect Roman piece of silver, perhaps fifteen hundred years old. Franc fished a half dollar out of his pocket and they swapped, each happy with his new acquisition.

That afternoon the road changed from gravel to cobbles, and the bus really began to shake us around. Ahead was an oval green mountain. Slowly we snaked up its side, and when we reached the top the grandeur of Ararat, 16,945 feet high and wearing a glistening cape of snow, greeted us. Exclamations of delight were uttered in four languages. We were not to lose sight of the mighty mountain for three days. The peak of Ararat is in Turkey, the north slope in Russia, and at that time an American expedition was being formed to seek the remains of Noah's Ark. Marco Polo had recorded the story when he spoke of Ararat as "an exceedingly large and high mountain, upon which, it is said, the ark of Noah rested." Noah really had a sense of the dramatic if he moored his boat up there. The Russians were protesting violently, saying that the climbers were nothing but high-altitude spies. And the Turks weren't enthusiastic about the expedition either, predicting that the Americans would be bitten by vipers or eaten by bears, and insisting that the ark really landed on a mountain in Armenia (a Mohammedan belief).

That day we made only a hundred miles in eight hours and at nightfall came to the village of Karaköse, an isolated cluster of mud-and-stone huts hiding in a lush and lovely valley. We came down into the valley just at dusk, into a scene straight out of the Bible. The rich meadows were strewn with wild flowers, and nomadic Kurdish tribes had pitched their low black goat-hair tents on the pasture land. Large herds of sheep and goats were grazing peacefully, tended by bearded shepherds with long crooks. Camel trains shuffled across the low hills. Donkeys were tethered near the tents, and nomads in brightly colored costumes sat around campfires. We rolled through the narrow, dusty streets of the ancient village as incongruous as a bus in the Old Testament. And then, as we pulled to a halt in front of the village inn, our attention was attracted by a loudspeaker fixed over the front door. From it came a shrill twangy voice, shattering my vision of the Biblical past: "Remember the Red River Valley, and the cowboy who loved you so true."

America, I am sure, has done much for Turkey. We have sent the Turks machinery and farm equipment and arms and technicians. But some things might better be kept at home.

The next morning our bus rattled past two small boys dragging the biggest bird I had ever seen in my life. It was very dead and the size of an ostrich, but unlike an ostrich it appeared airworthy. I knew it wasn't an eagle or a buzzard. "What kind of bird is that?" I asked Franc.

"Why, that's a roc," Franc said, as casually as if naming a meadow lark or a sparrow.

"I thought rocs were mythical."

"Then we have just seen a large, solid, dead myth," said Franc. "That was a roc, all right."

How could I argue with him? I had never seen a roc, nor had I ever met anyone who had seen a roc. But, after all, we were near the land of Sinbad the Sailor. So at this point in my travels I jotted down "roc?" in my diary.

At Dogubayazit, where we lunched with the commandant of the last army garrison in Turkey, the bus had dropped everyone except an elderly Iranian, Franc, and me. At mid-afternoon we three came to the border post, a square compound with courtyard divided by a low concrete wall. The Turkish flag flew on our side, the Iranian on the other. The Turkish side was neat and orderly, the Iranian side was a deserted, windowless mass of rubble. We handed over our papers to the Turkish customs and immigration authorities, and while waiting were served chocolate and crème de menthe with great ceremony, the office windows framing the magnificence of Ararat. Instead of prowling around in our luggage, the Turkish customs officers allowed themselves to be photographed with the Polaroid camera. On parting they gravely shook our hands, speaking words which we couldn't translate, except as friendship from a stranger which surmounts the formidable barrier of language. Turkey had been kind to us; leaving was like abandoning a safe port for a strange sea.

We crossed the courtyard to the Iranian side, staggering under the weight of our baggage, but we couldn't find any Iranians. We had to find some official, and quickly. Our Iranian visas were due to expire the next day. Struck by the singular informality of it all, we walked back to the Turkish side, leaving our luggage in Iran. The customs officials explained that the Persians sometimes didn't report at the border for work, but found it more convenient to perform their duties in the next village down the road, Maku, where diversions were to be found. There were two ways to get to the village. One was to walk the eight miles, and the other was to wait. At odd intervals, possibly today, an Iranian truck visited the border post.

Fortunately, the truck had been ordered to pick up the elderly, wizened Persian trader who had accompanied us all the way from Erzurum. The truck driver, to our great relief, had served eight years in the British army in Iraq and Palestine and greeted us in colloquial English. Certainly, he said, he would ride us to town, and he helped load our bags. These hospitable Persians, we thought . . . but that was before we met the governor of Maku.

Maku was a dismal place where half the inhabitants lived in caves burrowed into the base of a towering sandstone cliff and the rest inhabited shacks and mud huts surrounded by a semicircular wall of boulders and hewn stones. [Our truck driver stopped en route at the one-room customs house, where surprisingly we were cleared without incident.] There was no hotel in Maku, but we found shelter in the back room of a combination teashop and gambling house. I was exhausted, and my arms ached from carrying our bags, but the proprietor refused to let us sleep until we had been inspected by the police. The sympathetic truck driver took us to the police station, but the police, like the border officials, were not at home.

Back we went to the teahouse. The furnishings in our room consisted of two broken iron beds, with springs like sagging barbed wire, and no mattresses. Since the beds tilted crazily, we slept under them. It seemed to me that I had slept *under* more beds than on them. Franc was badly bitten by lice, and it was probably in Maku that he contracted the relapsing fever—similar to Rocky Mountain spotted fever—that was to threaten his life months later.

The armed local police greeted us next morning like long-sought bank robbers. Instead of taking us directly to the police station, they paraded us through the bazaar and then down the main street, showing off their catch. The ragged populace hardly seemed friendly, although I'm sure they didn't know whether we were Americans, British, or Russians, or whether we were held for smuggling, spying, or murder. We were ushered into the police station and ordered to sit on a bench. We sat there for an hour.

The governor arrived, wearing dirty striped pajamas that billowed around his middle and sagged in the rear. His unshaven, unwashed face oozed grease and looked as if it had just been raised from the soup. His lips were puffed and his mouth slack. When he sneered at us, which was often, you could see broken yellow teeth. We rose when His Excellency entered. He beckoned us into his office, and motioned us to another bench. Our passports fascinated him and he gazed at them frowning, his lips moving as if he were reading. But I noticed that he held one upside down. Then he tossed them into a basket on his desk.

Franc and I tried every language in which we had a working vocabulary. He didn't know any of them. He showed his contempt by an elaborate play at being busy, dictating letters, yelling into the telephone, ordering his subordinates in and out, drinking tea, and spitting on the floor.

The governor kept us on that backless bench for three hours before he condescended to send for an interpreter. He spoke sharply to the interpreter, in Persian.

"The governor wants to know why you are here, and where you are going?" the interpreter said.

"We are American journalists, following the route of Marco Polo from Venice to China," Franc replied quietly. "We are going next to Tehran."

"The governor does not recall any American named Marco Polo coming this way," said the interpreter, "nor does he see

why you should be following him. In any event, to pass through
Azerbaijan you must have a Red card. Where is it?"

"What's a Red card?" Franc asked.

"A special pass for travel in Azerbaijan."

"I didn't know we needed one," said Franc. "We have passports, and valid Iranian visas. Perhaps the governor will issue us
a Red card."

"Impossible. They can only be issued in Tehran."

"Well, then we'll go to Tehran to get one."

"Oh, no. You cannot go to Tehran without a Red card."

I thought wistfully of my copy of *Alice in Wonderland*. There
was something very familiar about this conversation. I saw that
Franc was near the point of explosion. "Perhaps we should return to Turkey," I suggested, "and cable Tehran for a Red card?"

The interpreter smiled. He knew the answer to that one without prompting by the governor. "Ah, but you cannot go back to
Turkey without an exit visa, and you cannot obtain an exit visa
without a Red card."

Franc looked up at the picture of the Shah over the governor's
desk. I could see the wheels turning behind the expressionless
face. Franc is a poker player of no mean skill and he sensed the
moment for a bluff.

"This is all most embarrassing," he said quietly, as if to himself. "We had planned to visit His Majesty in Tehran. In three
days we have an appointment for an audience with the Shah.
Now we will be late."

The governor looked startled, then contemplative. His eyes
ran over our dusty, travel-worn clothes. The familiar sneer returned to his unpleasant features. He snapped at the interpreter.

"His Excellency says you do not appear to him to be the sort of
people who would be granted audience with the Shah-in-Shah,"
said the translator, obviously embarrassed. "But since your lack
of papers makes it impossible to return you to Turkey, and since
he does not want people of your type in Maku, he will let you
proceed to Tehran."

He paused a moment.

"He also says," the interpreter continued reluctantly, "that in his opinion you are likely to spend much more time in jail in Tehran than in His Majesty's palace."

The interpreter helped us buy bus tickets for the next town, Khoi. After paying the fare, we had only five tomans (about one dollar) remaining in Iranian currency, an alarming state of affairs since exchange facilities were nonexistent, and we doubted that our credit would be much good in Azerbaijan.

The small green bus was an antique crate, with dirty windows, mounted on a Chevrolet station-wagon chassis. A picture of our —uh, acquaintance, let us say—the Shah was nailed over the windshield, where the rear-vision mirror should have been, and the interior was tastefully decorated with dusty artificial flowers, small bells that tinkled at every bounce, pictures of Oriental dancing girls, and Moslem amulets, mostly hands of Fatima.

The road to Khoi twisted under steep cliffs, offering glimpses of Kurdish tribesmen, indistinguishable from those on the Turkish side of the frontier, camped beside the streams. Every five miles the bus was stopped by soldiers, for we were in a strategic area only a few miles from the Russian border. Over and over we explained about the Red card, and our lack thereof. Fortunately, our little Persian trader was still with us, and he helped with our answers. The soldiers always tried to telephone back to Maku, or ahead to Khoi, to ask about us and buck the responsibility for our passage to higher authority. Luckily they never could get a connection, so they passed us along. Always we had to fill out forms before the bus could proceed. It was necessary to write our names, our birthdays, and the first names of our fathers. As we have the same birthday and our fathers have the same first name, the confusion was endless. Some of the soldiers thought we were acting smart, others thought we misunderstood, and a few believed we were twins. Our fathers' names, George Bowie and George Shor, and our birthday, March 24, can now be found on police blotters from one end of Azerbaijan to the other.

Had we known the fierce reputation of Khoi, we would not have been so relieved to leave Maku. For foreigners, Khoi is the most dangerous town in Azerbaijan. Religious fanaticism bubbles just beneath the surface and occasionally erupts in bloody display. A thousand Persian Christians were massacred in Khoi some years before our visit, and an American consular official was murdered there quite recently. The people of Khoi hate Christians and they hate foreigners. We qualified on both counts.

We jounced into the walled town just in time; the bus sighed and expired in front of the inn. Franc was trying to explain our lack of negotiable currency to the manager when a well-dressed man, a journalist from Tabriz, appeared as if from a lamp to come to our aid. He listened to our hopeless linguistic efforts, and then, in excellent French, said he would be glad to lend us whatever number of tomans we needed to reach Tabriz, the capital of the province.

"How will we repay you?" Franc asked.

"Just deposit it to my account in Tabriz," he said. He wrote down the name of the bank and the account number. His amazing generosity to absolute strangers, and the kindness of the Persian trader, more than counterbalanced the rudeness of the petty officials at Maku.

In the late afternoon we strolled around Khoi, noticing that guards had been placed in front of the inn, but never guessing that they were there for our protection against possible mob violence. Nor did we know that we were followed by secret police, for the same reason. We were only aware that the people were not in the least friendly.

Franc was carrying his Rollei, and when he saw a slim blue minaret, with a mother stork feeding her two babies in a nest balanced on top, he did what anyone else with camera in hand would have done—he snapped a picture. For this heinous crime, the commandant of the local garrison was waiting when we returned to the hotel. He was a most polite gentleman who looked like a small, thin edition of Eric von Stroheim, including the monocle. He spoke French, German, and Turkish—about ten words of each. We were in a restricted military zone, he said, and we had been making photographs. It was necessary to confiscate the camera. It would be returned to us after the pictures were developed.

"How long will that take?" Franc asked.

"Two days, perhaps three," the commandant said. Who could tell? Would we come with him, please? We went—to the jail.

There, I tried to explain to him that all Franc had photographed was a mother stork feeding its young on top of a minaret. I told him that we didn't have storks or minarets in our country, and that the picture would be of interest to Americans. I spoke in mixed French and English and he didn't understand a word. I didn't know the word for stork in *any* language he understood. The more I talked, the more it sounded as if we had been photographing all the tanks and guns in Asia.

Finally, Franc took over in sign language. We indulged in a game of charades we wanted desperately to win. It was ridiculous that our trip around the world should be delayed by a mother stork. First, Franc made motions with both hands outlining a minaret (I am sure the commandant thought he was describing a willowy woman with a large bosom), and finally the commandant caught on, pointing to a minaret near the police station. We enthusiastically nodded our heads. Franc made the imaginary minaret again, and pointed to the top of it. Then my big husband flapped his arms like a large stork landing in the imaginary nest. The officer nodded wisely. Franc made a scissors motion with two fingers, like bird babies stretching their beaks for food. Then he pecked at the scissors with his left hand, like the mother stork feeding them. Always the perfectionist, he again held up two fingers, repeated the scissors movement of the fingers, clearly showing that the mother stork on the minaret was feeding two babies.

Suddenly the commandant understood the whole scene, and we were all babbling and laughing and flapping our arms like mother storks. Another crisis was past. The commandant escorted us back to the hotel, and as we went inside he plucked a lovely Persian rose and handed it not to me, but to Franc. First prize, I guess.

The bus was supposed to leave at seven the next morning. When our luggage was carried to the front door, we noticed dour-looking men gathering in groups outside the hotel. We sensed our danger. The gathering of a mob is not peculiar to the province of Azerbaijan, nor to Persia.

Our journalist friend arrived, a little out of breath, and suggested politely that it would be nice if we would take a carriage ride with him *outside* the town. The bus, he assured us, would not leave until eleven. It would not only be a pleasant trip, he said, but a safe one. As a matter of fact, he grew quite firm and insisted that we leave immediately, and by the rear entrance.

The carriage was a Russian type droshky and the tour worth while, not only as health insurance but for the ruins. We saw remnants of city walls, abandoned caravansaries, and a half dome of a mosque. We returned just in time to catch the bus and a glimpse of soldiers intently watching a sullen crowd. The bus was strung with good-luck beads, along with other knickknacks and charms, and we hoped these covered Christians as well as Moslems. Not until we were well out of Khoi did we feel safe.

We stopped for the night at a village inn where we inspired no international incident until the following morning when the proprietor figured up the bill, on an abacus, for our two cots and a breakfast of tea and black bread. "Eight tomans," he said.

Franc glanced at the abacus. He hadn't spent all those years in China for nothing. "I believe," he said, "that your abacus reads three tomans, plus twenty-five reals."

"You know nothing of mathematics," the proprietor screamed. "Eight tomans. Pay!"

Franc called in our bearded driver, who spoke French, as a referee. The driver looked at the abacus. Franc was correct, he said. Three tomans and twenty-five reals.

The proprietor, caught, was outraged. His face grew red and he puffed up like an adder. He called upon Allah to witness that he was being cheated by a Christian dog. He screamed and cried out for vengeance. It was quite a performance. Rather than bring another mob down upon us, Franc settled for four tomans. When we left, the proprietor was staring down at his abacus in bewilderment and disgust, as if it had betrayed him.

Of Azerbaijan, Marco Polo wrote, "The inhabitants are treacherous and unprincipled. According to their doctrine, whatever is stolen or plundered from others of a different faith, is properly taken, and the theft is no crime."

ON OUR FOURTH DAY of travel from the Turkish border we suddenly left the eroded, dusty hills and entered a fertile plain. The cobbled road gave way to smooth city streets, and we were in Iran's second largest city, Tabriz, a city of more than 200,000, and the capital of Azerbaijan.

Marco Polo called Tabriz "a large and very noble city," and spoke of its commerce in silk and cloth-of-gold, and its "precious stones and pearls in abundance," which made me eager to see the bazaars. He also spoke of the "delightful gardens, producing the finest fruits," and indeed Tabriz seemed to have changed little, for each courtyard was a miniature oasis, and everywhere the city was fragrant with flower gardens and orchards. Baskets of rose petals were sold on the street corners. "The people of Tabriz like good odors," our driver explained. "They scatter petals around the rooms of their houses, and on elegant moonlight picnics guests are seated on piles of rose petals instead of cushions."

Next to our hotel was a wonderful Turkish bath, where we were shown into separate cubicles. Boiling water was splashed from huge caldrons onto hot rocks, and we steamed for an hour, and soaped and scrubbed and rinsed. Then we lay, wrapped in long towels, on wooden benches while tea was served. Afterward, feeling clean and relaxed in a cotton dress, I went for a stroll with Franc. But very soon I grew acutely uncomfortable. Everyone was staring at us. I realized, finally, that I was walking with my arm through Franc's, while all the other women were walking demurely a step behind their men. I disengaged myself and thereafter walked at a respectful distance behind Franc. My lord and master made much of the situation, imagining himself an Oriental potentate followed by a minor member of his harem.

At the American consulate the vice-consul in charge was astonished that we should be there. Travelers had to have special

permits even to come to Tabriz from Tehran, and it was unheard of that we should have crossed from Turkey. Even the consul had been denied permission to visit Maku. How had we
done it? Through a sound knowledge of poker and charades, we
answered. A little bluff and a lot of sign language.

We wandered through the covered bazaars, and found no pearls
or abundance of jewels, but in the alley of the moneylenders we
did manage to change traveler's checks for tomans, fifty of which
we left at the consulate to repay the trusting editor who had
staked us in Khoi. Recalling that the Three Wise Men had come
from the Tabriz area, Franc asked the vice-consul whether there
were any Persian Jews in Tabriz.

"Not any more," said the vice-consul. "There used to be some
Jewish merchants here, but they couldn't compete with the
shrewd Tabrizi traders."

What I remember best about Tabriz was the caviar—wonderful
Caspian caviar at two dollars a pound. We indulged at every
meal, spreading it like peanut butter on slices of dark bread. It
was especially good with light Persian vodka. But the American
influence was apparent (although few Americans ever saw the
city) in the bazaars where you could buy Baker's cocoa, Calumet
baking powder, Kraft cheese, and Pet milk. The local movie
house was showing "The Black Dragon," a ten-year-old thriller
in twelve episodes, and the three-piece hotel orchestra's favorite
piece was "Joseph, Joseph, Won't You Make Your Mind Up?"

On our second day in Tabriz we had a brief and strange encounter with a man, dressed in a neat business suit, who stopped
us in the street. "Americans?" he inquired.

"Yes," we said.

"We love you."

"Why?" I asked.

"I don't know," the man said. "We just do." And he walked
away.

IT WAS A HOT and dusty two-day trip from Tabriz to Tehran by
bus. This particular vehicle was not only decorated with the ex-

pected religious charms and blue beads but with celluloid birds
in cages and pictures of Hollywood starlets. These long-legged
ladies in bathing suits and high heels indicated that we were approaching an oasis of modern civilization. Despite the assur-
ances of the consulate at Tabriz that we would have no further
trouble on the road to Tehran, we were stopped at a police post
fifteen minutes out of Tabriz, found to be without Red cards,
and the bus was turned around and we were ordered back to the
city.

At the central police station (we were becoming *very* familiar
with the drab interiors of Azerbaijan police stations) the colonel
commanding the Tabriz garrison spoke good German, so for
once Franc could follow the conversation. The colonel said it
was remarkable that we were not rotting in jail in Maku. We
readily agreed. Ordinarily, he said, travelers without Red cards
were held in Maku for three weeks or a month. It took that long
for a Red card to be issued in Tehran. He was polite enough to
us, but we had a feeling that his subordinates back up the line
were going to catch hell for passing the Shors along to Tabriz.
He was the ranking officer in the province, and would have to
submit a full account to the capital of our unprecedented trip.
However, he told us with a weary resignation, since we had already passed completely through the restricted military zone, he
was forced to give us safe conduct to Tehran. There was no way
he could send us back to Maku without a Red card!

Back aboard the bus we apologized to our fellow passengers
for the delay. They were all sympathetic, and seemed genuinely
relieved that we had not been jailed. They pressed food on us
—cookies and raisins and cherries. A fakir smiled and nodded his
black-tasseled turban in approval. An old lady in black veil came
back to my seat, patted me on the shoulder and made clucking
noises. It was hot, and a thick cloud of red dust followed us,
walling us in whenever we slowed or stopped. I didn't mind. We
would soon be beyond the borders of suspicious Azerbaijan, and
into a more hospitable part of Persia.

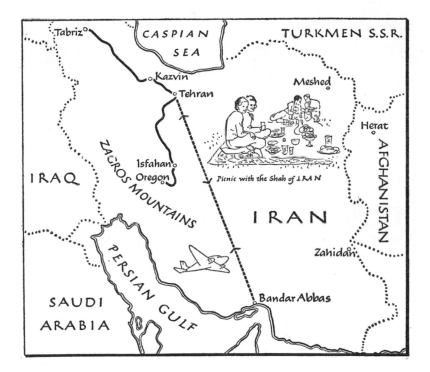

Picnic with the Shah of IRAN

# 5

# PERSIA AND THE SHAH

MARCO POLO brought to Europe the news of Hasan the Assassin, who in the eleventh century established his earthly paradise for the care, feeding, and training of murderers. On our two day journey from Tabriz to Tehran we passed a night in Kazvin, not far from that infamous valley.

Hasan Ibn Sabbah, a schoolmate of the wise and gentle Omar Khayyám, operated the Murder Inc. of his day. Whenever an Oriental prince or grand vizier wanted an undesirable heir or palace enemy rubbed out he called upon Hasan the Assassin. Our word "assassin" is derived from the arabic word *hashshashin,* meaning one who is under the influence of *hashish,* as the Assassins usually were. The Crusaders brought the word from Syria, where they fought a branch of the sect, and it became part of our language.

"The Old Man of the Mountain," wrote Marco Polo, referring to Sheikh Al-Jabal, the Assassin's powerful Grand Master, "caused a certain valley between two lofty mountains to be enclosed, and formed it into a luxurious garden, the most beautiful that ever was seen, filled with every variety of fruit. In it he erected pavilions and palaces, the most elegant that can be imagined, all covered with gilding and exquisite painting.

"And there were runnels too, flowing freely with wine and milk and honey and water; the inhabitants were the most elegant and beautiful damsels, accomplished in the arts of singing, playing upon all sorts of musical instruments, dancing, and especially those of dalliance and amorous allurement. For the Old Man desired to make his followers believe that this indeed was Paradise . . ."

Hasan would enlist young men from the surrounding mountains, Marco Polo wrote, and drug them. When they awoke, they would be within his walled garden, guarded by a fortress "strong enough to resist all the world."

"When therefore they awoke and found themselves in a place so delightful, they believed themselves assuredly in Paradise. And the lovely damsels dallied with them to their heart's content, so they had what young men would have, and of their own good will would never have quitted the place."

When Hasan picked an assassin for a job of murder, the young man knew that if the assassination was successful, the Old Man would permit his return to the garden. If the young man died in the attempt, the Prophet had promised him a Paradise equally lush.

"So he caused them to believe," said Polo. "And thus there was no order of his that they would not affront any peril to execute, for the great desire they had to re-enter Paradise."

Hasan's youngsters matriculated at the Paradise murder school and were taught the ingredients of subtle poisons and how to

introduce them, stabbing from behind, and the niceties of gar-
roting with a silken bowstring, a death usually reserved for
princes.

With such a tutored, fanatic band at his disposal, Hasan inspired dread through the East. History records a long list of Oriental potentates who fell under the Assassins' daggers, or quaffed
hemlock with their wine. The Assassins did away with an Egyptian caliph, and the princes of Aleppo, Damascus, and Mosul.
Raymond, count of Tripoli, was slain by the Assassins, as was
Conrad of Montserrat. The tribe maintained their Paradise and
continued to hire themselves out for courtly killings, even after
the death of Hasan. Eventually they made the mistake of mur-
dering a Mongol prince, and the vengeful warriors of Hulagu
stormed Paradise and obliterated the castle of Alamut. Everything was destroyed except a lonely section of stone wall, jagged
and gray on a promontory overlooking a lifeless gorge.

As we came close to Tehran, the road became smooth with
macadam. We passed a modern airport with new concrete han-
gars, and then through shady streets flanked by canals, actually
open water mains. We checked in at the Park Hotel, the best in
the capital. We have stayed in Park Hotels in Ankara, Istanbul,
Amsterdam, Shanghai, Delhi, and Tehran. Sometimes Franc will
wake at night and ask me: "Where are we?"

"At the Park Hotel," I reply.

"Which Park Hotel?" he grumbles.

This particular Park Hotel was the largest establishment we
had stayed in east of Ankara. There was an outdoor café set in
the center of a garden, and an orchestra whose favorite song was
"Silent Night, Holy Night" played in rumba rhythm. Inside there
was hot water and room service. These touches of luxury buoyed
up our spirits to contend with the truly difficult problems that
confronted us—the Afghan visas that weren't in our passports.
The Afghan embassy in Washington had cabled their foreign
office in Kabul asking that our visas be granted and that we be
allowed to pick them up in Tehran. The world being the way
it is, I had a hunch the visas would not be there and that our
journey would come to an abrupt and ignominious end.

Preoccupied with this problem, we went down to dinner. However, our attention was soon diverted by our fellow diners. Seated not far from us were thirteen Russians, rigid and grim, stocky men who looked so much alike they could have been brothers. They ate in silence and they ate much. They were Soviet agricultural experts, sent to Iran to aid in stamping out a plague of locusts. After they left the dining room, single file and unsmiling, like unhappy robots, our waiter whispered that every night the thirteen devoured the same menu: twenty-six bowls of borscht, twenty-six steaks, twenty-six orders of fried potatoes, twenty-six orders of eggplant, thirteen loaves of bread, twenty-six salads, and twenty-six desserts. Each washed down his dinner with a pint of vodka and two bottles of beer. I noticed that each one carefully tucked a few slices of bread into his pocket before he left the table, in case starvation threatened before breakfast, I guess.

Later, a harassed Iranian official who paid their food bills told us: "There is an old Persian proverb: 'Locusts are not fatal, for after the locust eats the grain, the farmer eats the locust.' But one cannot eat a Russian. They are worse than the locusts."

It was so hot in the mornings that we poured pitchers of water on the tile floor of our balcony to cool it while we ate breakfast. By 8:30 it was an effort to dress. Yet we walked in the sun, for it was on foot that we wanted to see the city. Along one street the merchants were opening their shops and "aging" Persian carpets. They dragged the new, brightly colored rugs, many of them magnificent in design and texture, into the busy street, and allowed all the traffic of the city to tramp or roll across them. Camels, donkeys, horse-drawn droshkies, decrepit taxis, and heavy army trucks all pounded the rugs. When traffic slowed, the shop owner ran into the street and quickly swept off the rug. In ten days a carpet's color could be so softened by the traffic and the fierce sun, and become so authentically worn, that an amateur collector or unsuspecting tourist might think it several hundred years old, undoubtedly the heirloom of a princely family.

A few days after our arrival, we visited the Afghan embassy. There our worst fears were realized. First the clerk, then the second secretary, and finally the first secretary assured us that no word had come from Kabul. We were thoroughly alarmed, and asked if we might have a word with the ambassador. We were not complete strangers to the ambassador as I had drawn him as a bridge partner a few nights before at the home of the American ambassador, John Wiley. One of our opponents had been the ambassador from Pakistan, not only a superior bridge player but a towering Pathan whose height and dignity were enhanced by a starched turban soaring at least eight inches above his head. The Pakistani had thoroughly intimidated me and I suspected that the Afghan ambassador shared my feelings. Perhaps, I thought hopefully, this bridge-table rapport would help us now.

Franc's card went into the private office on a silver tray and in a moment we were drinking tea with His Excellency and explaining our problem. He personally searched the files. There was not so much as the mention of the name Shor in any correspondence from Kabul, and we were despondent. The ambassador smiled and said, with mysterious confidence, "Come back tomorrow at five for more tea. Perhaps something will turn up."

What could twenty-four hours produce in the way of a visa that all those weeks had not? The next day we were back at five, promptly and nervously, to drink more tea. After several cups the ambassador said finally, "I think there must be a little mistake about your names. I find in the files authorization to issue visas to two Americans. One is Mr. Wagner, a businessman, who has asked permission to fly his own plane to Kabul. I am instructed to give him a visa, but he must leave his aircraft behind." He looked at Franc intently. "Are you sure your name is not Wagner?"

"I am positive," Franc said.

The ambassador sighed and turned to me. "The other visa," he said, "is to be issued to a Miss Flagenheimer, a social science teacher from Des Moines, Iowa, who wishes to study family organization among the Pashto tribes. Your maiden name wasn't Flagenheimer, was it, Mrs. Shor?"

"No," I said. "Not Flagenheimer. What are Pashtos?"

"Pashtos are very interesting," he said, "particularly their tribal rites. Americans are also interesting, but for other reasons." He seemed to be laughing at us. "You're still sure you're not Mr. Wagner and Miss Flagenheimer?"

"Absolutely," we said, missing the ball completely.

The ambassador sighed. "Well," he said, "to me it's a clear case of confusion in the cables. Obviously those authorizations were intended for you two. So if you will give me your passports I will have the secretary insert the visas. Now, how about some more tea?"

It dawned on us that the ambassador was a man of humor, determined to do us a great favor, in a somewhat Oriental manner. But for a moment, only a moment, I worried a little about Mr. Wagner and Miss Flagenheimer. "What will happen when they call for their visas?" I asked.

"Those authorizations have been in my file for months," said the ambassador. "Many people plan trips to Afghanistan and never complete them. Should these two come to Tehran I shall simply say, 'So sorry. Two Americans have been here already and we seem to have given them your visas by mistake.' Since all Americans know that all foreigners are stupid, they will not be surprised. They can simply wait here for a month or so while I cable for new authorizations."

The ambassador was thoughtful for a moment. "I'd rather help two people bent on a trip like yours—an adventure, you might call it—than a man who wants to buy karakul skins and a woman interested in the puberty rites of the Pashtos. There is too much organization in this world, too much exploiting and investigating, and not enough understanding."

We walked back through the crowded streets in a pink haze. Our first big hurdle was behind us, and through sheerest luck. Already I was beginning to love the Afghans.

But, as always, there was a slight hitch. The next day the ambassador summoned us back. I hadn't had time to amend my passport since our marriage, which meant that we were traveling in apparent sin under the names of Jean Bowie and Franc Shor. The ambassador feared his countrymen might take a dim view of our morality. Several hotel clerks and border officials *had* raised their eyebrows. I agreed to go to the U.S. embassy and have my passport amended.

At the American embassy, another complication developed when it was discovered that my marriage certificate was in Chinese. The embassy clerk complained, "You *say* this is a marriage certificate, but how can I tell? For all I know, it may be an invitation to a chop suey dinner."

It was therefore necessary to go to the Chinese embassy for a certified English translation. By this time the temperature was 120 in the shade. While we waited for a Chinese interpreter to ready the document, we were served our fiftieth cup of official tea, after which we plodded back to the American embassy where at last my married name was officially entered in my passport. Then we staggered to the Afghan embassy, dizzy but triumphant, and the visas were issued at last.


As KABUL had to be notified that we were en route, we could not leave for Afghanistan until the ambassador had cleared all lines with his capital, a matter of two weeks. But we did not fret, as Tehran had much to offer.

Franc wanted to write a magazine piece on the fabulous Major Lincoln, a legendary American spy who supposedly prowled the Middle East. We wished to visit the Bakhtiari country in southern Iran, where the nomad tribesmen were reputed to be especially fierce and primitive. And Franc wanted to photograph the famous crown jewels, the hard base of Iran's currency. Just as the American dollar is backed by the gold entombed in Fort Knox, so the Iranian toman is backed by the Pahlevi crown jewels safe in a vault at the Bank Melli.

Most of all, we wanted to photograph and interview the Shah, who, revered by his subjects, perhaps holds more power than any hereditary ruler alive today. At that time the throne was beset by dangers from within and without. The Shah had to contend with the machinations of the Communist Tudeh Party, the personal ambitions of relatives and tribal chieftains, that irascible old fox of a politician Mossadegh, and his Soviet neighbor

crouched along the entire length of his northern frontier. He
was in trouble with England over control of oil rights and the
great refineries at Abadan; revolt never ceased to simmer in
Azerbaijan; and his seventeen million subjects had found themselves suddenly in the midst of the struggle between Russia and
the West. No one was certain that the young, cultivated ruler,
despite his popularity, could hold his ancient kingdom together
and keep his crown, or even his head.

At the American embassy, we presented our problems to Gerry
Dooher, a sandy-haired Irishman who was special assistant to
Ambassador Wiley. Visiting the Bakhtiari tribesmen, viewing
the crown jewels, and photographing and interviewing the Shah
would all be difficult, perhaps impossible, he told us. But he
would do his best. The Shah had never been informally photographed, and an audience, rarely granted, seldom lasted more
than fifteen minutes.

"What about the Major Lincoln story?" I inquired.

Gerry Dooher chuckled. There was no such a person as Major
Lincoln! Major Lincoln was, in fact, his own invention, con-
cocted to confuse the Russians and make life more complicated
for the numerous secret agents busy in the Middle East. This it
certainly had done. Everything that went wrong between Istanbul
and Karachi, which was plenty, the Russians blamed on "Major
Lincoln, the notorious American spy."

The American colony for a long time had amused themselves
at cocktail parties and picnics by inventing fantastic new esca-
pades for the "major." He was not only a super-spy, but a great
ladies' man. He was sent on mythical missions to Moscow, Washington, or Tabriz, and returned with equally mythical tales of
counterplots and love affairs. He was a master at organizing
"spontaneous" uprisings.

Every time a Russian stubbed his diplomatic toe, the Americans would smile and whisper that he had been tripped by
Major Lincoln. Each satellite figure who defected to the West
anywhere in the world was credited as a coup to Major Lincoln.
The report spread that Lincoln was actually Lawrence of Arabia,
who had not died at all but had settled in Brooklyn and become

an American citizen. Major Lincoln was the shaggy dog of Tehran.

The Russians, bombarded with this imaginative barrage, decided that there must be a germ of fact behind all these whisperings. To them Lincoln became a very serious problem, though his name was never uttered officially, and there was no doubt he was wanted by the MVD.

Since Major Lincoln was obviously not the appropriate subject for an illustrated article, unless we could photograph spooks, we pressed Gerry Dooher for help in obtaining an interview with the Shah. Gerry whetted our appetites further by quoting an opinion on the importance of the Shah, and of Iran, by an eminent American diplomat who had spent much of his life in the Middle East. "The loss of Iran," he had written, "would knock the keystone out of the land bridge to the Orient. If the Russians take it, India and Southeast Asia will be flanked. The only force that can keep the Russians out of Iran is the Iranians themselves, and the only man in Iran who can mobilize that force is the Shah. He is the most important man in the Middle East. I hope to heaven he stays on our side!"

That decided the issue. We *had* to interview the Shah.

The Shah-in-Shah was born in 1919, the oldest son of Reza Shah Pahlevi, a fierce soldier, who founded the present dynasty. The elder Pahlevi seized power in 1921 when the prestige of Persia was at its lowest ebb, and electrified the country by promising to throw off the dual yoke of Russia and England.

The present Shah absorbed Western manners and knowledge at school in Switzerland where he was a fine student and athlete. He is the best amateur tennis player in Iran today. Surrounded as he was by Swiss, English, and French boys in his impressionable years, he learned something more important than their languages. He became a democrat, in thought, in spirit, and in action.

When he ascended the throne in 1941 (his pro-German father had been deposed) the Shah encouraged the Majlis, the national assembly, to take more seriously its constitutional duties. Every adult Iranian has the right to vote, but widespread illiteracy, lack of political consciousness, and difficulty of communications keeps millions from the polls. Political activity is largely confined to the cities, and vast outlying areas are still ruled by tribal chieftains.

In 1949 an attempt was made on the Shah's life. Of five shots fired at close range, two pierced his hat, another ripped his coat, and a fourth grazed his lips and creased his cheek. His assailant was killed on the spot by the royal guard. It was generally agreed that the attempted assassination was plotted by the Communist Tudeh Party, and his closest advisers urged the Shah to seize dictatorial powers and suppress all opposition groups. He refused, and thoughtful Iranians realized that the Shah was a determined follower of democratic ideals. Not until Mossadegh's attempted grab for power did the Shah show his strength. And even though Mossadegh was convicted of treason, his life was spared.

Basically, the Shah had staked his personal and political fortunes on the same theory that inspired the Marshall plan: a prosperous and contented people will not turn to violent revolution or heed the call of Communism. He sponsored a seven-year plan to increase agricultural production, modernize villages, and raise the standards of public health and education. He placed his younger brother, Harvard-educated Prince Abdor Reza, in charge. To spark the plan, he gave nearly all of his own large estates to needy peasants, hoping to set an example for other wealthy landlords.

This was the man we wanted to visit and photograph, not to talk politics, but to see how the King of Kings lived when not engaged in official duties. Gerry Dooher presented our application for an interview according to protocol through the foreign office, and for days we heard nothing. Meanwhile, we blundered into the crown jewels.

We were invited by Ambassador Wiley to a garden party and tennis matches at the American embassy. During the tennis we sat next to Mr. A. B. Eptihaj, director general of the Bank Melli, the national bank of Iran. He talked to us about the country's finances, and then Franc casually asked, "Would it be possible to come to the bank sometime and photograph the crown jewels?"

Eptihaj, a slim, straight, cultivated man, was equally casual in his reply. "Certainly," he said.

I could hardly contain my amazement. By the accident of seats at a tennis match, we again had enjoyed wonderful luck. What had seemed difficult and perhaps impossible a few days before was suddenly ours for the asking.

"When would it be convenient?" Franc asked.

"Give me two days," said Eptihaj in his excellent English. He explained that the vault could only be opened in the presence of the minister of finance, the attorney general, the inspector general, the director general of the bank, and three members of parliament. It might take a while to round them all up.

Two mornings later, at ten o'clock, we accompanied the grave group of officials into the bank's basement, where armed soldiers guarded every corridor and stairway. In a room with heavily barred doors, which contained only one small safe, the attorney general produced a key, opened the safe, and lifted out a sealed leather case. From the case he lifted another heavier key. Then the minister of finance produced a similar one, and the inspector general drew a third from his pocket. It took all three keys, two in the possession of trusted officials and one kept at the bank, to open the vault where the crown jewels were cached.

With immense solemnity the seal to the great vault was broken. The three keys were inserted in the massive door, then turned in unison. The three officials pulled. The door didn't budge. They braced their feet against the steel and pulled again. This time the door sighed and opened.

We found ourselves in the treasure room, a subterranean chamber eighteen feet wide and thirty-five long, lined on three sides with glass cases containing swords and crowns. The fourth wall was curtained entirely with ropes of pearls hanging from ceiling to floor. Real pearls, bigger than moth balls, in yard-long strands. In the middle of the room were five showcases, each heaped with unmounted jewels—emeralds, rubies, diamonds, sapphires, and turquoises. The number of stones was unbelievable, and the sight too much for anyone to absorb or appreciate. I caught myself thinking of five-and-ten counters at Christmastime.

Eptihaj told us the history of some of the historic treasures of Persia. In one case were the relatively modern Pahlevi crown and the older crown of the Kajar dynasty, whose reign of a century and a half ended with the rise of Reza Shah. The Kajar crown, encrusted with huge rubies and crudely cut diamonds, was so heavy that no man ever wore it. At coronation time it was suspended over the head of the new Shah-in-Shah by a silken harness. The Pahlevi crown was adorned with a belt of diamonds increasing in size from rim to top. The center stones measured more than an inch in diameter.

The hills of green stones in the emerald showcase glistened like the Irish countryside. With them stood the famous royal snuffbox, the top a deep and flawless emerald three inches long and two inches wide. As I stared at it, my own emerald engagement ring shrank to pinpoint size. When Parisian jewelers came to Tehran to appraise the crown jewels two years before, they refused to attempt an evaluation of the snuffbox. "There is no stone in the world that remotely compares to this perfect emerald," they said. "It is unique. No other will ever be found, for it undoubtedly came from Indian mines which have been worked out for three hundred years. Colombian emeralds are not of the same quality." Without question, it was the most beautiful thing in the collection and the only jewel there I truly coveted.

In the diamond case, stones were piled up tall as a man's hat —brown diamonds large as golf balls, saucers full of canary diamonds, platters of white diamonds, boxes heaped with bright blue-white stones. In a case by itself was an aigrette plume pin set with the famous Daria-i-noor (Sea of Light). Once the Persian collection also contained the Koh-i-noor (Mountain of Light), now the most precious stone of the English crown jewels.

There is a fascinating legend about how the Persians acquired the Daria-i-noor and the Koh-i-noor, both mined in East India centuries ago. They belonged to an Indian Mogul king whom

At a picnic on the grounds of the summer palace in Tehran, the Shah of Iran feeds his Saint Bernard a lamb bone while servants pass platters of food.

The Shah-in-Shah, Mohammed Reza Pahlevi, poses for a picture with me. I wasn't so much petting that huge Saint Bernard as trying to keep him from pushing me over the porch rail.

Seated at his desk in Kabul, the King of Afghanistan, Mohammed Zahir Shah, discusses our proposed trip with his uncle, General Mohammed Omar Khan, Minister of War, and Mr. Rishtya, the Press Director and our "friend at court."

Pitiful Wakhani (Wahki) women study us as we ride through their village. The children wear only a covering of dirty rags, the older women are more thoroughly covered, but no cleaner. Their windowless house stands behind them.

Nadir Shah defeated in battle. Naturally, to the victor belonged the spoils, including royal ladies and crown jewels. Nadir Shah ordered the defeated king to appear before him. Just before the poor man's arrival, an Indian minister to the Mogul informed Nadir Shah that the defeated king had secreted the priceless Noor stones in his turban.

At the end of his last interview with his vanquished foe, Nadir Shah told the Mogul that as a bit of parting courtesy they would exchange turbans. Unable to refuse, the Mogul handed over his turban—and the two great jewels.

As with all fables, this one has its moral. As Nadir Shah prepared to lead his army back to Persia, the Indian minister asked for a reward for his information. "You will get the reward that treachery merits," Nadir Shah told him, and cut off his head.

I looked at the steely blue Daria-i-noor for so long that it began to have an hypnotic effect, and appeared to grow in size. It seemed blinding, even in the yellow light of the vault's dim bulbs. On one edge of the 170-carat Daria, in the most minute Persian characters, is engraved the name of Fath-ali-Shah, a ruler who once wore it.

I nearly skipped the turquoise table entirely, until Mr. Eptihaj educated me on the subject. I had scorned the New Mexico Navajo turquoise, much of which was an unattractive green color flawed with matrix and sold in lumps to tourists. In the Middle East, Eptihaj explained, people consider turquoise the finest semiprecious stone. The best quality stones, mined in northern Afghanistan, are a beautiful pale blue, and are most attractive when set in gold. The royal jewels were mostly unmounted, but on the turquoise table was one golden bowl, with small round turquoise pressed into the metal in a spiral design. Seldom have I seen anything lovelier.

By the time I got to the rubies, many of them large as the end of my thumb, I was sated. The royal treasure was valued at more than $600,000,000, not counting the unique orbs and mugs, swords and ornamental chains and antique Oriental jewelry, on which no value can be placed. Gold bricks stacked in a nearby room supplied the rest of the backing for Iran's currency. After seeing the jewels we didn't want to look at it. After all, it was only gold bricks.

After the vault was carefully locked and resealed, we walked up Ferdowzi Street, window shopping, and stopped before a candy-store window, piled with rock candy, fruit drops and jelly beans. They looked exactly like the mounds of diamonds, rubies and turquoises we had left in the vault. Feeling magnanimous, Franc took me inside and let me buy any "stone" I liked.


FOR THREE SUCCESSIVE DAYS I visited a small shop loaded with antiques and junk, where a primitive amulet in the shape of a man's head, of black stone flecked with gold, had caught my eye. The merchant wanted thirty cents for it. After many sessions of spirited bargaining, I ultimately bought the amulet for twenty-three cents. A year later in a New York museum, I was told that it was at least two thousand years old and of considerable value. I might never have bought it had the dealer refused to come down that last cent.

Ferdowzi was the street for shopping. On display were fine rugs, Greek coins, Persian miniatures on ivory, the most beautiful and elaborate old harem costumes, and Luristan bronzes. Amulets of all sorts were for sale, including carvings of wise-looking little ibexes. The international market was also represented—by French perfume, Swiss watches, English gin, Italian anchovies, and old American comic books. There were wonderful counterfeit products—"Lifegirl" soap, "Fix" soap, and "Wrigglers" chewing gum. An American trademark with a slightly scrambled name seemed enough to sell anything.

On the side streets I noticed black-veiled girls, obviously prostitutes despite their demure and modest dress. Men approached and occasionally pinched them as if testing for youth and firmness. What their faces looked like seemed of no particular importance.

After the unveiled women of Turkey, I was surprised to find that most Persian women still wore the veil, called a *chador*.

The *chador*, a half circle of printed cotton, worn like a head scarf but much larger in size, is a graceless and unattractive garment. A country woman's *chador* may drag on the ground, while her more "modern" city sister may wear hers to the knees.

Traffic in Tehran was even worse than that in China. Drivers came from all directions, on both sides of the streets, turned anywhere, and invariably traveled at high speed. Taxis saved gasoline by cutting their ignition switches and coasting down the hills, a dangerous practice since brakes were rarely in good condition. The topography of the streets themselves added to the confusion. Lone telephone poles were set in the middle of some streets, and others were flanked by the open water mains called *jubes*. Each morning the *jubes* were filled with water which people used for every possible purpose, from drinking to washing their feet. By evening the water was covered by a scum of oil, filth, and garbage.

Iran's system of *bastee,* or sanctuary, interested us greatly. Anyone accused of a crime or fleeing from an enemy, personal or political, can find sanctuary on the property of the Shah. The most popular place of *bastee* among the poor was the telegraph office, called "the ear of the Shah." Often refugees come prepared for a long stay, with food and cooking utensils, wives and children. Outlying telegraph offices are occasionally jammed like hotels in a convention city, and one must step over sleeping men or across children and chickens in order to reach the clerk's desk. All are allowed to remain until the dispute is adjudicated legally.

ONE EVENING a messenger intercepted us on our Tehran tour with a note from Gerry Dooher. "Tanya and I are at the Park Hotel Restaurant," it read, "with an important message for you. Could you come to our table?"

We ran all the way, and the message was worth the exertion. The Shah would see us at ten o'clock the following morning, Gerry said. He didn't know whether photographs would be permitted, but advised us to take our cameras anyway. Our audience was scheduled for twenty minutes. The Shah would give us a clear indication when the interview was at an end, we needn't worry about overstaying our allotted time.

At seven in the morning I awoke doubled up with pain. I had an acute case of "Tehran tummy," and gloomily admitted to Franc, after several attempts at rising, that I would never make the palace. All my life I had wanted to meet a real-life potentate and now I was being robbed of that opportunity by a few tiny bacteria!

Franc was sympathetic. He comforted me with sulfa pills and promised to remember everything that was said, and how the palace interior looked. Gerry Dooher was sending his car to take us to the summer palace—one of five residences the Shah uses in Tehran—and when the car arrived at nine-thirty I was still in bed, moaning.

Franc bustled about the room, bright-eyed and eager, gathering up the camera equipment. Jealously I watched him, feeling worse each minute.

"Well, good-by, darling," he waved. "Tough break. I'll give your regrets to the Shah."

I couldn't stand it. I had never met a Shah, and how many other chances was I going to have? I scrambled out of bed, shouting, "Franc, don't you dare go without me!"

He stopped halfway out of the door, astonished.

A woman can dress in a hurry when she has to. In seven minutes I had on my gray linen suit, had snatched up my hat, shoes, bag and gloves, and we were in the car. I fixed my face and combed my hair on the way to the palace, no doubt convincing the Iranian chauffeur, once and for all, of American informality.

We were greeted on the steps of the white stucco palace, which was about the size of the White House, by M. H. Pirnia, a dapper little man educated in Italy, who was Iran's chief of protocol. Pirnia led us down a wide corridor, and an army officer opened the doors into the reception chambers. The Shah was waiting just inside. Two enormous police dogs, crouched at his side, instantly charged us—but not in anger. They leaped all over us, licking my hands and face. The Shah laughed and ordered them down, the dogs obeying instantly, which seemed entirely proper. The fact that the Shah kept dogs as pets was in itself somewhat remarkable, and an indication of the many changes he is working toward within his country. For centuries Persians regarded dogs as unclean. Everything a dog touched with its tongue was washed seven times, and it was believed a carpet was defiled by its feet.

The Shah was a handsome, lithe and slender young man, much more attractive physically than I had imagined from his news photos. He was dressed in fawn-colored riding breeches and a tweed jacket. He shook our hands genially and seated us around a low table inlaid with pearl and ivory. Servants silently padded across magnificent carpets to serve tea. I was happily soaking up every detail.

The Shah, speaking English with a few French words dropped in for precise meaning, asked how we were enjoying his country. We told him of our favorable impressions and that we had delayed our departure for Afghanistan to learn more of Persia.

This seemed to please him. "But I heard you had some sort of trouble in Azerbaijan," he said.

Really nothing, nothing at all, we lied. The principal thing was that we had reached Tehran, and we had our visas to continue our journey.

The Shah, too, was fascinated by the travels of Marco Polo, and began to question us about our trip—what we had seen so far, and what we expected to see. After a few minutes I began to wonder who was interviewing who. Then the Shah asked, "Precisely why do you want to interview me, and what sort of photographs do you want to take?" Obviously he was experienced in public relations.

Franc answered carefully, having prepared his "presentation" the night before, that America knew little of the Shah and his ambitions for his country. To Americans, the Shah was simply a Middle Eastern caliph. We wanted to show them how a Shah really lived, and to tell them of his plans for the future of Iran.

"That might be helpful," the Shah agreed. "How about starting with pictures in the garden? You've got color film, haven't
you?"

We assured him that we had, and from there the Shah took
over, suggesting that we go outside. I was greatly relieved; our
audience was obviously going to be longer than the scheduled
twenty minutes. I had noticed that the Shah's servants and
aides bowed and backed out of the room when leaving his
presence, and I was suddenly confronted with this hurdle of
royal protocol. Shouldn't we let him go out first? Did we back
out? I stepped back as we approached the door. He stepped back
and bowed. I stepped back and waited. We were doing a little
dosey-do. The Shah smiled, "Please, Mrs. Shor," and I went
out first.

He led us first to a magnificent bed of Persian roses, celebrated in verse for two thousand years. They are among the
largest and most beautiful in the world, and surely the roses of
the Shah were the loveliest in the land. He picked some of the
finest blossoms and gave them to me.

After a dozen informal photographs in the garden, the Shah
said casually, "I'm having a family luncheon today—a sort of
picnic. Would you care to join us?"

Would we! Franc said we would be delighted; I was busy
trying to restrain my enthusiasm and hide my expression of
incredulity. But could we make pictures as well as eat?

"Certainly," the Shah said. "You want informal pictures, and
there is nothing so informal as a picnic. Meanwhile, I'll show
you the palace grounds." He sounded like a Westchester County
squire eager for his guests to see the greenhouse and barbecue
pit.

A fire-engine-red Packard convertible appeared, by magic I
am sure, and with the siren wailing we toured the grounds,
which occupied as much space as a New England village. In
addition to the Shah's palace, each member of the big Pahlevi
family, male and female, had a private palace. Everyone within
sound of the siren—gardeners at work, relatives out horseback
riding, soldiers on guard—stopped what he was doing and bowed

as the Shah drove past. Franc sat in front with the Shah and I sat in the back seat in lonely grandeur, firmly resisting my impulse to give a Queen Mary nod and gracious wave to the bowing subjects.

We stopped in front of a palace, smaller than the others but serene and lovely, constructed of multicolored marble and surrounded by pools and woods. This was the highest point in the Shah's preserve, and from it he could see all of Tehran below him. "I come here to meditate," the Shah said. "When there are problems of great importance that only I can decide, I come here alone. I listen to all advice, true; I hear all sides of a question. But when the time comes for decision, I must be my own counselor, for final responsibility is mine alone."

No one was in attendance, and the door was locked. To our amazement, the Shah climbed in through a window to open the place so we could see the interior. I had visions of being arrested for palace-breaking, but no guard appeared. As serious problems requiring meditation are frequent in Iran, I suppose the Shah used his lonely palace a great deal.

At his stables, the Shah showed us a wonderful string of horses—twenty Arabian thoroughbreds and crossbreeds with Arabian blood. I patted their sleek sides while Franc knowledgeably praised their lines and conformation. A servant appeared bearing a big silver bowl filled with sugar and I solemnly went down the line feeding each horse a lump. Then another servant appeared with a bowl and pitcher of water so that I could wash my hands.

The Shah was delighted by our enthusiasm over his stable and interested in Franc's years of riding in the cavalry and of mine in Texas. We photographed the Shah vaulting into the saddle—he didn't use stirrups to mount—and riding his favorite white stallion. Then he drove us back to the first palace and left us, saying, "See you for lunch" in his best American idiom.

We sat over tea in the palace drawing room until the Shah, having finished his ride, led us to the picnic site.

On a plot of lawn in the center of a formal garden, shielded on three sides by plane trees and edged by a swimming pool on the fourth, incredibly fine Persian carpets had been spread. Satin pillows were scattered around as seats. In the middle of the carpets was laid a beautiful cut-work linen cloth with a tall centerpiece of roses, white, pink, and deep maroon. Flanking the flowers were bowls of cucumbers, cherries, apricots, plums, apples, and peaches. Nine places were laid with cream-white china, gold-bordered and bearing the royal cipher, and rows of heavy hand-wrought silver.

In a moment we were introduced to the Shah's brilliant, strong-willed twin sister Ashraf and her Egyptian husband; to Prince Ahmed Reza, his second brother, and to Ahmed's pretty wife; and to his principal military aide and his wife.

I didn't know exactly what protocol called for when you picnicked with the King of Kings so I watched the others. They all waited for the Shah to sit down, and I stood with them. But he turned to me and said, "Please try this pillow, Mrs. Shor," placing me at his right. Luncheon was served by ten waiters in black uniforms with more gold braid than a Brazilian admiral. Each wore white gloves, for it is considered sacrilege for a servant to bare his hands before the Shah.

It was the best and biggest lunch we'd eaten since we left Paris. It started with cream soup, then tender broiled chicken served with potatoes, green beans, fresh carrots, and a green salad. The Persian national dish, *cheloh-kebab* (rice with charcoal-broiled strips of lamb and chopped meat molded onto long skewers), came next, with a raw egg yolk. I wondered what to do with the yolk until I saw the others mix it with the hot rice, a delicious dish that we ate many times thereafter in Iran. Then came coffee ice cream, huge platters laden with juicy melons, Turkish coffee and, oddly enough, tea. I wasted not a single thought on my "Tehran tummy" of the early morning hours but seriously wondered whether I was going to be able to rise from my cushion unaided after such a feast.

I am an ardent admirer of fine china, and at the picnic I couldn't resist trying to read the markings on the bottom of the plates. Franc shook his head sternly in disapproval, but as the dessert plate was laid before me, I saw that the Shah was talking to

Ashraf. Stealthily, I turned it over. Before I could read the name, the Shah, without turning his head, said, "It's Haviland, Mrs. Shor." My embarrassment was balanced by his amusement.

Between courses, as I photographed the Shah reclining on his side, eating while resting one elbow on a satin pillow, he remarked: "I guess I'm not your idea of a Middle Eastern potentate."

"I don't understand," I answered.

"All potentates are supposed to sit cross-legged on cushions, and I can't." He explained that an old polo injury had left him with a stiff knee, and added, "I hope you're not disappointed."

While the Shah and Franc discussed the economic and political problems of Iran, I talked with Princess Ashraf about domestic life. Very few Persian women, she said, had any modern conveniences whatsoever. Procuring a refrigerator was a tremendous problem, involving foreign exchange and interminable waits for transport, even for the very rich. However, I suspected that Ashraf had everything *she* wanted, including iceboxes.

Franc had heard that the Shah had a fast sports car, "a Frazer-Nash with triple carburetion" (whatever that means), and for quite a while they talked a mechanical jargon that didn't mean a thing to the rest of us. A few moments later the car arrived at the picnic lawn, an underslung yellow two-seater shaped like a torpedo. The Shah opened the hood, and he and Franc disappeared first into the engine and then into the interior. Next thing I knew, the motor roared and they sped away, siren screaming. Around a hairpin turn at sixty, they vanished in a spray of gravel, leaving me with visions of being without a husband and Iran without a ruler.

(A few days later, when I collected our pictures from the local photo shop, I was horrified to see an enlargement in the store window of Franc and the Shah seated like old pals in the royal roadster. I asked the shop owner to remove it, suggesting His Majesty might disapprove of this display showing him rubbing elbows with a foreign journalist. The proprietor agreed. The picture was back the next day, however. The Shah sat alone at the wheel. Franc had been touched out completely.)

At five o'clock we left, after seven hours at the palace, with an invitation to return the next day "to discuss our Seven-year Plan further," said the Shah, "and perhaps you'd like to make more pictures." As far as Tehran was concerned, we had "arrived." Back at the palace the following afternoon, there was more political talk and later we watched the Shah play tennis against a professional, and beat him. The referee was completely impartial, but I'd hate to have to call "out" or "foot fault" against the Shah. Not in Persia, anyway.

As we were preparing to leave, we told the Shah about the next leg of our journey. In order to follow Marco Polo's footsteps exactly, it was necessary to journey south to Bandar Abbas, which would be as useless a junket for us as it had been for Polo. Polo had gone south in the mistaken hope that he could find a boat to take him to China. He had been told that seaworthy boats were available on the Persian Gulf. Like so much information given freely in the Middle East—then and now—it was wrong. He had to return to northern Iran and enter Afghanistan through Meshed, as we planned to do.

In late summer the trip south would be anything but pleasant. It would be horrible. It was so hot near the Persian Gulf that buses traveled only at night. We would see little of the countryside, mostly arid plains and eroded mountains.

The Shah thought the whole thing foolish. He counted up the number of days we would lose, and predicted, gallantly, that I wouldn't be able to stand the heat. Franc said he had less doubts about my surviving the heat than about his own chances. Still we didn't want to renege on our map of Polo's wanderings and clung to our original plan.

"Why don't you fly south?" the Shah suggested.

We had already tried the commercial lines, and all flights had been canceled until autumn. Passengers would bake in a metal plane standing on the desert airstrips in July and August.

"Would a private plane do?" the Shah asked. "If you can go on short notice, I'll fly you south over the Polo route, and back again."

I was too stunned by the generosity of his offer, put so casually, to express my thanks. Franc found his tongue, however, and I am sure our pleasure was evident in our ready acceptance.

That evening I wrote in my notebook, "Persia is still the land of magic carpets."

We had just finished dressing the next morning when a servant came to our room with a message. Though the Park Hotel was the biggest and the best in Tehran, there were no room phones, and calls had to come through the lone instrument in the lobby. It was a call for Franc, said the boy. Would he please come down? We both went to the lobby.

Franc picked up the phone, listened to the voice of the caller, inhaled audibly, and said, "Yes, Your Majesty."

The desk clerk dropped his pencil and stood at respectful attention. Two porters seated on the call bench quickly arose. At Franc's next "Yes, Your Majesty," all three bowed slightly from the waist.

Franc was now thoroughly enjoying this unexpected performance. I am sure that even after the Shah was off the line, he said, "Yes, Your Majesty" a few extra times.

We had been invited to fly the next day.

By this time we had acquired much face, not only in the hotel, but throughout the foreign colony, because of the interest the Shah had shown in our journey. In a Middle Eastern capital like Tehran, always seething with gossip and intrigue, people look for an ulterior motive. Perhaps the Russians thought Franc was the mythical Major Lincoln. After all, we *had* come through Azerbaijan.

We arrived at the palace early, to find the Shah playing chess with an aide-de-camp, using porcelain chessmen fashioned as creatures of the sea. Squids were castles, sea horses knights, the king and queen were tall spires of coral topped with sponges, and the pawns were small octopi.

The Shah, in the uniform of commander-in-chief of the air force, drove alone to the airport in his sports car, a loaded revolver on the seat by his side. We followed in the red convertible.

At Mehrabad we met the Shah's two copilots, both American-trained Iranians, and his crew chief, Wayne Livingstone, of Junction City, Kansas.

His B-17 was a flying palace, with Imperial crowns painted under the wings, and the royal insigne—lions upholding a crown—on the nose. Even the royal flag was painted on the tail, along with the golden initials H.I.M.—His Imperial Majesty. Inside, it was beautifully fitted, with pale cream leather covering the fuselage, maroon carpets, beige seats, and maroon silk curtains.

In the pilot's seat, the Shah revved up the engines with a professional ear and treated us to a smooth take-off. We flew south over the badlands and desert, passing over Isfahan, Shiraz, and then Bandar Abbas. We turned at the sea's edge, and returned over the lifeless desert. Circling Tehran, the Shah lovingly pointed out features of the city before coming down in a perfect landing.

Back on the ground, we remembered to tell the Shah how a predecessor of his had furnished an escort of 170 horsemen for Marco Polo on his return through Persia, when the Polos were bringing one of Kublai Khan's daughters to wed the Persian king.

The Shah looked amused. "You say the king gave Polo an escort of a hundred and seventy horsemen? I believe I've done a bit better by you two." He looked up with pride at the B-17. "I've given you an escort of forty-eight hundred horsepower."

Thus did the Shah of Iran help us keep faith with Marco Polo, whose footsteps we followed even where they erred. And yet I couldn't still a twinge of conscience that told me we were cheating ourselves of knowledge. For a view from the air is not like travel on a four-legged beast. I wanted to know more of the people of the Persian desert, the tribes whose territories Marco Polo crossed on his long journey from Bandar Abbas to Meshed. Particularly did I want to visit the Bakhtiari, fierce horsemen and famous warriors whose tribal lands lay like a scimitar between Kirman and Isfahan. Their ancestors had roamed the Dasht-i-Lut, and the Polo party must have encountered them.

And their way of life, we were assured, had changed little since the days of our predecessor.

The luck which had placed me across the bridge table from the Afghan ambassador and next to Mr. Eptihaj at the tennis match dropped me into a seat next to Supreme Court Justice William O. Douglas at a dinner that night. Burned red by a rugged climb up Mt. Demavend, the wandering Justice was full of enthusiasm for Iran and its people. Unlike most travelers, he shunned the capitals and bright lights of far-off lands and sought out the remote areas and people.

Justice Douglas looked like Spencer Tracy, and had the dry wit of Will Rogers. Epigrams flowed effortlessly from his tongue, and I remember particularly his remark that "I would rather set a precedent than find one." But what brought me half out of my chair was his answer to my question about where he planned to go next.

"I'm going south," he said. "I've been invited to visit the Bakhtiari tribe."

A lady can't invite herself to accompany a gentleman on a journey, but a journalist can always try to cover a story.

"I think *Life* magazine would love pictures of that," I said. "Would it be all right if we cabled for the assignment?"

"I'd be delighted," smiled the Justice, his good manners concealing his surprise. "We leave in about a week."

I couldn't shout the news across the table to Franc, but the minute the ladies rejoined the gentlemen I blurted it out. He composed a cable as we rode back to the hotel, and sent it at midnight.

"INVITED BY JUSTICE DOUGLAS ACCOMPANY HIM ON VISIT PRIMITIVE SAVAGE TRIBE IN SOUTH," it read. "WILL YOU GUARANTEE EXPENSES FOR COVERAGE."

Approval came in twenty-four hours. Disillusion came in forty-eight.

Justice Douglas invited us to tea with Majid Samsam Bakhtiari, a tribal chief of the area we were to visit. We expected to meet a bearded barbarian. Instead, we were introduced to a suave, clean-shaven young man, London-tailored and speaking

Oxford English, who had left his tribe that morning and flown his own Beech Bonanza to Tehran. If the Bakhtiari were all like Majid, we thought, we'd have a terrible time explaining that "primitive savage tribe" to *Life*.

"Don't worry," he reassured us. "My brothers and I were educated abroad, but our people have not changed. And frankly, I like their way of life. Everyone in Tehran seems to want to make a million dollars and go to America. I've *got* a million dollars, but I prefer to stay home. Must be something wrong with me, what?"

Part of Majid's land, flanked by the towering Zagros Mountains, is considered the most inhospitable area of Iran. It is a rolling desert covered with a hard layer of black shingle, and lacks landmarks of any kind. Its water holes are frequently more salt than the sea. Its heat in summer is insupportable, while in winter it is swept by icy blizzards. Much of it is uninhabitable, even by the hardiest tribesmen.

Each powerful tribal khan is legally subservient to the Shah, but for all practical purposes the khans are their own rulers. The Bakhtiari number about two hundred thousand. Their livelihood is that of sheep herdsmen; they live in tents and migrate with the seasons to better grazing lands. Every Bakhtiari is a horseman, and every man carries a rifle. "You will find my land," said Majid, "something like your Wild West."

OUR FLIGHT to Isfahan, aboard an Iranian Airways DC-3, took us over cities built wholly of mud, and watch towers and oases on what had once been the silk road to the Persian Gulf. Of Isfahan, where we landed, it is written, "Isfahan is half the world." For centuries it was a bright jewel in the crown of the Caliphs of Baghdad, the Abbasids who were descended from the elder uncle of Mohammed. It fell to the Mongols in 1221, but was once again the capital of the Eight Kingdoms when Marco Polo came to Persia. It was captured, plundered, and almost entirely destroyed by Tamerlane in 1387, but was rebuilt into one of the most magnificent of Oriental cities by the great Shah

Abbas in the seventeenth century. When we came to Isfahan it was no longer "half the world," but a city of a quarter million that still retained much of its splendor.

For instance, we saw there the largest polo field in the world, 560 yards long and 174 wide, big enough to accommodate the two hundred horsemen who played there. Along one side of the field Shah Abbas erected a palace pavilion of marble, connected to the seraglio by a balcony. From behind the lace stonework of the balcony the women of the harem, unobserved, could watch the game, while the Shah himself viewed it from the third story of the pavilion. His throne, set exactly at the center of the field, was probably the most expensive fifty-yard-line seat in history.

In the middle of the field had once stood a twenty-five-foot marble mast. On feast days archery contests were held, with the archers shooting from the backs of galloping horses at targets set atop this mast. Commoners shot at melons, but the khans and shahs and nobles shot at cups of silver and gold. It is recorded by the Persians (as we keep our old records in the pole vault and shot put) that in 1516 Shah Ismail hit seven of ten silver cups, and Shah Safi scored three out of five. It is thought that polo originated in Persia. When Tamerlane took Isfahan he also played the game—using human skulls as balls.

Lowell Thomas, Jr., the modest, friendly son of a famous father, joined the party at Isfahan. He was in Iran filming a travelogue. When we set out for Shalamazar, the "capital" of the Bakhtiari, late in the afternoon, it was quite a caravan. There was a new Studebaker for Justice Douglas, an old Hudson taxi for us, Thomas's custom-built jeep, and a weapons carrier loaded with luggage. Majid, flying to the tribal area ahead of us in a light Cub, buzzed us twice as we bumped along the road. Plenty primitive, these Bakhtiari, I thought enviously.

We reached Shalamazar after seven hours and 120 miles of driving through almost trackless country in the dark. Sometimes our drivers lost the road entirely, and had to circle until our headlights picked up the ruts again. Our taxi got hopelessly stuck in a shallow, sandy river and there we sat—until a jeep-load of tribesmen arrived with shovels and dug us out. At last we came to the rock walls and tiny winding alleys of Shalama-zar, fully expecting to sleep in a mud hut, or a goat-hair tent. But at the far side of the town we turned into a wide avenue lined with poplars, at the end of which stood an imposing mansion. There the old chief lived.

When we walked up the richly carpeted stairway our way was lighted by uniformed serfs, standing rigid and holding long candles. I felt like Scarlett O'Hara ascending the stairs of Rhett Butler's mansion. We were taken to a long room where servants brought silver bowls filled with perfumed water, and soft towels. Later, on a veranda overlooking a garden and the snow-capped Zagros peaks, we were presented to the seventy-five-year-old khan, Ghulam Bakhtiar Bakhtiari. He seemed to have many sons, all of whom spoke good English, although the chief himself spoke only Persian. He had been to Europe once. What did he do there? "I met Queen Alexandria," he said through his interpreter, "and a lot of other pretty girls."

Sixteen of us sat down to dinner that night by candlelight, heightening the illusion of being guests in an old Southern manse. As usual there were no other women present and I was placed at the right of the host.

Middle Eastern wives, except for royalty, seldom eat with their men, and almost invariably, at banquets formal and in-formal, I was the only woman present, and, seated as the guest of honor, was served first. Frequently I would have exchanged my place for a seat below the salt, for I had to figure out how to handle strange dishes properly and, when possible, gracefully. For instance, when offered an enormous mountain of *kebab* (rice and meats) does one act dainty and spoon rice off the top, or disturb the whole mass by digging around for the chicken, partridge, or lamb undoubtedly hidden inside? I learned to dig.

Often yogurt, called *mast* in Iran, was mixed with the rice. One of the finest dishes was a yogurt soup, called *ab dough,* in-vented centuries ago without the aid of Gaylord Hauser, and eaten by generations of people who didn't know it was good for them. The yogurt was put into a big tureen, big cubes of ice

added, then sliced cucumbers, a few white raisins, and fresh
dill scattered on top. Stirred until it had the consistency of
cream soup, it was wonderfully refreshing when served on a hot
day. Since the Iranians liked to copy other peoples' trademarks,
the best yogurt had a picture of Mickey Mouse on the label,
and was called "Mickey Mast." Appropriately its closest com-
petitor was called "Minnie Mast."

After dinner, Franc and I lugged our sleeping bags to our
room, expecting that nomads slept on the floor. Instead, we
found beds spread with lovely linen, embroidered pillow cases,
and blankets with a lion crest. The whole room was draped,
tent-fashion, in a fine white mosquito net. Beside each bed stood
a silver water pitcher, and in the glasses was clean snow brought
fresh from the mountains each day. "A nomad's life for me,"
murmured Franc as he sank six inches into the soft mattress.

But that was the life of a chieftain, not a tribesman. In all
of the Bakhtiari country there were only three doctors to
serve 200,000 people. The only cash crop besides wool was pop-
pies, which means opium. The chiefs assured us the opium was
grown only for export.

We went by jeep, next day, to the tiny village of Oregon,
which in Persian means "Cloudy Hill." A delegation of elders
was lined up to greet Justice Douglas. Customarily, the Bakh-
tiaris sacrifice a cow in honor of distinguished visitors, and when
we arrived the cow was readied, a knife poised at its throat. The
young khan, Majid, ran ahead and stopped the slaughter, explaining that Justice Douglas didn't wish such a large sacrifice. A chicken was killed instead and thrown under the lead
car. This satisfied Justice Douglas perfectly, but disappointed
the tribesmen, who undoubtedly had planned on gorging themselves with beef that night.

Oregon was the center of the tribe's summer pastures. Our
party was housed in tents in a walnut grove beside a clear bubbling stream. The Justice was given a glistening white tent,
partitioned into several rooms. Ours was gaily striped in orange
and green. All the tents were floored with the famous Isfahan
carpets.

It was while we camped in Oregon that I unwittingly con-
tributed my small bit to the Major Lincoln legend, although it
was Justice Douglas who set the stage for me. One afternoon
the Justice went out riding alone, and when he returned, the
Bakhtiari chiefs, courteously curious, inquired as to what he had
seen. Without ever saying so outright, the Justice intimated with
a straight face and solemn manner that he might have been meeting Major Lincoln for a conference.

That night I was bothered by mosquitoes and got up to
search for the DDT. Wandering around in the dark, I tripped
and fell against the side of the tent. This upset our tripod, which
I had leaned against the outside tent wall, and it tumbled into
the mountain stream with a splash. Dressing hurriedly in Franc's
pants and shirt, I slipped out to rescue the equipment. I stayed
in the shadow so as not to alarm the guards, but it was necessary to wade into the icy stream, and I was pretty noisy about it.

The next morning at breakfast one of the Bakhtiari chiefs
told us solemnly that a guard reported that a man slipped into
our camp in the middle of the night and waded across the
stream. The intruder had not been shot, he continued, because
everyone knew that Major Lincoln was in the area, and no doubt
wished to contact one of the distinguished campers.

I didn't say a word, even when Franc wondered out loud
how his trousers got so wet during the night.

On another evening we listened while Justice Douglas and
the tribal chiefs sat cross-legged in a circle, and discussed the
problems of the Bakhtiari. The chiefs spoke of roads, schools,
and medical attention needed by their people. The Justice
pointed out that the United States was aiding Iran, and that no
doubt the tribes would share in this aid. He urged them to send
some of their smartest young men to America to study medicine
and agriculture. Through all his visit to the Bakhtiari the
Justice was a tireless seeker for facts. He was invariably courteous to the most humble herdsman, and while I doubt that the
tribesmen had any realization of the power and importance of
his position, they regarded him as a great man simply because
of his presence, his friendly dignity.

The next evening we watched the famous Bakhtiari stick dance. Perhaps it would be better to call it a stick fight, a pretty rough pastime which is played only by men, thank goodness. One tribesman was armed with a heavy pole, for defense, and his opponent with an inch-thick willow stick. The idea was that the man with the stick should knock the other's legs from under him. If a leg was broken, that proved the man with the stick was really an expert. Reedy instrumental music accompanied this weird dance, and it was fascinating, in a sadistic way. The tribesmen loved it. Justice Douglas and young Thomas tried a modified, bloodless version to the delight of the crowd.

I had often wondered why Persian carpets were so expensive. I found out when we returned to Isfahan and accompanied Justice Douglas on visits to several factories. Children did most of the work on the rugs. A child should be under ten to work on the very finest, a foreman told us, for after that age their fingers are too large to tie the delicate knots. We watched them sitting cross-legged on long planks at their looms, their fingers working so swiftly that they seemed a blur.

We talked, through an interpreter, to three children who had been working on an eight-by-six-foot carpet for a year, and had just reached the center. They were tying 600 knots to the square inch, and the rug was progressing at the rate of less than a quarter of an inch a day. They were being paid twenty-five cents for a twelve-hour day, which was more than they received before the Shah ordered some regulation of the industry.


When we returned to Tehran we had a last visit with the Shah. While leafing through our photographs, all of which he approved for publication, the Shah said, "Remember your friend in Maku?"

We certainly did. We had entertained the Shah and his family, at the picnic, with an account of our adventures in Azerbaijan, and the pajama-clad governor of Maku had been the villain of the story. Still, I was surprised that the Shah should think of it.

"I feel he needs a lesson in manners," said the Shah, selecting from the pile of photographs, one showing himself and Franc standing side by side on the palace terrace, inspecting a book, and looking for all the world like old school chums.

The Shah rang for a secretary, had an envelope bearing the royal crest addressed to the governor of Maku, and dropped the picture into it. No message, just the picture.

"Send this immediately," said the Shah.

Occasionally we think of that poor man of Maku just sitting in his filthy office, in his splotched pajamas, waiting for the ax to fall.

I wish I could bring myself to feel sorry for him.

# 6

# TEHRAN TO KABUL

THERE ARE ALL SORTS of conveyances that can transport you around this world, and I have traveled in everything from Bengali jungle dugouts to a Mediterranean yacht and to trans-Pacific airliners, but the bus that carried us east from Tehran was in a class by itself. It seemed designed for torture rather than travel. The springs were lifeless, and the narrow, upright seats were splintered. An Indian fakir would have adored them. Furthermore, the seats were not designed for longish Americans. The tops caught us just below the shoulder blades, the sharp edges cutting into our spines with every jounce, while our knees banged against the seats in front of us. And that bus did nothing but jounce over what Franc called a "corrugated obstacle course." Occasionally, the bouncing became too monotonous even for the driver, who would then turn off the "highway" and steer through plowed fields or across rocky pastures. We decided that Marco Polo, on horseback, was a lucky gent to have predated the "conveniences" of modern transportation.

Aboard was an English-speaking Persian, an employee of the Anglo-Iranian Oil Company in Abadan, who volunteered his help as guide and interpreter. He, his wife, and two small children were en route to the holy city of Meshed on a pilgrimage. For the same reason, the mighty Shah Abbas once walked from Isfahan to Meshed, but I think our modern Persian friend did more penance by riding the bus.

That evening we found a back room at the inn in Shahrud and went to bed early, knowing that the bus would leave at two in the morning. It is usual for Persian buses to start at three or four A.M. to avoid the heat, and to take a long noon halt out of the broiling sun. But two A.M. seemed a bit extreme.

We were awakened not at two, but at one. I was dehydrated from the heat, and parched. I reached for the jug of water on our table but Franc stopped me. "Let me put a halazone tablet in it. It's probably full of bugs."

"I don't care," I said, "unless I can see them."

I poured a glass of water and Franc flashed his light on it. To my astonishment, I *could* see the bugs, wriggling like mad along the bottom. I waited until I could get boiled water.

After noon we halted at a town with a magic name, Nishapur, where both Omar Khayyám and Hasan the Assassin were born, and where Omar is buried. Nishapur is only a half-hour gas stop, so we hurried to see the little blue-domed mosque in the courtyard of which rest the bones of the poet.

The Persians consider Omar only a minor poet, the Edgar A. Guest of their day, popular and prolific but hardly great. The Fitzgerald translation, they say, is far superior to the original verse. When Persians recite poetry, which they will do at the drop of a hexameter, they quote Saadi, Hafiz, and Ferdowzi, all natives of Shiraz, "the city of wisdom." The Persian poets are beloved by the people because of their rebellion against the austere dictates of the mullahs. Celebrating this theme, Hafiz sings of himself:

> *"Drink, Hafiz! Revel, all your cares unbend,*
> *And boldly scorn the mean dissembling knaves*
> *Who make religion every vice defend."*

In Tehran a scholar had told us that Omar's works were being translated from the Fitzgerald version *back* into Persian. "When that is completed," the professor had predicted, "Khayyám may take his place alongside Hafiz and Saadi, and suitably be honored as a poet in his own land. Now, he is famous as the scientist and astronomer who devised the Persian calendar."

It was there in Omar's Nishapur that our real camera trouble started. In most of Asia a camera is regarded as a secret weapon, and anyone who carries a camera is a probable spy. Our route to Kabul lay close along the Russian border, and military governors and police were allergic to fair-skinned photographers.

With our Polaroid camera I made a picture of one of the women aboard the bus, and produced a print a minute later, to the applause of my fellow passengers. Instantly a policeman appeared and rudely snatched the print from my hand. There must have been some military objective—such as a ragged recruit riding sideways on a donkey—in the background.

Franc lost his temper and snatched the picture back. He is always smiling and polite when dealing with even the pettiest official—until someone gets rough with me. More police arrived, and people began to crowd around us. Before we knew it, an ugly situation had developed. A little more heat and this murmuring crowd would have become an unreasoning mob.

The police yelled for our passports. Franc produced his, and when the angry official opened it, he jumped as if he had seen a snake. He saluted and returned the passport case immediately. Inside, and not by accident, my wise and far-sighted husband carried a photograph of himself and the Shah, standing together on the terrace of the royal palace. The police consulted excitedly

among themselves, but didn't bother us further. They ordered
the belligerent onlookers to disperse. The home of Omar Khayyám, who sang of love and wine and roses, had become a dusty
crossroads of hostility and suspicion from which we were relieved
to depart. I wondered whether Hasan was buried there too.

The next day at dusk we reached Meshed, the holiest city in
Iran and third holiest in the Moslem world. We had arrived
during Ramadan, the Moslem period of fasting, when the faithful are forbidden to eat or drink between sunup and sundown.
Thus all who can, stay indoors during the day. But in the
evening the streets were crowded with people going out to dine,
and with pilgrims thronging to the Great Mosque. Tempers
flare easily during the long period of fasting, and the bus driver
drove gingerly. At one point he carefully turned aside to avoid
the body of a woman, a pilgrim, I guessed, whose journey had
ended short of the mosque. Moslems who make the pilgrimage to
Meshed may prefix their names with "Meshadi," just as those
who reach Mecca may use "Haji." In the distance we could see
the giant gold-domed mosque, garishly lighted by strings of raw
electric bulbs that outlined its curves and ascended the minarets.
We were anxious to get off the streets, for the city has a reputation for anti-Christian feeling.

We took a droshky, adopting as a guide a small boy who
claimed he knew the whereabouts of the American missionary
hospital where we hoped to sleep. As soon as we rounded the
corner he leaped off and asked directions of a passer-by who
obviously had never heard of the mission. This was repeated
several times, until finally an English-speaking Armenian di-
rected the driver. We immediately fired our guide.

Our droshky rattled through twisting alleys and stopped at a
barred doorway. Franc knocked, a servant appeared, and led us
through a labyrinth of halls and arches, and into a large living
room where two couples sat chatting. Nicely furnished mission, I
thought. We introduced ourselves, and one of the men arose and
said, "I'm John Waller. You're just in time for a drink."

Very strange missionaries, I told myself. Franc asked, "Is this
the American mission?"

"No," said Waller, laughing. "This is the American Consulate."

We were caked with the dust and sweat of miles, and, as we learned later, could not have arrived at a more inopportune moment. The Wallers had just opened the consulate, Mrs. Waller was about to have a baby, most of their furniture was still unpacked, and the British consul and wife had come to dinner that night for the first time, so the Wallers were anxious to make a good impression. Nevertheless they invited us to join them at dinner and offered us a comfortable bedroom. Not until the next morning did we learn that the Wallers had slept on cots on the terrace. Ours was the only bedroom in the house.

That was by no means all. The British consul, a stuffy pillar of Empire, and very pukka sahib, thought our intrusion highly improper and showed it. Franc wasn't exactly in black tie, but I *was* ravishing in my dusty khaki slacks. When the Black Man's Burden learned that we were following the route of Marco Polo he announced that he was something of a Marco Polo scholar himself and insisted that we were on the wrong road.

We had verified the route by reading everything written by and about Polo, and consulting the maps and documents in the museum in Venice. He simply snorted at this and said, "I'll wager you didn't set foot in the British Museum!"

Later in the conversation Franc mentioned that we had spent some time in Acre and had found Israel interesting.

"Israel? Israel?" said the consul, as if the name somehow escaped him. "Oh, yes. *We* call that Palestine." Victoria could not have used the imperial "we" more loftily.

Franc, bless him, remained unabashed. "And what do *you* call Pakistan these days?"

The party broke up shortly afterward, and we enjoyed a nightcap with the Wallers and discussed transport to the Afghan border. John said that an Anglo-Iranian oil truck made occasional trips, and one was scheduled to leave in about three days. Then he laughed. "Once in a while," he said, "they lay on an extra truck—make a special trip—when I want to get rid of someone."

It was just a passing remark without significance until the next morning when, to our surprise, John awakened us at six. Anglo-Iranian, he explained, had found it necessary to run a special truck to the border.

"When does it leave?" Franc asked sleepily.

"In thirty minutes. You can just make it. Breakfast is ready downstairs."

We made it. As we jounced out of the outskirts of Meshed I asked the driver why the special trip. "I'm not sure," he answered, "except it was an emergency. They called me after midnight and told me to be ready to go out. The manager said something about doing a favor for an American friend of his. That's you, I suppose?"

A few hours out of Meshed the road abruptly widened into what seemed the main street of a modern town. "Maybe we can stop here for tea," I suggested hopefully to Franc.

"But I don't see any people," he answered.

Our Persian driver, who had learned English in Abadan too, leaned over and said, in his British accent, "Sorry, old man, but this town is not truly a town at all."

When I looked more closely down some of the side streets, I saw that the buildings were only façades. The back walls had never been finished. Even the most handsome were empty shells.

The Persian explained. During the reign of Reza Shah funds had been allotted for the construction of a new city called Farimun on this desiccated countryside, and a deadline set for its completion. Czechoslovakian architects and Meshed carpenters went to work. But when the date neared, the funds were exhausted and only the fronts of the buildings completed. There was no permanent population in residence and not likely to be one.

The authorities were properly fearful of telling Reza Shah the truth. On the day set for inspection by the hot-tempered ruler the false fronts were cleaned and painted, and an imported throng of "happy townspeople" cheered as the Shah was driven down the wide paved street. It was hoped that Reza Shah thought the town completed, but I trust that he was too observant to be deceived. However, if he accepted the construction of the sham town as an accomplished fact, then it would be accepted by the whole country, and he would be credited with another step toward a modern Iran. The story reminded us of the Potemkin villages thrown up for the edification of Catherine the Great on her tour of the Volga basin. On the way out of town I saw a few rubble shacks hidden behind the imposing shop fronts. That was the true "city."

Eighty miles east, in the village of Turbat-i-Jam, for the first time we found ourselves out of communication, written or oral, with the world. There the truck driver delivered us to the home of another Anglo-Iranian employee, and left. By and by, he predicted, a postal bus would come this way, and undoubtedly would take us farther toward the Afghan border.

Neither our new host nor anyone else in the village spoke any language we knew. Yet he was quite hospitable, fed us tea and fruit, and then led us to a surprisingly elaborate guest bedroom, with linen slip covers on the chairs, embroidery counterpanes on the bed, and an arch of draperies over the head of the bed. Just before we sat down, our host, obviously embarrassed, rushed into our room with two stiff cane chairs. He demonstrated that we should sit on them rather than on the overstuffed chairs. Then he motioned that we should spread our sleeping bags on the floor. Perhaps his wife, though we never glimpsed her, had studied us from behind the curtains and decided that we were too grimy for her best linens.

To our great relief, the very next day a postal bus rumbled into Turbat-i-Jam and the turbaned driver welcomed us aboard as formally as if he captained a ship. This Persian postal bus not only carried mail and people but baskets of melons, cans of goat's milk, boxes and parcels of all varieties. Once it stopped to give a lift to a tribesman leading a sheep. The tribesman swore he had no money to pay the fare. Our driver searched him, found no money, and let him ride free. The sheep was lifted into the bus and stood quietly in the aisle.

As we entered Youssefabad, the last town before the border, we could see dust rising from a bus, just leaving and headed east. We had missed a vital connection by a matter of minutes. As the next bus for Afghanistan would not leave for four days, the situation was at once exasperating and ridiculous. Every day was precious to us, if we were to reach the Wakhan before the snows. The Afghan frontier was only two hours' drive away, and yet without transport it was as inaccessible as the moon. We wandered through every street in town trying to hire a means of conveyance, any means. Two camels would have been fine. We had no success.

There was no inn of any kind in Youssefabad, and no Americans or friendly Anglo-Iranian employee to befriend us. At the Iranian customs shed, where we asked for a place to sleep, a tall, handsome customs officer introduced himself in passable English. He was studying English by linguaphone, and insisted on taking us to his own home. This would give him a chance to practice, he explained, and would give him great pleasure. We assured him that a place to sleep would give *us* great pleasure.

Gholam Hossein Shakibai's wife did not eat with us that evening nor the following two. She came shyly to sit with me, however, while I unpacked, but we could only smile at each other. We had no words to share, yet a smile is common currency the world over, and before I left we were friends.

Shakibai and Franc sat in the evenings and engaged in long discussion of politics and history. Shakibai had an alert, receptive, logical mind, and he picked up English phrases and American colloquialisms with astonishing facility. A year later, when we flew back to Tehran, we found Shakibai promoted to chief customs inspector at Mehrabad Airport, the most important post of its kind in the country. We were pleased and surprised that superiority in a remote post would be so quickly rewarded.

Our host set up cots for us in the dining room, but we preferred to sleep on the roof. It was the dark of the moon, and nowhere in the world are the stars so bright as in Persia, as her renowned poets have so often noted. Indeed, it seemed that a prodigal giant had flung all the Shah's diamonds against the soft velvet dome of our tent, while the planets hung low and fat, like bright baubles that you could reach out and grasp. Counting stars is a lovely way of finding sleep.

On the third day of fretting in Youssefabad, our luck changed. A Persian diplomat traveling to Herat, the first large Afghan city on the other side of the border, was driven up to the customs post in a feeble British Ford fitted with a luggage rack on top. With him were his wife, grown son, and three small children. When he generously offered to give us a lift to Herat we were dumfounded. We could not figure out how even one of us, without barracks bags, sleeping bags, camera case, and all the rest of it, could possibly squeeze in. Yet we could not afford to lose another day. We accepted, waiting to see how this miracle could be arranged. We were seated in the front with the driver, with our bags piled to the roof on our laps. Another mountain of luggage was thrown up on the top and strapped securely. In the back seat the diplomat, his wife, and oldest son each took a small child on his lap. And we were off.

In an hour and a half we were at Islam Qala, the border, and since we were traveling with an official, formalities were kept at a minimum. The guard officer asked for our passports and Franc accompanied him into the bleak shack while the visas were checked. The rest of us baked silently in the tiny car.

Inside the shack, while Franc watched, the guard carefully read our passports, page by page, upside down. Then he nodded wisely, reached for his rubber stamp and pad, and turned to a clean page. He ground the stamp on the pad, then on the passport. No print. The ink pad was dry as the desert. He tried again, leaning all his weight on it. Still no imprint. He sighed, and, as if this was not unusual, licked the passport page thoroughly, and whammed the stamp on it. A perfect impression! He handed the passports to Franc, and we were safely in Afghanistan.

The Persian diplomat dropped us at the largest inn of Herat, one of a chain of guest hostels built about 1930 by the assassinated king, Mohammed Nadir Shah, the first of Afghanistan's modern rulers. It had fallen into disrepair, since so few travelers have been admitted in recent years; yet, wonder of wonders, we were given a room with bath. Quite a unique bath, as it turned out. When you pulled the stopper in the tub, the water drained out on the floor. The American toilet was appropriately named "The Real Niagara." When you pulled the flush chain a cascade of water descended on your head.

Soon after our arrival, the Afghan manager came to our room and spoke the magic word "Police!" The word must be the same in every language. How typical, I thought. Here we were, dirty, tired and hungry, and before we could even wash our hands we would have to contend with the police.

Not so. The "police" was on the office telephone. When Franc answered, a pleasant voice said in English, "This is Rafik, chief of police. I know you must be tired from your trip. What time would it be convenient for me to call in the morning to check your passports?"

Franc could not keep the surprise out of his voice. "Make it ten o'clock and thanks for the consideration." This gentleman seemed so out of character for the Middle East.

Promptly at ten Rafik arrived, a rotund, forceful-looking man dressed in a Western suit but wearing a karakul hat. He welcomed us to Herat, rapidly and efficiently checked our papers, and then asked what he could do to help us.

"The first thing you can do," Franc said, "is tell us where you learned English."

"Sure," he smiled. "For two years I served with the Royal Canadian Mounted Police in Saskatoon, Saskatchewan."

We told Rafik about our Marco Polo trip and our desire to follow the northern route, as Polo had, to Kabul. Rafik looked worried. All modern travelers to Kabul used the southern route through Kandahar, he answered, which took only two days, or the central road, which took four. There was, he warned us, no real transportation service whatsoever on the Polo route, there were few inns, the mountains were high, it was on the Russian border, and we would find no one who spoke English. We had heard all this before. Rafik tried another tack. He himself had traveled through Badakshan nearly to the Wakhan and he warned us that winter came early. Anyway, he frankly doubted that we would be allowed into that area at all. We refused to be discouraged and Rafik finally gave up. "I'll do what I can for you. I'll get you seats on the next bus headed northeast and have it call at your hotel."

He didn't need the red coat and Boy Scout hat to look like a Mountie to me! "How long will that be?" I asked.

It was hard to tell. There was no such thing as a regular bus "system" in northern Afghanistan. Buses ran between the larger towns, but they maintained no schedule.

Was there any other means of transportation to Kabul? Nothing but camels, said Rafik, and Kabul was nine hundred miles away. We reluctantly settled down in Herat, sight-seeing in a droshky by day, when we weren't plaguing Rafik to find transport for us, and playing gin rummy every night. I lost a thousand dollars to Franc, a debt I airily canceled with an I.O.U.

Herat, a city of 85,000, was once twenty times as large, a great commercial and communications center for all of Asia. It was also known as the artistic capital of the Middle East, the home of the finest miniature painters. Its origin is lost in antiquity, but some believe it as old an inhabited place as there is on earth. Around the present city are many square miles of rubble and ruined walls, the debris of forgotten civilizations. Because of its strategic position at a crossroads between Russia, India, and Persia, Herat was overrun by conquering armies time and time again, pillaged, looted, burned, but always rebuilt. In 1232 Genghis Khan stormed its enormous earthen walls—250 feet wide at the base—and in the resulting massacre only forty inhabitants of a population of more than a million survived. Tamerlane overwhelmed Herat again in 1383 and slaughtered nearly all its inhabitants. Yet it was his descendants who decreed Herat should be their capital, and who inspired its age of splendor.

In Herat I first saw women wearing the burka, an outer garment shaped precisely like a tent, and almost as attractive. These tents, completely covering the wearer, had small eye holes covered by lattice-work embroidery, which allowed whoever was under the burka to look out, without even her eyes being seen. Most burkas were drab in color, but a few were green, pale blue, or deep red. The American male might imagine that the brightly colored burkas covered shapely Afghan debutantes, but it would be strictly a wild guess.

One afternoon while we were drinking tea at a side-street café, a crowd began to gather, muttering and gesturing. The omnipresent police drifted our way and one, who spoke a little English, said, "I think madam move now."

"I think madam finish her tea," Franc answered.

Now what had I done wrong?

"Madam will move now—now!" the policeman screeched.

"But why?" I demanded. "Why?"

"Madam's face is showing," said the policeman.

Thank goodness Franc didn't think it that bad. Feeling absolutely naked, I left.

The burka is worn mostly in the cities and towns. In the countryside, where women must work in the fields, thresh grain and tend herds, such a garment is impractical. Countrywomen always veil their faces when they see a stranger, however. Women like me, who left their faces naked, had terrible reputations. After the experience in the teahouse, I always wore a large scarf over my head, and stayed away from crowds.

Once again we were arrested for photographing ancient minarets, some of them two hundred feet high, leaning as crazily as the Tower of Pisa. Rafik rescued us, but warned that we had better put our cameras away and forget them until we got out of Herat.

"Surely," Franc said, "a minaret is not a military installation."

"No, but it is a crime to photograph any slum area," Rafik said.

"That minaret wasn't a slum area, was it?"

Rafik made a broad gesture. "All of Herat, except the city parks, is a slum area."

One night late in July a bus decided to travel northeast. Rafik shook our hands, wished us luck, and, obviously somewhat relieved, put us aboard. For most of the next eleven days and

Dressed in a *chapon*, here I sit beside a warm mineral spring near Nurss, in the Wakhan corridor. The mountains in the background are in the U.S.S.R.

Above Baroghil in the Wakhan. we rode for long hours to get to this bridge before dark. The stick and stone construction groaned and swayed under each horse and man, and one overloaded yak fell partly through. This bridge spans the Shor River, and in the rapids at the lower right, Franc took his unplanned dip.

This *yurt* is in the Pamir Plateau 'village" of Langar, which consisted of only two *yurts*. Our party slept here with this Kirghiz family in their clean neat home. The interior construction of a nomad shelter shows clearly here: lattice frame with reed matting placed behind it and bent poles overhead.

This *yurt* sits in the edge of Rahman Qul's encampment at Bozai Gumbaz. The reed door and a hole in the top are the only means of ventilation. Bedding and mats air in the sunshine.

nights we traveled on the world's most haphazard transportation system, a succession of Afghan buses. Afghanistan is one of the few large countries in the world in which there are no railroads. At the end of the first eight days we had traveled only 510 miles from Herat to Mazar-i-Sharif, the holy city of Afghanistan.

Our route ran very close to the Russian border, and often we saw blue-eyed, blond children, indicating that there had been traffic of some kind across that closed border. We glimpsed, occasionally, the fortifications of Afghanistan, which included field guns of Civil War vintage and one bronze, bell-mouthed, muzzle-loading cannon—manned and ready. Aimed north, too.

An Afghan bus runs by no schedule, nor is there such a thing as "making a connection." Each time a bus reached the end of its particular line and turned back west again, we were left stranded in some public square. Franc, the linguist in the family, frantically began learning Afghan.

The buses themselves consisted of homemade bodies wired to decrepit truck frames. They were always overcrowded and overloaded. All luggage except what each passenger could hold on his lap (in the case of the Afghans: children, melons, baskets, chickens) was tied to the top. On some occasions overflow passengers also rode on top. Almost always the buses left from an hour to six hours late.

Because of the unremitting heat of the day, most of our traveling was done by night. But while the days were suffocating, the nights were frightfully cold. Frequently we rode sitting up in our sleeping bags. The Afghans wore their warm woolen *chapons*, or hooded sheepskin coats, extending to the heels, with sleeves so long gloves were unnecessary.

A typical day's ride started at, say, seven P.M. After perhaps seven hours of travel, there was a stop for the night, or what remained of it. If we happened to be in a village, we slept in public parks, on some hospitable citizen's porch, at the curb, or infrequently at an inn. If we happened to be out in the country we slept either in the bus or out on the fields. Once, a nervous citizen trying to sleep on top of the bus had insomnia and walked up and down most of the night, keeping everyone inside awake. These "stops for the night" usually lasted three or four hours, and we would be off again until daylight, when we'd stop for tea. When the heat became unbearable at noon we'd halt for the rest of the day, sometimes in a village, sometimes at a farm where we could find shade, and occasionally in an expanse of desolate dunes where we'd have to crawl under the bus for shelter.

On this part of our journey we began to eat with our fingers. Here, too, we were introduced to clarified butter, called ghee, with which the Afghans drench many dishes. We had taken the precaution of buying two spoons in Tehran, but found it difficult to compete when using them. The person using his fingers would always get the choice chunks of meat.

The technique of eating, Afghan style, was to grab a handful of rice, mold it into a ball and dip it into any side dishes that looked tempting. The side dishes were beans and ghee, tomatoes and ghee, squash and ghee, or peppers and ghee. Ghee, made by melting butter and skimming off the foam, was a yellow liquid which never seemed to resolidify. Fresh ghee was rather like an old dressing, but rancid ghee was quite another thing. Most of the ghee we ate was rancid. Our Afghan friends seemed to take no notice of its state of preservation. Learning to like ghee, I guess, is like acquiring a taste for sea slugs, hung game, and octopus. Only harder.

Once the rice had been dipped in the side dish it became more difficult to hold on to, and the safest thing to do was to pop it into the mouth as quickly as possible. Our meals were served on the floor or on the ground as we squatted in a circle with the Afghans. The center dish was a mountain of rice covering lamb joints or roasted chickens. The side dishes were in bowls set in a ring around the huge central tray. There were no plates, napkins, or forks. Lucky Afghan housewives!

As Moslems eat with the right hand only, and we did not wish to appear impolite or unsportsmanlike, we followed their custom. For a time it placed me at a disadvantage as I found it quite difficult to tear chunks off a leg of mutton, or the wing from a fowl, unless the person next to me volunteered to reach in and hold the meat down. But the main objection to this style of eating was the excess of ghee. I found it impossible to finish a meal without grease dripping from my elbow. The Mongols, who serve in the same manner as the Afghans, had a solution for this problem. At a nomad meal, when the right hand becomes so greasy as to be unusable, it is considered *de rigueur* to wipe it on your dinner companion's shoulder. This not only solves the grease problem but waterproofs his coat.

From Meshed to Kabul we never saw Western food, and our manners were permanently impaired.

We stopped in towns with names like Qaisar, Andkhui and Agchah where no one spoke English, French, Turkish, or any other language that we knew. At first we didn't speak a single word of Pashto, and were walled in by our linguistic short-comings. In Afghanistan, even the sign language was different. Early in our travels, Franc had compiled a list of one hundred words and phrases necessary no matter what the country or language. As soon as he could, after entering a country, he would learn the local equivalents. First, how to count from one to ten. Then, "Where is the—" and a list of nouns such as hotel, food, bus, water. Next came "How much?" Then, "Too much!" We put his system to good use crossing the wild sections of Afghanistan.

Our buses stopped for everything. They stopped for tea six times a day, and also at odd hours throughout the night. They stopped for Moslem prayers even more often. Moslems regularly pray five times a day, but as our passengers belonged to two different sects, Sunnites and Shiites, who didn't agree on prayer hours, there were ten stops daily for foot washing, then prayers. We also stopped for hitchhiking shepherds, burned-out headlights, flat tires, clogged gas lines, no oil, or simply because the engine wouldn't run.

On the last lap to Mazar-i-Sharif the bearings burned out in a desert area where the dunes rolled away to the horizon like the sea. The driver disassembled the motor, and then went to work with a pair of shears and a strip of metal, to shape a new bearing. Franc shook his head and murmured, "It'll never work." Three hours later when the homemade bearing was in place, the motor didn't even cough. The driver made a short speech, indicating that if we all pushed, the motor might turn over. None of the Afghans seemed enthusiastic. Two Uzbek tribesmen wandered by, and were promised a ride to the next town if they'd help. Franc and the Uzbeks and the Afghans began to push, Franc and the Uzbeks straining and heaving, but the Afghans merely leaning against the bus. At this Franc lost his temper, calling the Afghans all manner of things in a number of languages which I was glad they could not understand. Then he booted each Afghan rear, just once. This they understood instantly. They all pushed hard, the motor sputtered, the bus started, and we scrambled back aboard as it lumbered across the desert. The makeshift bearing lasted about fifty miles before it burned out again, this time fortunately in a village where we could eat melons while the driver, resourceful fellow, cut a new one.

A bus driver is an elite technician in Afghanistan, considerably higher up the social scale than the first pilots of our largest air lines. While they make repairs under conditions, and with tools, that would cause an American mechanic to throw up his hands in despair, they are utterly disdainful of the comfort of their passengers. One ingenious driver would amuse himself during our night runs by waiting until all the passengers were asleep, and then switching on the interior lights and slamming on the brakes. He'd watch, chuckling, as the passengers disentangled themselves, grumbling a bit. Then we'd be off again only to have the performance repeated thirty minutes later. Another driver delighted in rushing us into the stifling bus, then sitting in the inn over a leisurely cup of tea. If anyone else ventured out, he would chase them back in with threats of a sudden departure.

Mazar-i-Sharif, the Holy City, where the fourth caliph, Hazrat Ali, is buried, was a sizable oasis with 30,000 inhabitants. We had been warned that the population disliked Christian infidels, and not to go near the mosque. The local inn seemed hospitable enough, and the proprietor, who was porter, waiter, room clerk and laundryman as well, showed us to a room with two bed frames and a table. Real luxury. Across the hall was a bathroom, of which he was inordinately proud. All it lacked was water pipes; there were none anywhere. We admired the porcelain fixtures, however, so as not to hurt the manager's feelings and suppressed our smiles when we saw the toilet. The seat had been put on upside down, and three rubber knobs adorned the wooden circle. "Nonskid," Franc commented.

The next morning at breakfast, we were once again frustrated by our ignorance of the language. Franc explained in his limited, newly acquired Pashto that I wanted my eggs hard-boiled. No reaction. He made motions of boiling water, thumping the table to show how hard I liked my eggs. Then he showed the proprietor the teapot, indicating that the eggs were to be boiled like the water for tea. A light dawned. The proprietor grinned, shook his head vigorously, yes, and was off to the bazaar.

He returned with a tray holding a teapot and bread, but no eggs. The proprietor beamed, proudly lifting the lid from the teapot, and there were the two eggs floating near the bottom among the sodden tea leaves. The eggs, placed in the tea after it was made, were barely warm and decidedly raw. We could only nod in approval.

In the bazaar we bought a beautiful piece of lapis lazuli the size of a lemon for a dollar, remembering Marco Polo's note that there were mountains nearby "in which are found veins of lapis lazuli, the stone which yields the azure color (ultramarine), here the finest in the world."

We were not so lucky in our search for a balas ruby. Of these stones "of fine quality and great value," Polo had written, "they are imbedded in the high mountains, but are searched for only in one, named Sikinan. In this the king causes mines to be worked, and through this channel alone they are obtained; no person daring, under pain of death, to make an excavation for the purpose unless he obtains his majesty's license. Occasionally the king gives them as presents, as they are not procurable by purchase from others, and cannot be exported without his permission. His object in these restrictions is, that the rubies of his country, with which he thinks his credit connected, should . . .

maintain their high price; for if they could be dug for in-
discriminately, so great is their abundance that they would soon
be of little value."

Today's diamond syndicate, I decided, wasn't being very
original.

Overhead, as we wandered toward the mosque, we glimpsed
its huge, dark-blue dome, like lapis, rearing from a garden.
Wherever we stopped to make photographs we attracted crowds,
and thought it best to move on. Near the mosque, a group of
ugly-looking boys began to follow us. The crowd grew, and the
boys hooted, yelled, and finally threw a few rocks. The oldest
made rude signs and gestures of throat-slitting. We hurried back
to the hotel, where the manager explained that since I was the
first American woman to visit Mazar-i-Sharif, their "curiosity"
was understandable.

He comforted us with a bowl of peaches, for which the area
is world-famous. They were bigger than a teacup, flushed pink
in color, and so juicy that it was best to eat them while leaning
over the balcony rail.


IN CONTRAST to the boys who had stoned us in Mazar-i-Sharif,
our fellow passengers on the bus to Kabul were helpful and
pleasant, although few of them had ever seen any Americans.
Whenever one of them split a melon, we were handed a slice.
Grapes and apples, sometimes dried fruits and raisins, were also
pressed upon us. And as our bus bounced across the desert between Tashkurgan and Kunduz, a burly, bearded Afghan inched
his way down the aisle to our seat, reached into a pocket of his
baggy trousers, and brought out a round chunk of crystallized
sugar, about the size of a tennis ball but much stickier. Bits of
wool clung to it. He extended it to Franc.

Franc smiled and tried to indicate that the delicacy was the
most enticing treat he had ever seen, but that he had just eaten
and could not fully savor such a treasure.

The Afghan smiled, and insisted. Franc smiled, and declined.

"I bet you lose this set," I murmured, looking determinedly out the window for fear the Afghan might press it on me.

With a quick motion the Afghan grabbed Franc's hand, pressed the sticky ball into it, pounded Franc on the shoulder with what he meant to be a friendly pat, and sat down on the knee of the man in front of us—keeping his eyes on Franc to be sure he enjoyed the present.

Franc conceded the point, took out his knife, cut a slice off the primitive candy and ate it. The Afghan was delighted. But what was to be done with the remainder? Obviously, on a sweltering day, Franc couldn't just sit there for miles holding it, nor could we drop it out the window, which was jammed shut. So Franc, Afghan fashion, shoved the gooey lump into his pocket. That night we pried Franc's knife, some paper money, and our key chain from its surface, and disposed of it. *"You* will eat the next present!" was Franc's ultimatum.

During many noontime siestas all the passengers relaxed and rested—except the Shors. We were curiosities. In these remote villages, where foreigners perhaps had never stopped, we attracted as much attention as a traveling zoo. Our bus drivers could have sold tickets. Occasionally Franc, chivalrous fellow, would leave me as a decoy for the crowd, while he slipped off for a bath in an irrigation ditch, or a nap under a shrub. Unfortunately I was never able to curl up and take a nap in a public park, teahouse, or roadside shelter. A dozen people standing around and staring kept me wide awake.

As we learned more of the language and the customs of the country, we found we made friends easily with the Afghans. Basically, Afghans are not so extraordinarily different from many Americans. Afghans are of Aryan stock, fair-skinned with dark hair. Nearly all the men wear beards. They are a handsome race in a rugged way. One of the Afghans who stands out in my memory was a big, kindly mullah who escorted Franc back to our inn near Agchah, when a holiday crowd began to jeer the foreigner.

"With your beard, you might be a fellow Mussulman," he

commented, putting his arm protectively around Franc's shoulder, silencing the crowd by his gesture.

Another Afghan friend was the police chief in Shirim Tagas, who insisted that we rest in the barracks compound while the bus was being "rebuilt" one afternoon. Tea and hard-boiled eggs arrived, and as we squatted on the carpet the chief picked up a pebble, cracked the shells of each egg thoroughly all around, rolled them a moment in his palms, and the shells fell off in one piece. I thought of all the eggs I had mutilated at picnic lunches. I had to travel ten thousand miles to learn to peel an egg!

When we departed, this same policeman strolled to the bus with us, a huge melon under each arm. We thought he had come to see us off, but instead he got on the bus. As mile after mile passed, we guessed he must be going to the next village, but just as the meter turned seven miles, he commanded the driver to stop, presented us with the melons, and got off. We were in the middle of a wide valley, with no houses or means of transportation in sight. He turned and walked back toward Shirim Tagas. It was not until we reached Kabul and learned more of Afghan courtesy, that we found the chief had only done what custom requires for departing guests. The host rides with them seven miles on their journey, gives them a gift, and returns to his home.

Everywhere along the route, history was mute before us, frozen in stone. Ruined castles perched in impossible places. These, the Afghans said, were "Kaffir-ha," meaning pre-Moslem, and we would speculate how the tides of successive invasions must have swept around them, and of the long-forgotten battles that destroyed them. Near ancient Balkh were endless, magnificent first-century walls, and the crumbling half domes of ruined mosques. Of Balkh, Marco Polo had written that once it contained many marble palaces, "still visible, although in a ruinous state." And it was in Balkh, according to Polo, that Alexander the Great "took to wife the daughter of King Darius," though historians refute the statement. We passed mounds of adobe that marked the sites of caravansaries. Occasionally we overtook long camel caravans winding through the dunes to the sonorous accompaniment of their bells. Our bus crept at a steady twenty-mile-an-hour pace across deserts, around hairpin turns ascending high mountains, and along the ditches of irrigated valleys. Marco Polo's descriptions still fitted the route perfectly, and his book read like a recent dispatch, accurate even in detail, for this land had changed little in seven hundred years.

And there was a wondrous procession of faces, varying by tribe and locale. Strong, handsome, fierce faces—but men only. Only occasionally did women ride the buses, and when they did appear they were heavily veiled in burkas, and pointedly chaperoned by father, husband, or brother. It was impossible to guess either age or general appearance.

One morning a veiled woman carrying a young child, accompanied by her husband, got on the bus. They settled themselves across the aisle from us, and shortly afterward the baby began to cry. The mother reached through a slit in the front of her burka, drew out an ample breast, and nursed the infant. Soon the baby slept, and perhaps the mother too, for her breast continued to hang out as we journeyed on. The Afghans did not even notice, but had she lifted her veil an inch to show her nose it would have been a public scandal.

I saw unveiled tribal women later in Badakhshan, but even in Kabul, where members of the government entertained us, their wives and daughters were never present. I was introduced to only one Afghan lady in the whole country. She was the wife of the provincial governor in Maimana.

While we were waiting in Maimana between buses, a teen-age boy came to the inn with a note for me, written in pink ink on paper decorated with rosebuds. It said, "Please come to tea at four." I looked puzzled. "It is from my mother," explained the neat youngster in English. "She heard you were in town. She went to England once. She doesn't speak English. I will talk for her. Please come."

After changing into my best khaki slacks and a clean plaid cotton shirt, I walked with the boy to his home. In the parlor he introduced me to a short woman, weighing perhaps a hundred and eighty-five pounds, overflowing out of baggy pantaloons and an overblouse. Her short black hair was brushed straight back.

The palms of her hands were stained with a bright-red dye which didn't come off when we shook hands (I sneaked a look). She nodded for me to sit down on a pile of cushions.

The son excused himself and turned to leave the room. "But wait," I protested, "how can I talk to your mother without your help?"

"I will have to sit outside the door," he said, "and interpret for you. I cannot remain here, for some young ladies might come for tea also."

A maid brought tea and local sweets and English fruit drops. I visited with my hostess as best I could, our questions and answers being relayed by the boy from behind the door.

"Excuse me," said madam suddenly. She left the room only to return a few moments later wearing a brightly printed American house dress, sturdy English brogues, and lisle stockings rolled just under her bulging knees. I complimented her on her fetching outfit, and we had more tea.

She excused herself again, and this time returned wearing a tweed suit, low-heeled pumps having replaced the brogues. I was both confused and impressed by this impromptu fashion show, and wondered what was coming next.

By this time I was repeating what I had already told her, that I liked Afghanistan and the cookies were good and her taste in clothes excellent. She popped out of the room a third time, and came back wearing a dark-blue crepe dress with a scarf tied around her hair. I had glimpsed a series of veiled faces passing by the door as I chatted with my hostess, but her other guests were apparently too shy to enter and bare their faces to a foreigner. Ultimately my appetite for English fruit drops and small talk was more than satisfied and I bade her good-by.


MELONS ARE Franc's favorite food, and everywhere the markets were piled with mounds of yellow, green, and white ones. But we looked forward to Shibarghan which, Polo had stated, "is plentifully supplied with every kind of provision, and is particularly celebrated for producing the best melons in the world . . . they are eagerly sought for, being sweet as honey."

Conveniently our bus broke down in the Shibarghan bazaar, and Franc bargained for an assortment. We sampled every kind, and drove away lauding the accuracy of our reporter friend.

At one o'clock one morning our bus pulled into the completely darkened square of the town of Pul-i-Khumr. The driver and the Afghan passengers got off and wandered away into the night. The square was surrounded by low mud buildings with arcade-style porches in front. People were sleeping on many of them, and we stumbled around looking for a place to spread our bags. On one of these porches stood a low, narrow wooden frame with rawhide thongs stretched across, making a primitive bedstead. "Just the thing," Franc said happily, and spread his bag from head to foot, then mine in the opposite direction. We put our cameras and exposure meters around our necks for safety's sake, and wormed our way inside the bags, boots and all. There were too many barefoot Afghans who might be tempted with stout GI shoes. Except that a partridge hanging in a cage near my head kept making whirring noises, I slept soundly. Some man, I was vaguely aware, kept shaking Franc from time to time and muttering things. Franc, irritated and half asleep, ordered him off.

At dawn the bus honked, and we reluctantly crawled out. At the head of our bed sat a big, sad-looking fellow who nodded glumly at our greeting. He rose, shook his finger in Franc's face, and in eloquent sign language made us understand that we had been sleeping in his bed. He had left it briefly at one A.M. to go around the corner on private business, and on returning had found two foreigners occupying his domain. I wondered whether there was an Afghan version of "The Three Bears." Franc gave him two afghanis, which he understood, and I promised to recommend his place to Duncan Hines and the AAA, which he didn't.

The gateway to Kabul is the awesome gorge of the Shibar River. The cliffs rise three thousand feet straight up from the edge of the roaring river, and the road, a masterpiece of engineering, is carved from the living rock. It is the most spectacular scenery in all Afghanistan. We came the length of it on a bright, clear night with a full moon.

The gorge narrowed, the stream grew thinner, and we climbed steadily until we stopped for a moment atop the spectacular Shibar Pass, 8,379 feet high. We had crossed the Hindu Kush divide. The terrain dropped swiftly thereafter, and we picked up a new stream running in the opposite direction. Soon we entered a land of fruit trees and fertile fields and irrigation ditches. The character of the people changed as well. The country Afghan wears baggy trousers, shoes with turned-up toes, long-tailed shirts, black waistcoats and turbans. Now the men we passed, although similarly clad, seemed better dressed, taller, stronger. To understand the fierce fighting qualities of the Afghan all one need do is to look at him—or ask the British.

On the outskirts of Kabul the houses changed in style from the small country homes of stone and mud. We saw two-story gray stone buildings of European architecture, government bureaus and offices, and a movie theater which advertised a Tarzan picture. Afghanistan's capital is a city of 120,000, but there was only one hotel that catered to foreigners, the Kabul Hotel. We stuffed the potbellied stove in our bathroom with wood and waited for the luxury of hot water, reveling in our brief respite from travel.

After weeks of struggling with Pashto and sign language, it was a pleasure to meet fellow Americans in the dining room. One, a visiting professor at an Afghan college, had been staying at the hotel for a year. Three others were young and bearded American archeologists preparing to go on a "dig" in the Helmand River Valley. The six of us chatted together at meals, feeling terribly garrulous, for three silent Russian technicians ate at an adjoining table. They never glanced our way, nor uttered a word.

The Russians entered the dining room single file at the instant it opened for a meal, the tallest one in front, a medium-sized bald one in the middle, and a little fat one in the rear. They looked comical, but I never seemed to have the right words to describe them until one evening Hap Hart, one of the archeologists, began to whistle softly as they marched into the dining room. The tune was:

> *"Heigh ho, heigh ho,*
> *It's off to work we go . . ."*

Our big task, perhaps the most difficult of all, confronted us now. We must somehow persuade Afghan officialdom to let us travel through the Wakhan. As a preliminary step, Franc asked to meet the American ambassador, only to be told that the ambassador was very new and very busy, and could not see us. However, we could call on a vice-consul in the afternoon.

The vice-consul was not new in Kabul, nor busy, but he was very young, rather bored, and quite supercilious. I had the definite impression that he considered visiting American journalists a nuisance. He asked what had brought us to Kabul, and Franc casually laid it on the line for him. "Only two things," Franc said. "We want permission to cross the Wakhan, and we want to photograph and interview the King."

The young man was horrified. From his expression you might have thought that we had asked permission to assassinate the King, not just to photograph him. As for the Wakhan . . . "It is absolutely impossible to get permission to enter the Wakhan," he said. "Sensitive military zone, you know. Many people have made the same request. Have, for years. Not one has been granted. Even archeologists, historians, and geographers with the official backing of our embassy have been turned down. The British, Germans, French, and Danes have all tried. They all have been refused.

"As for seeing the King, why that's absurd! He never, never gives interviews. Even our ambassador only sees him when he presents his credentials. Photographs, of course, are absolutely out of the question."

The young man said "photographs" as if it were a dirty word. We would not only get no help here, but might actually be hindered. Since the embassy had made the request for others, and been turned down, its pride would suffer if Americans with no official backing succeeded. I began to wish we'd followed Amundsen to the Pole, or Cortez through Mexico, or something else easy.

That evening we dined with David Wharton, the commercial attaché, and his wife Toby. Wharton was blunt, though pleasant, and just as discouraging. "If that's what you came for," he said, "you might as well forget it. Nobody can get through the Wakhan. We won't even ask officially on your behalf. No use to be rebuffed."

Toby Wharton temporarily distracted me from gloomy conjecture by modeling a costume she'd bought in the bazaar. It had yards and yards of cotton in the pantaloons, an embroidered jacket, and a filmy blouse. With turned-up shoes and ropes of junk jewelry we decided she would be a sensation at a Halloween party—or any kind of party—back in the States. It was interesting to see what was really worn under those ungainly burkas, and I recalled that Marco Polo had reported on ladies' fashions in Afghanistan, and evidently the styles, like the countryside, had remained unchanged. "A peculiar fashion of dress prevails amongst the women of the superior class, who wear below their waists, in the manner of drawers, a kind of garment, in the making of which they employ, according to their means, an hundred, eighty, or sixty ells of fine cotton cloth; which they also gather or plait, in order to increase the apparent size of their hips; those being accounted the most handsome who are the most bulky in that part."

Back at the hotel, Franc unpacked his map case. I could see that he was as discouraged as I. "There's one other way," he said. "We could go through the Khyber Pass into Pakistan, then travel north from Peshawar to Gilgit. From there we'd pass through the Hunza Valley, and enter Sinkiang from the south. That way, we'd avoid the Wakhan entirely."

"And leave Marco Polo's route," I wailed, "after all the trouble we've taken to follow it?"

We talked late into the night, ultimately agreeing that we would make every effort to follow the exact trail. However, just in case we had to digress a bit we secured Pakistani visas the next day. In any event, we would not turn back.

The one favor the uncooperative vice-consul did us was to refer us to Syed Kasim Khan Rishtya, the chief of the Afghan Department of Press. Mr. Rishtya was a pleasant surprise. He spoke excellent English, was cordial and well-informed, and he not only had time for us, but seemed genuinely sympathetic and interested. It did not seem so strange to him that we should want to follow the trail of Marco Polo through Afghanistan and beyond. Rather it seemed a fine adventure. The West had learned many things about Afghanistan through Marco Polo, Rishtya reminded us. He added that he too had always been intrigued by the *Travels.*

Rishtya asked us a thousand questions about our travels through the military zones of Iran and Turkey, and our journey through Afghanistan to Kabul. He wasn't surprised at our difficulties. We must remember that his country, isolated as it was, found it difficult to keep up with the West. Afghanistan had been a great and powerful nation sustained by trade from the Silk Road until the voyage of Vasco da Gama around the Cape of Good Hope doomed the ancient, tortuous land routes between China and the Mediterranean. After a self-centered life for centuries, he was confident that Afghanistan would emerge as a great nation again.

He asked what magazines we wrote for, and when Franc mentioned *The National Geographic* Rishtya seemed extraordinarily pleased. "His Majesty," he said, "is a member of the National Geographic Society. It is just possible—"

I took a deep breath, held it, and waited. "It is just possible," he continued, "that His Majesty will receive you. He likes *The Geographic* very much."

"And the Wakhan?" I ventured.

Rishtya smiled speculatively. "I don't know. But I'll do my best . . ."

Hope springs eternal. We floated out of Rishtya's office on the wings of optimism.

We assured each other that everything was going to be all right, and readied ourselves for departure. It was mid-August, and the days were growing perceptibly shorter. As an ominous sign we had our first cloudy day since leaving England. Franc bought a black karakul hat. With the black beard he had grown, neatly trimmed, he truly looked like an Afghan.

Sir Giles Squire, the British minister, was of much help to us in the anxious days that we waited for word from Rishtya. He made available his legation's library on Turkestan and the Middle East, one of the most comprehensive we had seen anywhere on that area. We reread the account of Lieutenant John Wood's exploration of the Wakhan, 110 years before, and of Lord Curzon's journey to the Pamirs and the Oxus, and Sir Henry Yule's analysis of the travels of Marco Polo. These were the best sources available, practically the only reference works on the rugged wilderness we hoped to cross. We pored over the British maps. Much of the territory over which we were to pass was simply marked "unsurveyed"; the mountains, "height unknown."

There was no civilian telephone service in Kabul. Messages were carried by "bearers" who trotted around the city. Finally, such a uniformed government bearer brought a note to the hotel. Rishtya wished to see us immediately.

As soon as we walked into his office we could tell that the news was good. Rishtya's eyes twinkled behind his horn-rimmed spectacles, and he was smiling. "I think," he announced, "that you are on your way!"

"Through the Wakhan?" Franc said.

"You have a chance. I have talked with the minister of war, the minister of the interior, and the prime minister. They raised the usual objections. But I pointed out that you had been allowed to pass through military zones in Turkey and Azerbaijan, and indeed had passed along our own frontier with Russia on your way here. So they are agreeable—at least with the consent of the King."

"The King has assented, then?" Franc asked.

"The King will give you an audience. He will permit photographs. He wants to talk to you, and you can present your case directly to him. After that, we shall see."

The audience had been arranged for August 21. On that day, the King would have us for tea. It wasn't until we returned to the hotel that we realized that the King, in his generosity, had placed an obstacle in our path. If we didn't leave Kabul until after August 21, we would almost certainly be trapped by the snows in the passes. There was only one thing to do—ask that the date of the audience be advanced by nearly two weeks.

This was a most delicate and embarrassing situation. "All we have to do," Franc sighed, "is insult the King by seeking an earlier audience and then ask an enormous favor of him."

We called on Rishtya the next morning and presented the matter frankly. I sensed a coolness, as he explained that we had already been greatly honored, and that it was unprecedented for anyone to ask the King to change the date of an audience. But Franc was wearing his diplomatic hat that day.

"In that case," he replied politely, "we will take our chances with the snows. We would not wish to impose upon your kindness, which already has been much greater than we had any right to expect."

Rishtya thought this over, staring intently over our heads. Then he smiled. "I also will take a chance, and convey your request to His Majesty."

As if by magic—Rishtya's magic—the doors swung open and we saw the King the very next morning.

Rishtya drove us to the palace, a great, gray stone pile on the outskirts of the city. We waited a few minutes in the vast, two-story reception hall. Franc named for me the trophies on the walls; the heads of ibexes, antelopes, stags, and the prized *Ovis poli,* the long-horned mountain sheep first described by Marco Polo, and named in his honor.

Then we were escorted into the office of His Majesty, Mohammed Zahir Shah. The room was frighteningly large, larger even than Mussolini's office in the Palazzo Venezia in Rome. It seemed as if we walked a mile across the regal red and gold carpeting before we reached the King's desk.

His Majesty was as gracious as the room was forbidding. He stepped from behind his desk, shook hands with us, and introduced his uncle, General Mohammed Omar Khan, the minister of war. The present King's able father, Nadir Shah, had installed his four brothers in key positions of the government. After Nadir Shah's assassination in 1933, Zahir Shah ruled under the guidance, but not the domination, of his uncles. The King led us to nearby leather chairs, tea was served, and he questioned us quietly about our journey.

While he talked to Franc, I studied the King, who seemed a very formal man, much more reserved than the Shah of Iran. I recalled what someone at the embassy had said of him: "If the King puts his hand in his pocket, he thinks he's being informal." He wore a flawlessly tailored English suit and a golden karakul hat. He was almost as tall as Franc, though slender and angular. His eyes were piercing black, but had a friendly sparkle. The King was a graduate of the French Military Academy at St. Cyr, and spoke French perfectly. He could speak English also, but preferred to have Rishtya translate our answers into Persian, a process that gave him more time to study us.

The King particularly wanted to know how his friend, the Shah of Iran, was faring. We told him of our visits. The problems of the two countries, particularly that of having Russia as a neighbor, are somewhat similar, though Afghanistan has no oil to add to her troubles or to her treasury. Then the King told us of his own tour, a year before, through Badakhshan, the most northern province, almost to the Wakhan. When he began making suggestions as to how we should travel, I knew that approval of our journey was only a few minutes away.

We photographed the King at his desk, and when Franc explained that informal pictures were preferred by United States publications, the King invited us to his summer palace at Paghman that afternoon to take photographs, in the gardens, of him and his young son, Prince Mohammed Nadir Khan. If the Shah of Iran permitted informal pictures, the King of Afghanistan would do likewise.

We returned to the hotel for lunch, by which time Franc had a violent and alarming chill, which took the edge off our elation. We sent for Dr. Mohammed Yusuf who, we learned, had studied in the United States at the Long Island College of Medicine. He examined Franc and quickly diagnosed malaria. "In Afghanistan," the doctor added casually, "everyone has malaria."

I explained that we had to be at the Paghman Palace that after-

noon for as important an appointment as we had ever had, and
that Franc simply had to keep it. Dr. Yusuf injected a potent
anti-malaria serum into Franc's arm. "You'll make it," he predicted confidently. Though Franc was groggy, and had a high
fever, we managed to arrive on time to photograph the King and
prince in the vast and beautiful formal garden of the summer
palace.

The eight-year-old prince, named for his grandfather, Nadir
Shah, was dressed in a magnificently embroidered Afghan coat
of red and black, with white pantaloons and elaborate shoes. For
centuries Afghan princes had dressed thus, but probably the brilliant costume had never been exposed to a camera before. The
King wore a summer-weight blue suit, a golden karakul hat, and
a tie which looked somehow familiar. I did a double take. It
was exactly like Franc's.

When I mentioned it, the King asked Franc, "Where did you
get that tie?"

"I'm not sure," Franc hesitated.

They gravely inspected the labels. Both had been purchased
in the same Parisian shop. After that, the King became much less
formal than before. Old Sulka tie, I thought.

As we left the palace, I acted on a sudden impulse. I liked the
King. He was receptive, intelligent, and friendly, and he had con-
ferred an enormous favor upon us. He alone was giving us the
chance to continue our journey. I wanted to give him something
in return, so I handed him our Polaroid camera. It was certainly
the first one to reach Afghanistan.

He seemed a little startled at the gift, but he took it graciously
enough. How was I to know that kings customarily accept presents
only from other kings?

Mr. Rishtya called at our hotel the next morning. He spoke
like a drama critic, rendering verdict on our performance. "The
King," he said with great enthusiasm, "was much impressed with
your manner and bearing. His Majesty has given orders that
everything be done to facilitate your journey."

We were a "smash hit."

Rishtya would assign a young journalist to accompany us as our interpreter. The prime minister had issued an order to all government officials to help us. This was equivalent to an act of parliament. The minister of war would provide a military escort for the most dangerous part of the route, when motor roads came to an end and we would travel by horse and yak. The minister of aviation had ordered an altimeter removed from one of his antique biplanes so that we could check the altitude as we progressed through the land of unconquered mountains. A station wagon had been secured for the trip to Faizabad.

That night chills and fever returned to Franc, and he became extremely ill. Dr. Yusuf rushed to the rescue with more shots, and predicted that the attacks would end in forty-eight hours. But Franc was on his feet next day, Tuesday. There was much still to do, for we had decided to leave on Friday.

The Roof of the World—the High Pamirs—awaited. All the petty man-made obstacles lay behind us. Only the mountains themselves, the snowy passes, the wilderness, could stop us now from following the footsteps of Marco Polo to China. This was the challenge we had come halfway around the world to meet.

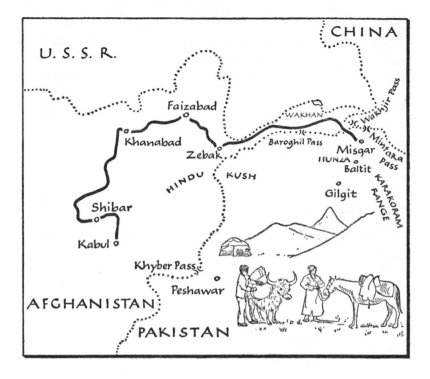

# 7

# THROUGH THE WAKHAN

THE WAKHAN corridor is a long, gnarled finger of Afghanistan held in a vise between Pakistan, on the south, and Soviet Russia, to the north. Its eastern tip digs into Chinese Turkestan, of which Urumchi, where I first thought of following the trail of Marco Polo, is the capital. To reach the Wakhan from Kabul we would be aided by gasoline for the first five hundred miles, retracing our path north across the Shibar Pass, then swinging east to Faizabad. A road was under construction for forty-five miles beyond Faizabad. From there on it was "Indian country." We would travel by horse and yak, or on foot.

Some seventy miles of our route, once we entered the corridor, would run along the south bank of the River Oxus, now called the Amu Darya. The north bank was Russia. Our ascent toward the headwaters of the Oxus, and the divide beyond, would take us into a land of unnamed peaks and untamed peoples, and beyond the protection of any sovereign or law. Our only exits, unless we were forced to turn back, would be the 16,000-foot Wakhjir Pass into Chinese Turkestan, or the even higher passes that dropped from the southern tip of the finger into Pakistan. Marco Polo had done it, and Lieutenant John Wood had gone as far as the Pamir plateau 110 years before. I would be the first woman to traverse it.

Of the pass ahead Marco Polo had written: "So great is the height of the mountains, that no birds are to be seen near their summits; and however extraordinary it may be thought . . . fires when lighted do not give the same heat as in lower situations, nor produce the same effect in cooking victuals."

The narrow Wakhan Valley was guarded by an imposing array of peaks and ranges. South of us, walling off Pakistan, would be the mighty Hindu Kush, with 25,000-foot peaks soaring above. To our north, rising abruptly from the Oxus, was the Nicholas range, the ramparts of the Tadzhik S.S.R. To the east clustered the Pamir Knot—the Karakoram, the Kunlun, the Tien Shan, and the Pamirs. We would be in the midst of the most magnificent mountains in the world.

We were too elated over having surmounted the political difficulties, and too busy with last minute preparations, to worry over the formidable physical obstacles that lay ahead. In the bazaars we shopped hurriedly for supplies. In addition to cheese and chocolate—food that would give us maximum energy with minimum bulk—we found tinned meats, Bovril, and candles. We put together a small medicine kit; a friend from the embassy presented us with a bottle of bourbon, scarce and valuable as liquid gold.

We took along real gold too. We had been told that paper afghanis would be acceptable until we reached the Wakhan, and that we could buy Chinese silver taels in Faizabad. But for an emergency, we decided to obtain gold pieces. No man yet has ever refused one. Here we ran into another snag. Afghanistan does not permit the export of gold, and no money-changer would sell us coins to take out of the country. We appealed to our guardian angel, Rishtya, for a special permit and immediately we were able to buy beautiful English gold sovereigns, at fifteen dollars each. The money-changer told us that very rarely was he permitted to sell them, except to local dentists who melted them down for fillings.

How many pounds can a yak pack? Never having seen a yak, I didn't know. We had been advised not to take more than two yak-loads of supplies. I destroyed batches of letters that had joined us on our travels, and it was like severing threads tying us to home. I parted reluctantly from "Alice," Franc from Housman. I gave away two dresses, Franc a London suit. Cosmetics were not exactly a "must" since I was unlikely to meet another lady who had ever smeared anything on her face except ghee. I threw away my last box of powder and last bottle of nail polish. The despair of Elizabeth Arden, I headed for the High Pamirs equipped with one used lipstick.

Press Director Rishtya provided an interpreter, Ghulam Hazrat Koshan, a young journalist who turned up at our hotel protesting that he would much rather stay at home. Koshan was nicely dressed, well-educated, and spoke excellent English. His face was pink and round, and his hands soft. For an hour he sat and told us the reasons why only the King's order (which could not be disobeyed) compelled him to accompany us. He was married and had a son. He and his wife were building a new house, the construction of which must now be left under the supervision of his father. And Koshan's father was old-fashioned, he would certainly make a botch of it. "I want a modern house," Koshan wailed. "I want a house with furniture in it!"

Was it possible, Franc intimated delicately, that Koshan was afraid?

Koshan was indignant. He had never heard anything so ridiculous in his life. Did we not know that all Afghans were courageous, all Afghans brave?

Franc assured him he was aware of these national traits. "But can you ride a horse?"

"All Afghans can ride," Koshan said.

"Have you ever done any mountaineering?"

Koshan didn't answer directly. All Afghans were gallant men who feared nothing, particularly heights, he said, and naturally all Afghans could climb mountains.

We reserved judgment, although we had misgivings from the first about Koshan. "He's a city boy," Franc said, "and I'm not sure this trip is the place to re-educate him."

But we were assured that he was the best interpreter in Afghanistan.

For the trip to Faizabad we hired a station wagon and driver. Rishtya told us that the government would provide yaks and horses, along with an armed military escort, from Faizabad to the Chinese border. Everything seemed set. We wrote letters to our families telling them to expect to hear from us in Peiping in four or five months. We were that optimistic.

On our last evening in Kabul, Dave Wharton of the American embassy called to say good-by. A few minutes later two Afghans appeared at our door, one of them carrying a rug folded over his arm. Thinking they were rug peddlers (Kabul was full of them), Franc was about to order them out when the second man spoke in resonant English: "A gift from His Majesty the King!"

With a flourish, he unrolled the rug at our feet. It was a magnificent Royal Tekki Bokhara, so soft that it could be crumpled in your hand like a silk scarf, and yet so strong of texture and tightly knotted that its life expectancy was hundreds of years. Its design, one traditionally reserved for the royal household, was done in dark red and black, with delicate touches of yellow and white.

Wharton had been one of those who had said that we would never be able to see the King, must less gain permission to attempt the Wakhan. Now he just sat and stared.

The Afghans explained that our rug had been presented to the King by Herat Province, as the finest example of their weavers' art. It had been on display at a crafts show, but the King had personally ordered it taken down and given to us. We thanked the bearers, and wrote the King a grateful note. We had much, indeed, to thank him for.

The rug was far too valuable to risk sending home through the mails. We didn't know where we were going to put it, but we took it along anyway. Later we had to hire an extra yak at times, for with the rug we had more than a two-yak caravan. It was worth it. It was a real treasure.

We left Kabul on August 19—one jump ahead of the diplomatic sheriffs. News of our permission to enter the Wakhan was received with bad grace by two embassies—the Russian and the American. A few days after we passed through Faizabad, the Russian embassy filed a formal protest. Franc was a journalist, and therefore in Moscow's eyes a spy, and he was to be allowed to peek across the Oxus into Russia. Someone at the American embassy was miffed because official requests on behalf of others, no doubt better qualified to the diplomatic eye, had been refused. So the American embassy protested as well, though not formally. But neither protest came in time.

Our Afghan driver was a wiry little man dressed in a tweed coat and the customary black karakul hat. The station wagon was a fairly new Chevrolet. To the luggage rack on top were lashed extra tires and tins of gasoline. There were no service stations on our route.

On the night before our departure Mohammed, the driver, visited us. Would we be so kind as to allow him to take a small boy as far as Shibar?

"There is hardly space for our luggage," Franc protested.

"But this little boy is an orphan," said Mohammed, a tear in his eye, "and in Shibar is a family that will take care of him."

Franc looked at me. Such pathos! How could we turn down a poor little orphan? Furthermore, we would be ill advised to alienate the driver before we started. I nodded.

Franc capitulated. "All right, but he will have to sit in front with you and Koshan."

At seven in the morning we gathered in front of the hotel to load. Koshan dumped his huge roll of bedding, suitable for a four-poster, in the luggage section, half filling it. The driver tossed in his own numerous bundles and boxes. We had to strap our bags on top with the tires. The "poor little orphan" appeared. He was about five-feet-nine, sported a few days' growth of straggly beard, and was old enough to claim children of his own. But since he was only going as far as Shibar it didn't matter too much. We were off.

We set out to make the five hundred miles to Faizabad in three days, a tremendous feat over Afghan roads. Outside Kabul the road twisted upward, and it began to rain, cooling us off for the first time in weeks. We crossed the Shibar Pass for the second time shortly after noon, and stopped for lunch at a delightful seven-thousand-foot altitude.

Mohammed the driver, discovering our basket of sandwiches and cakes, helped himself generously, climbed into the back seat and promptly began to snore. Koshan spread himself over the front seat and also prepared for a siesta. I recalled that the governor of Pul-i-Khumr, two hundred miles north, had been notified that we would be there at nine o'clock that night, and we didn't want to keep him waiting. Franc shook Koshan and told him to order the driver to get started.

Mohammed waved Koshan aside. "He says he does not wish to drive any more today," Koshan explained. "He does not feel well." I was not surprised. He had stuffed himself with half of our picnic lunch.

"O.K.," said Franc. "I'll drive. Tell him he can have his little nap in the back of the car."

The discovery that Franc could drive came as a horrible shock to Mohammed. Driving is a rare skill in Afghanistan, and like all Afghan chauffeurs and truckers, he fancied himself a demigod who controlled transportation. When Franc took the wheel Mohammed groaned and muttered predictions of disaster. But as soon as he discovered that Franc could drive at least as well as himself, he made an amazing recovery, and begged to be allowed to resume his job.

The rain grew to the proportions of a cloudburst, and our progress slowed. When night came we were nowhere. At eleven o'clock Mohammed slammed on the brakes and began to swear. Peering through the rain-blurred windshield, we could see that a dozen yards ahead the road disappeared in a muddy torrent. A flash flood had swept down the gullies, and this little stream was on a rampage. We would have to wait for it to subside.

Mohammed glared at us, and unloosed a string of words that I am sure were not complimentary. "He says," Koshan interpreted diplomatically, "that this is what comes of interfering with the will of Allah. It was Allah's will that we not reach Pul-i-Khumr this night. Had we allowed Mohammed to sleep and rest and recover his health, back at the Pass, none of this would have happened."

At this point we were not inclined to engage in any theological arguments. Koshan, the driver, and the "little boy" announced that they would sleep *in* the car. So, as the rain had stopped, we stepped out and spread our tarpaulin in the mud, unrolled our sleeping bags, and as a touch of elegance spread the king's rug over them. We crawled in and slept soundly.

Before dawn the flood had run off and we were able to start again. Koshan complained of a stiff neck, the first in a long line of laments that was to last until we parted. We reached Pul-i-Khumr at breakfast time, and found a banquet awaiting us. It was the dinner the governor had ordered for our arrival the night before, rewarmed, and very tired. We breakfasted lightly on roast chicken, lamb *kebab,* eggplant with sour cream, rice with saffron and raisins, and sweet, crisp melons.

At noon we were halted for four hours by another stream on the rise. Mohammed grumbled that this was what came of driving for infidels. He predicted that wherever we were going, we would never get there. If we were smart we would turn back, for Allah was against us. Koshan, sitting glumly in the front seat, took a morose delight in passing on to us Mohammed's awful prophecies. When the dirge got too monotonous Franc and I explored the little canyon, and chatted in sign language with curious nomads who forded the stream on horseback. It was a beautiful day, even if Allah wasn't on our side.

That afternoon, on a desolate stretch of road, we passed an Afghan carrying an automobile radiator. He waved us to a halt, and engaged in animated conversation with Mohammed. "He needs a lift to Khanabad," Koshan explained. "He must get this welded."

Although we had passed no stalled vehicle, it was difficult to say no. He rode on top—sitting on the flash bulbs, we discovered later. When we dropped him off that evening on the outskirts of Khanabad, Franc leaned out and inquired, just for the record, exactly where the hitchhiker had left his truck.

"Oh, he doesn't own a truck," Koshan reluctantly translated. "This is a secondhand radiator. He says he can sell it for a higher price if it is welded."

We were beginning to learn that Koshan's basic characteristic was evasiveness. He had a maddening habit of refusing to interpret questions and answers directly, and seemed to delight in our delay and embarrassment. Later we discovered that in any argument he always sided against us. Being an unusually well-educated young man, he looked with contempt upon his less fortunate countrymen, and hesitated to accompany us into their mean dwellings and tents. Yet he was fiercely chauvinistic, and never spoke of Afghans without the prefix of gallant, or noble, or brave. He himself was frightened a good deal of the time. He didn't know how to mount a horse, light a fire, wash his clothes, or pack his bedroll. Certainly, he was not the explorer type.

Since the whole trip was not to his liking, and he lived in a state of mounting apprehension, he constantly tried to eavesdrop in the hope, perhaps, of hearing that we wished to turn back. Having an interpreter with you, day after day, has its disadvantages. How could we discuss matters which we didn't want him to hear or repeat? How could we comment on the people along the way, or the quality of the food, or the condition of the roads, without offending his pride? Ultimately, we resorted to good old pig Latin, using it during the weeks that followed. Poor Koshan never caught on. When curiosity got the better of his manners and he asked what language we were speaking, I could be evasive too. "One of the more difficult American dialects."

Khanabad was a peaceful town set in a rolling sea of rice paddies, the greenest valley I had ever seen. Marco Polo wrote of Badakhshan that between the mountains were "wide plains clothed with grass and with trees, and large streams of the purest water."

Few of the women of Khanabad were veiled. They had fine faces, and were friendly, but they turned their backs on our cameras. The unmarried women wore red pantaloons, the married, black. This sharp demarcation keeps the social life of Khanabad on a proper plane.

On our last hot and dusty day on the road to Faizabad we crossed fertile valleys and rugged hills broken by deep gorges and rapid, foaming rivers. The Badakhshi tribesmen in their gaily colored costumes and heavy silver jewelry were on the move in their fall migration, coming from the high valleys of the Hindu Kush to the warm pastures of Bactria. The women and children were picking cumin seeds, an aromatic spice that grew wild on dwarf plants and which, Koshan explained, is exported in quantity from Afghanistan.

By noon our road began to parallel the Kokcha River, and it deteriorated until it was little more than a goat trail, narrow and twisting, with tall grass growing in the ruts. The bridges spanning deep gorges were precariously balanced on rocks and spliced poles. Some were so frail that we walked across, Mohammed following in the lightened station wagon. On steep hills we pushed, and on very bad hills Koshan helped, if we really insisted.

As we neared Faizabad the road snaked upward along the side of a crumbling cliff, our wheels running beside a sheer drop of a thousand feet. Koshan took one look, wrapped a sweater around his head, put his head on his knees, and began to shake and moan. Mohammed called repeatedly upon Allah. On hairpin curves he stopped the station wagon and walked around the corners to be sure there was still a road ahead. He would return shaking his head ominously, his teeth actually chattering. I am sure he would have insisted on turning back, had there been any place to turn around.

The "little boy" went all the way with us. He was the driver's cousin who just wanted a ride. He got more thrills than he bargained for.

Just at sunset we rounded the shoulder of the mountain, and beneath us lay the neat little town of Faizabad, its white clay houses gleaming in green fields. Mohammed turned to us and made a speech. "He says that if he is fortunate enough to return to Kabul," Koshan interpreted grimly, "he swears by the Prophet that he will never drive again."

Near Faizabad, the capital of Badakhshan Province, were many nomad encampments, with hundreds of sheep and camels milling around the black goat-hair tents. The streets of the village itself were lined with poplar trees, the streams running into the Kokcha were clear and sparkling, and the high air was clear and cool and smelled like the Alps. Marco Polo reached Badakhshan ill and worn, and "having been confined by sickness for nearly a year, he was advised to change the air by ascending the hills; when he presently became convalescent. On the summits of the mountains the air is so pure and so salubrious, that when those who dwell in the towns and in the plains and valleys below, find themselves attacked with fevers or other inflammatory complaints, they immediately remove thither, and remaining for three or four days in that situation, recover their health."

We were to find Polo's reportage increasingly accurate as we traveled eastward, and penetrated deeper into the land where time stands still.

We had been told in Kabul that Faizabad was the last outpost of civilization, but it seemed more like a mountain resort, remote but pleasant. We were billeted in the government's comfortable guest house, on beds which had wire springs but no mattresses. We were greeted by Mohammed Wajid, editor of the provincial weekly and a friend of Rishtya, who told us, in excellent English, that the governor, Sawar Khan, was waiting to receive us.

Sawar Khan was a gray-haired man of considerable distinction. He wore a blue business suit, but he carried himself like a soldier. By the telegraph line that ran from Kabul to Faizabad, he had been informed of our coming. Franc formally presented to him the edict, signed by the prime minister, authorizing our passage. It was an impressive document, inscribed on heavy, blue, gold-crested paper.

The governor informed us he would have to keep the document for his official files. I hated to give it up, wondering whether it might not be essential at some point farther along, far beyond the reach of telegraph. The governor insisted it would not be necessary, since we would be accompanied all the way to the Chinese border by an officer and several soldiers of his command. To be on the safe side, we photographed the permit before leaving it behind.

At dinner the governor told us what he knew of the way ahead, predicting that we would have no trouble. A band of Chinese pilgrims just in from Kashgar and bound for Mecca had recently crossed the passes on camels, and reported the trails in fair condition. The snows might not come for another month. Also, we would not have to worry about horses and pack animals, for these would be furnished by village headmen along the route. This had been ordered in the edict from Kabul.

It all sounded too good to be true, and we were to discover that none of it was true, but through no fault of the governor's. It was simply that east of Faizabad the law of the land grows weaker and more tenuous with each mile. And misinformation, freely given, is the rule rather than the exception in the Middle East.

Sawar Khan advised all of us to buy *chapons,* the wonderful outer garment of Central Asian mountaineers, and *chamooses,* the native shoes. He especially requested that we wear them when within sight of the Russian border. It would also be a good idea to camouflage our camera boxes, and tie old saddle bags over our aluminum cases. For safety's sake we should look as much as possible like local traders.

*Chapons* can best be described as a combination coat, blanket, and tent. They are so long that they touch the ground, and the sleeves extend eighteen inches beyond the fingertips, thus eliminating the need for gloves. The cloth is woven in herringbone design on twelve-inch looms. The *chapon* is without buttons or fastenings, but is held together by a large square red bandanna knotted around your middle. In Afghanistan a man's wealth can be judged by the color of his *chapon.* The lighter they are, the more expensive, and the harder to keep clean. High officials wear snow-white *chapons.* Poor farmers wear brown *chapons.* Ours were cream-colored, indicating at least upper middle class, and cost twenty dollars each.

*Chamooses* are high boots with heavy rawhide soles and soft tops. They are not laced, but tied by ankle thongs. The Afghans are good-sized men, but a national characteristic is their small feet. The *chamoose*-maker was shocked at Franc's size elevens. No feet of such size had ever been seen before in Faizabad, he assured us. He called in fellow shoemakers so that they could witness the marvel. He measured Franc's feet, and then measured them again. Still unbelieving, he cut Franc's *chamooses* two sizes too small. Franc could not wear them, and we left them with the sorrowful shoemaker, a souvenir of his skepticism.

To complete our costumes we bought knitted socks and Afghan stocking caps, the work of elderly Badakhshi men who had little regard for the shape of foot or head, and trousers fashioned from soft antelope wool, light but warm, which were made to order in three hours.

In the bazaars the people were more than normally curious about me, even for Afghanistan. Women trailed in groups behind me, talking and giggling. By this time I should have grown accustomed to my role as a sideshow freak, but I hadn't.

"It is only that you are the first American woman who has ever been to Faizabad," explained Wajid. "Word has passed through the town, and the people wish to see you. Please don't think them rude."

I suddenly realized that the people of Faizabad were receiving a warped impression. They would surely think that all American women wore slacks, plaid shirts, and pigtails. I yearned for a pretty cotton dress and a new hair-do.

The governor sent for the Chinese pilgrims, but they were of little help to us. They had reached Faizabad, it developed, by a circuitous route through Pakistan, not over the trail Marco Polo had followed. The governor questioned them concerning rumors of trouble among the Kirghiz tribesmen who inhabit the Pamir plateau at the extreme tip of the Wakhan, and who respect no rulers or boundaries, but the pilgrims professed to know nothing of it. No information, or misinformation, seemed to be our lot.

But at least we were able to buy Chinese taels from the pilgrims. A tael is a boat-shaped piece of silver, money that would be useful when we crossed into Turkestan no matter what paper currency was in circulation. As to the Afghan money we might need in the Wakhan, Mr. Wajid assured us there would be no expenses except for tips. We should carry, he said, perhaps 100 afghanis, the equivalent of $7 50. Franc decided to keep 1,000 afghanis, to be safe. The gold bought in Kabul we would keep for reserve.


WE LEFT FAIZABAD on August 23, the eve of Afghanistan's independence day, after Sawar Khan entertained us with a farewell luncheon plus an hour-long exhibition of local music and dancing. I was particularly fascinated by the drum dance, which is actually an endurance contest. Four men, while spinning at top speed, beat an intricate rhythm on ancient drums hung by straps from their shoulders. One by one they grew dizzy and collapsed. The last man on his feet was the winner, a dubious honor, for he was exhausted and staggering.

At the luncheon we met for the first time Cadet (comparable to the rank of second lieutenant in our own army) Syed Rashid, who was to command our escort, and who would be responsible for our safety. Rashid greeted us with a haughty look and a tired handshake. He wore a stiff, visored cap, brightly polished cavalry boots, and a uniform coat heavily padded to hide his narrow shoulders and cinched tightly with a Sam Browne belt to accentuate his wasp waist. He looked like one of the chorus in "The Student Prince."

We left in the governor's station wagon. Franc and I sat in front with the driver, Koshan and Cadet Rashid in the center seats, and two very young, unkempt, amiable soldiers sprawled on the barracks bags and equipment in the rear. The freshly laid road ascended a narrow valley, and we frequently had to get out and push on steep grades. All but Cadet Rashid, that is, pushed.

Rashid let it be known immediately that he could not be expected to push, pull, haul, or carry. All this was beneath the dignity of an officer and gentleman of the Afghan army.

At the end of the forty-five miles the road ended abruptly against a formidable wall of rock. Ahead, as far as Zebak, the road was under construction. It would progress, we judged, at scarcely more than a mile a month, for it was being chiseled out of sheer cliff by villagers laboring with sledge hammers, crowbars, and baskets. Ours was the third car to try this new road. Only the King and the minister of war had been before us.

This was as far as gasoline would take us. The next five hundred miles or more would be on foot, either our own or an animal's. Horses awaited us there at the end of the road, and an hour after dark we reached a temporary camp of the road engineers. We dined, squatting Afghan-fashion, around a tray of chicken and rice. They ate with their fingers, and we followed suit. Ominously it began to rain; our summer weather was behind us.

In the morning Rashid revealed more of his character and temperament. Before the pack animals were loaded, he had picked and mounted the largest and best riding horse. Franc's horse was thin, old, and sickly, scarcely thirteen hands high. The stirrups on the Mongol-type saddle were so short that Franc's knees stuck up higher than the horse's withers. Soon this posture became so uncomfortable that he was forced to kick away the stirrups, and then his feet almost trailed the ground. My horse was a somewhat healthier specimen, although again the stirrups were uncomfortably short.

Koshan's horse looked as if he'd live out the year, and his saddle was padded with so many blankets that it resembled a bed; yet he groaned and winced and bumped along in agony, clutching the saddle horn.

"Are you ill?" I asked him.

"No," he said, "but to tell the truth I'm not accustomed to riding."

"You've ridden before, haven't you?" I remembered that all Afghans, according to Koshan, were expert horsemen.

"Only once," he said.

"When was that?"

"Last night," he admitted.

Poor Koshan had ridden only long enough to start blisters. I pitied him, but no one could help him now. He would learn to ride—the hard way.

Before dusk it began to rain again. Franc's horse became so weak that he was forced to dismount and lead him. Completely disinterested, Rashid galloped ahead and disappeared from view. It was still raining when we dismounted and led our horses across the deep and swollen Kokcha, and labored in darkness up a rocky hillside to the village of Zebak. We had been in the saddle for thirteen hours.

At Zebak there was no food, and we could not locate Rashid. Zebak's altitude was 8,400 feet, and we were cold as well as wet. I brewed tea for Franc, Koshan, and the two soldiers, and we bedded down for the night in a half-ruined mosque. I recalled a sentence from Barger's letter: "In Afghanistan people will treat you courteously but you'll never be allowed to enter a mosque." There in Zebak no one seemed to mind, which was fortunate as there was no other shelter.

Koshan could not sleep. He moaned, complained of blisters, of pains and aches in every bone and muscle, and protested that he must be very ill, perhaps dying. I explained to him that discomfort must be expected, since he had never ridden before. "In a few days your muscles will harden, and then you'll be all right," I assured him.

When I used the word "muscles," Franc smiled.

Koshan was difficult to convince. "I doubt that I shall survive," he said.

This should have sounded amusing, for our journey through the Wakhan would not properly begin until we passed Ishkashim on the Oxus, still a day's ride ahead. But at that moment it wasn't amusing at all. Koshan was our ears and tongue. If he did not "survive," neither would we.

We awoke at dawn to find Rashid still missing. Koshan wandered off disconsolately in search, and found the cadet—warm, well-fed, and comfortable— in the home of the local mullah.

Rashid was irritated at being awakened so early. As for the party he was "protecting," we could have drowned in the Kokcha for all he cared.

But our troubles were only beginning. Koshan informed us that our horses must be returned to the engineers' camp, and the rental on them would be 150 afghanis, please. We told him of Mr. Rishtya's assurance, confirmed by Mr. Wajid and the governor, that the government would supply the transportation. Koshan appeared surprised. He said that neither he nor Rashid had been informed of this arrangement.

We were furious, as well as worried. We had only 1,000 afghanis with us, and at the rate of 150 afghanis a day rental for transport, we would need much more. We paid, as there was no alternative, but we wondered what obstacle Koshan would think of next. We didn't have to wait long. Soon it became evident that Rashid had not procured horses to continue our journey. Obviously, nobody but the Shors wanted to penetrate the Wakhan.

Rashid's attitude was one of an honored guest on the trip; he was not to be bothered with such minor details as transport, food, lodging, or the whims of infidels. The soldiers acted as little more than his personal servants. They prepared his bedroll each night, pulled off his boots, helped him dress and undress, brought his tea, and tended the fire under his Afghan water pipe. Rashid liked to sleep late, and always insisted on a last hookah before taking to the trail in the morning. His personal conveniences and luxuries cost us as much as four hours' traveling time each day.

Upon Franc's insistence, Rashid finally sent for one of the village elders, who kissed the cadet's hand and knelt at his feet while our needs were explained. The old gentleman went off to try to find horses, and Rashid relaxed in the mosque with his hookah.

In Zebak lived the first Wakhis we met on our trip. They were the poorest people we had ever seen, poorer even than the villagers of China. The men wore goatskins across their shoulders, and the women were clad in filthy rags. The children wore nothing at all. The men, who wore no shoes in summer, waded barefoot through the icy streams and could travel all day over the rugged, rocky

terrain at a pace equal to that of a horse. The women aged very
rapidly. At thirty they were toothless old crones, and they rarely
lived beyond forty. It looked as if neither men nor women in
Zebak had ever cut or combed their hair. Except that they carried
no clubs or spears, they could have stepped out of a cave—100,000
years ago.

Three teen-age girls stopped us in the narrow street, knelt and
kissed my hand, and invited us into their windowless, one-room
mud dwelling. They looked upon me with wonder, for by their
standards I was very tall, and they touched my face to see whether
the whiteness would rub off. The Wakhis are Aryans, with prominent noses and eyes often gray or blue, but their skin was much
darker then mine, and wrinkled even in early life.

We found fifteen men, women and children living in that tiny,
smoke-filled room. There were no rugs, or furnishings of any kind.
A fire burned in the center of the floor, the smoke escaping
through a round hole in the roof. Over the fire an iron kettle
steamed.

We were offered tea in wooden bowls. In return, I presented the
elders with a pound package of sugar and the children with a
handful of fruit-flavored hard candy wrapped in Cellophane. Before I could explain, through Koshan, that the wrappings should
be removed, they popped the candy into their mouths and swal-
lowed, Cellophane and all. This was quite probably their only
chance in a lifetime to taste candy—and they hadn't tasted it!

Through Koshan, I inquired what they thought of America.

"America?" they replied. "What is America?"

I tried to explain, but it was useless. They had heard of Afghanistan, China, Pakistan, India, and Russia. Beyond these, for them
the world ended.

During our passage of the Wakhan, I showed various Wakhis
magazine pictures of our country. They could not comprehend
New York at all, nor would they believe that people lived in, or
on, those tall peaks that I claimed had been constructed by man.
They doubted that such a place really existed. The photographs
to them were simply fanciful drawings. Our appearance and clothing and equipment was as strange to them as if we had landed

from another planet. When I produced pictures of Kabul, they wouldn't believe them either, although they did know the word.

We were only twenty-four miles, a day's journey by horse, from the mountain where the motor road crept slowly toward them from Faizabad, yet none of them had ever seen an automobile, and many had never even seen a wheel. On the precipitous, narrow, boulder-strewn trails of the Wakhan, wheels would be useless.

One of the soldiers brought word that the horses had been found, and we hurried back to the mosque. Rashid was already mounted on a fine-looking animal, and Koshan's bedroll was going up to cushion the ribs of a fairly respectable horse. For me there was a spavined mare with a nursing colt at her side, and Franc had drawn an ancient, lame bag-of-bones without a saddle. The packs were loaded on equally sad animals.

I watched Franc trying to keep his temper. I hoped he wouldn't explode, sensing that both Koshan and Rashid would like nothing better than a good excuse to turn back. Their help, little as it was, remained crucial. Franc became icily polite.

"Please thank Cadet Rashid," he said to Koshan, "for finding these mounts for us. Tell him I am sure that he has done the best he can, but obviously we cannot ride these horses. Tell him that you and he shall ride, while my wife and I will walk."

This was not what Koshan and Rashid had expected. As the meaning of Franc's speech sank in, I could almost see the gears revolving in Koshan's head. Word would go back to Faizabad that he and Rashid were compelling the Americans to walk, while they rode. Mr. Wajid would relay this word to Rishtya, who would inform the prime minister. The King himself might hear of it, and then what would happen to Koshan, the brilliant young journalist? He hurriedly summoned Rashid to a private conference. Rashid glared at us. Franc smiled sweetly. Rashid mumbled several phrases in Afghan, and galloped off. In half an hour he brought back two passable horses with iron scoop saddles such as European knights used in the Middle Ages. Naturally, he and Koshan stayed on the best mounts, while Franc and I climbed into our metal seats.

The recurring problem of securing good riding horses made us particularly regret an incident recorded by Marco Polo. "Not long since there were still found in this province (Badakhshan) horses of the breed of Alexander's celebrated Bucephalus. The whole of the breed was in the possession of one of the king's uncles, who, upon his refusal to yield them to his nephew, was put to death; whereupon his widow, exasperated at the murder, caused them all to be destroyed; and thus the race was lost to the world."

I was exasperated with that widow.

The twenty-mile ride from Zebak to Ishkashim, the strong-point of Afghan defenses on the Oxus, took us up a pleasant valley between 15,000-foot peaks. On our right, in the distance, soared an unnamed monarch of the Hindu Kush, more than 24,000 feet high. In the changing light it was beautiful to watch, and my spirits lifted.

We stopped for lunch at Zarkhan, called "The Place Where the Salt Ends." No salt is found in this area, or anywhere in the Wakhan. Since centuries of inaccessibility and absolute poverty have discouraged its import, the Wakhis live entirely without salt. Their diet consists chiefly of goat's milk, crushed dried peas, and a flat, crisp bread of whole wheat. Springs and glacial run-off supply adequate water, but the soil is thin, producing poor crops of wheat and barley. Plowing methods have not changed in two thousand years. A sharp stick is pulled through the pebbled earth by a decrepit horse, and if the family owns no horse, by two men. There at Zarkhan we saw our first flock of the famous midget sheep of the Wakhan, perfectly formed but barely eighteen inches high. These animals are highly prized; they regularly produce twin lambs, and their wool is of the finest texture.

Before we left Faizabad the governor of Badakhshan had given us a batch of Afghan cookies, called *kolcha,* or travel bread, hard and heavy as lead, two inches in diameter and an inch thick. Every morning we each put one in our pocket and munched on it as we rode. They were delicious and, more important, filling.

They were rich with sugar, fat, flour, and the salt which had suddenly become so rare. I could imagine strength oozing back into my blood after I ate one.

Few villages in the world are more beautiful, at a distance, than Ishkashim, or more strategically located. It sits atop a low cliff overlooking the silvery ribbon of the Oxus. Its Beau Geste fortress commands the principal bend of the river. Half a mile to the north is the Tadzhik Soviet Socialist Republic, while less than twenty miles to the south is the border of Pakistan. Set at the base of the crooked finger that reaches all the way to China, it is the key to the Wakhan.

A military telephone ran as far as Ishkashim and we were expected there. Rasul Khan, administrator of the Wakhan district, the local mullah, and the garrison commander greeted us on the edge of the village, and we were shown to the governor's two-room guest house. Rashid and the soldiers were to sleep in the barracks.

By this time I had grown weary of the continual company of Koshan—day and night. All day long he recited endless stories of the brave, courageous, and fearless Afghans. The Afghans, he assured me, had humbled British, Russians, Chinese, and Persians in one war after another. Only the treachery of international politics prevented Afghanistan from becoming a great power.

And every night Koshan slept in our room. Sometimes we had Rashid and the military escort as well, but always we had Koshan. So it was with sheer delight that I found that we would have a room to ourselves, even though it was mud-walled and bedless. Franc told the packers to put Koshan's bulging bedroll in one chamber, and we carried our sleeping bags into the other.

At last we were alone.

Fifteen minutes later in came Koshan, bent under the weight of his bedding. He dumped it on the floor next to ours and began to unroll it. "What are you doing?" asked Franc, dismayed.

"Getting ready for bed," Koshan replied calmly.

"But, Ghulam," Franc protested, "we thought you'd like to

have a room to yourself for a change. It must be very boring for you, being with us all the time."

"Oh, don't worry about that," said Koshan. "Besides, it would be very cold sleeping in a room alone. We will all be more comfortable here."

"You have plenty of bedding," Franc said, "and so have we. I insist that you be allowed a room of your own." Franc gathered up Koshan's bedding, carried it into the next room, and spread it neatly on the floor.

Koshan sighed and followed, his shoulders drooping. Franc returned to our room and closed the door.

At last we were alone.

Minutes later the door creaked and slowly swung open. Koshan was back, his bedding on his back, his round face sorrowful. "My brother," he said, almost in a whisper, "I must tell you something. I am a grown man, and I have a son, and I am respected in my country. But—but"—he looked unhappily at the floor and his voice faltered—"I have never slept in a room alone in all **my** life, and I am afraid!"

What could we do? Koshan slept in our room that night, and every night thereafter. This situation had one small compensation, for Koshan's vocabulary subtly altered. Afghans became "noble Afghans," "great-hearted Afghans," and "generous Afghans." The words "brave" and "courageous" never again passed his lips in our presence.

We dined with the army commandant, the mullah, and Rasul Khan, the civil administrator. It was the moment to speak of the horses and the money. We had to straighten out our finances before we left Ishkashim, for beyond that point there were no military telephone lines, or any other means of communication.

Rasul Khan assured us that it would be very simple. Koshan should call the governor of Badakshan Province in Faizabad, who would vouch for us, and then the village treasurer would cash a $100 check and give us 1,400 afghanis, enough to rent animals as far as the Chinese border. We went to bed, feeling confident that our problem was solved. We should have known better. The Afghan thinks like an Oriental. When you are his guest, he tells you what you wish to hear and what will make you happy.

In the morning Koshan was very embarrassed. He had called the governor, as requested, and Sawar Khan had authorized the village treasurer to cash our check. But the village treasurer, a suspicious character, had asked, "Who will vouch for this Koshan? And even if Koshan is truly what he pretends, how do I know he actually talked to the governor? And even if the person on the other end of this instrument said he was the governor, how would this Koshan know he was the governor?"

Franc produced credentials and credit cards by the pocketful, but the village treasurer could read none of them, and anyway they signified little on this particular continent. Then Franc displayed a letter signed by the prime minister. The village treasurer wavered, and then wondered aloud whether it might not be a forgery.

"This man is like a stone," Koshan whispered to us. "If we only had a letter from the King. He is afraid of the King, and would not dare refuse."

"What about the Shah of Persia?" Franc asked.

"I think he might also be afraid of the Shah of Persia."

Franc produced the autographed photo of himself and the Shah standing side by side. The treasurer examined it closely. At last he nodded his head. "Since this man is a friend of the Shah of Persia," he said, "I will accept his check. Assuredly a friend of the Shah is good for 1,400 afghanis."

It took six months for the check to emerge from Afghanistan, pass through clearing houses on three continents, and finally be honored by our bank in New York. I'll bet the treasurer was worried every minute of the time.

We were scheduled to leave at eight in the morning, and the pack animals were loaded at that hour. The soldiers in our escort now numbered four, although only two of them had rifles. Since for the next three days we would be within sight of the Russian border posts, the commandant had assigned us this added protection.

Rashid turned up an hour late, circles under his eyes and face more pinched and sour, if possible, than usual. We had made good use of his tardiness. For once we had the best horses and decent saddles. He was infuriated, but there was nothing he dared do or say in front of a superior officer.

Beyond Ishkashim the valley is only a mile in width, while the river itself narrows to two hundred yards. There is a motor road on the Russian side, and we saw numerous trucks rolling over it. On the Afghan side not even a wheeled cart moved. Ordinarily, in such a remote area, national boundaries have little meaning to the natives, but here there was apparently no intercourse between the two banks of the river.

Despite the 8,600-foot altitude the sun was blistering hot. To our surprise the heavy wool *chapons* deflected the heat, and we were quite comfortable, although our exposed faces were badly burned by the penetrating rays. My nose and lips became painfully swollen and Franc's skin literally cracked along the cheekbones. Koshan's face was puffed and red. I passed ointment around each night, but it did not do much good.

If the Russians were studying us from across the Oxus, our party looked impressive—at least in length. First came two soldiers, a sort of advance guard. Then Rashid, Franc, me, and Koshan, in that order. After this "main body" came four or five Wakhis leading pack animals. The two other soldiers rode rear guard.

That first night out of Ishkashim we stopped at a nervous Afghan military post, Shikhan. We slept in a tiny hut with our permanent chaperone, Koshan, while armed guards walked post outside the door. Everything was suddenly quite military. Rashid even lit his own pipe and removed his own boots. I asked Koshan why everyone was so skittish.

"There is a Russian military post only two hundred yards from here," he said. "We are afraid the Russians will cross the river tonight and catnip you."

The Russians didn't "catnip" us, but the bedbugs attacked in waves. Between the crunch of the sentries' boots, the dire predictions of Koshan, and the bites of the bugs, we had little sleep.

We came, the following noon, to the village of Urgund, and

were amazed to find fields bearing a heavy crop of barley at that altitude. The grain, known locally as *kaljaw*, requires only forty days between planting and harvesting. It is irrigated three times weekly with icy, glacial water, produces a fine yield, apparently is impervious to cold, and thrives in the thin air at 9,000 feet. We filled an old sock with seed, and when we returned to Washington sent it to the Department of Agriculture. Experiments are now being conducted to decide whether *kaljaw* can be grown in mountain areas of the United States.

In the evening we reached the mountain fastness of Pigash, where we found our first evidence of ancient civilization, a ruined fortress set atop a hundred-foot mound near the town. The inhabitants called it "Kaffir-ha," pre-Moslem, which meant that it was more than a thousand years old. We spent an hour measuring the crumbling walls and taking photographs, while Koshan and Rashid growled about how dangerous this was, for the Russians could see us. We did not find even one potsherd; it was impossible to say whether the ruin antedated Alexander or was of Greek origin.

That night we slept on the courtyard floor of the home of the local member of parliament. This mansion of the Wakhan was a two-story affair and I noticed a door set high on the outside wall, opening into the second floor. This was the entrance, I was informed, during the heavy winter snows.

"What happens," I asked, "in all the other houses—where they have only one floor?"

"The people crawl through the smoke hole in the roof," I was told, "and come down a ladder inside." From then on I carefully observed the houses. I never saw a window, or more than one door. Darkness and smoke were endured to frustrate winter's frightful cold.

From the time we left Faizabad, no day in the Wakhan passed easily or uneventfully, without arguments and delays. The hostility of nature and the obstacles of the trail did not hamper us as much as the reluctance of our companions. No one else in our party even wanted to be in the area, much less push ahead to the border. Koshan and Rashid, and later the commandant at

Sarhad, would have insisted that we turn back if at any time
we ever had admitted being ill, or tired, or if our enthusiasm
and resolution had once relaxed. Neither Rashid nor Koshan
really believed we would dare go all the way.

Each day was a struggle to reach the next village, invariably
a day's ride ahead, like the camel stages in China. Once these
villages must have been caravansaries; centuries ago this had
been a much traveled, although always dangerous, pathway to
the East. Now the Wakhi villages had degenerated into scabby
collections of ten to twenty stone-and-mud huts, with piles of
refuse rotting in the lanes between the habitations. As we progressed east, and reached ever higher altitudes, the standard of
existence—it could hardly be called living—deteriorated even
below that of Zebak. As a matter of fact we never saw another
mosque, even a ruined one, after Zebak. The deterioration was
spiritual as well as physical. As we penetrated deeper into the
rocky wilderness, ignorance gave way to complete apathy. The
villagers, after staring at us for a bit, would wander back into
their huts, or return to their primitive farming. They were like
listless animals, devoid of spirit or even curiosity.

For eleven dollars a day (in afghanis) we had the use of three
riding horses and three pack animals. Rashid and his soldiers
requisitioned their horses from the villagers without payment.
The Wakhi owners accompanied their stock to the next village.
There, they impassively accepted payment and returned to their
homes. Although the money we paid represented the only hard
cash they were likely to receive in a year, it never seemed to please
them. In the Wakhan, there is no place in which to spend money,
and nothing on which to spend it. The villagers always seemed
anxious to get rid of us.

Except on rare occasions, we ate off the country. We bought
tea and coarse wheat bread for our morning meal. The tea, the
poorest quality exported (sticks, twigs, and tea dust pressed into
bricks), was strong and bitter. For lunch we simply brewed our
own tea and gnawed at bread saved from the morning, or at a
travel cake.

At the end of a day Rashid would order the villagers to bring a sheep and slaughter it for the evening meal. We would sit around a fire while the liver, kidneys and heart were grilled on long skewers. These tasty hors d'oeuvres quieted our hunger while the sheep stewed in a huge pot. The sheep, hacked into chunks of about two pounds each, was served in a communal bowl swimming with ghee, with slabs of bread on the side. I never acquired a taste for ghee, but it supplied strength to keep me going.

Although our stomachs were filled each night, we were daily growing weaker from the combination of unremitting physical effort and a diet to which we were not accustomed, and which lacked essential vitamins. Certainly we became thinner. I did our necessary washing in the frigid glacial streams, and hung our clothes on bushes to dry. Our long woolens and cashmeres did not seem to shrink a bit—and then I realized that while they probably actually *were* shrinking, so were we.

Nearly every day Koshan fell off his horse. After the first day it no longer scared him speechless, but it never failed to give Rashid a hearty and malicious laugh. Once my horse slipped in a stream bed, and down I went onto the muddy bank as he lurched to right himself. Franc was riding close behind, so while Rashid looked amused, he didn't dare laugh.

Ropes broke and packs had to be reassembled and reloaded. Much of the time we progressed on foot, when the trails were too steep to ride, or the horses too exhausted to carry us. And our days in the saddle, and on foot, were long and arduous. Stretches of nine, ten, and twelve hours were common, while one day we were on the trail sixteen hours.

When there was no accident or crisis, we rode on like automatons. One day, when I had exhausted all possible lines of conversation, I amused myself by swatting flies on my horse's neck, using a flat loaf of bread and keeping score. I had killed sixty-four before Franc made me stop.

We noticed that Rashid and Koshan often held long, private discussions with the elders in the villages. When I inquired about the palaver, Koshan would reply: "We were discussing the price of yak tails." We knew he was lying. They were grousing about the crazy Americans.

As a party we progressed with complete ignorance of what might lie ahead. Franc and I had never before set foot in Afghanistan; Koshan had never before been in northern Afghanistan; the soldiers, patient and good-natured country boys, had never been beyond Faizabad; Rashid had never been beyond Ishkashim; the villagers had rarely been more than a single day's travel east of their own homes.

I pitied the people. Though they were treated like chattels by Rashid and Koshan, they never protested except as an animal protests, by moving slowly and reluctantly. Their flinty environment had worn away all human feeling, even anger and resentment. I recalled that in Kabul I had asked a high government official what we should take along as presents for the Wakhis, thinking he would suggest sugar, tea, salt, or candy. He had answered, abruptly, "Opium." I was shocked, and thought him callous. But after seeing the people, and the subhuman manner of their life, I could appreciate his response.

There were endless compensations, however, for the hardships. The scenery was fantastically beautiful—jagged mountains and wild rivers, roses and buttercups defiantly displaying their loveliness in rocky crevices, a valley of purple rocks, a hill of garnets, and lonely floating eagles. Often we heard the merry whistling of marmots along the trail. Every day had some delight for our eyes and ears.

There were even exceptions among the miserable people. We found one on our third day along the Oxus, when we came to Khandut, where dwelt the judge of the Wakhan district. The village was called "the place of the Judge." He administered Koranic law, which is the law of Afghanistan.

The judge had a magnificent white beard. At seventy, he was certainly the most respected patriarch of the Wakhan, and probably the oldest. He sat cross-legged in his combination living hut and courtroom, served tea, and questioned us, through Koshan.

The old judge said that he had heard that sometimes in Kabul people were seen with skin as fair as ours, but we were the first he himself had ever seen. We tried to explain to him how far we had traveled, and by what means, but we were immediately stumped when we spoke of flying the Pacific, since the judge had never seen an airplane or an ocean. When one spoke of far travel, the judge naturally thought in terms of camels and yaks. But he was pleased that we had chosen to visit this area.

The Koran, the judge said, urged all good Moslems to travel widely in order to know the other peoples of the earth. He himself had never traveled, though a few people of the Wakhan had been to faraway Kabul. He was certain our mission had the blessing of the Prophet Mohammed, and to make doubly sure he chanted a prayer for us before we departed. We gave the judge our genuine thanks. In a land where foreigners are often greeted with suspicion, if not actual hostility, his friendship and his blessing were refreshing.

We rode hard to reach Qala Panja, called "Fort of the Oxus," before dark that day. At Qala Panja two branches of the Oxus meet, one flowing from the Russian border and Lake Victoria, while the other comes down the Wakhan, from the great glaciers and passes of the Pamir plateau.

Though we had been led to expect a large and well-armed garrison there, the post actually housed only fifty poorly equipped soldiers, captained by one Mahbob Khan, who wore a U.S. Army jacket, and baggy Afghan trousers tucked into Russian boots. The fort itself, situated at the confluence of the two rivers, must for ages have commanded the whole area. It was ancient, but in excellent condition. Its walls were five feet thick, and inside were stables and cisterns. Just outside the garrison compound were the ruins of an earlier fort, and a few hundred yards beyond rose a mound which was undoubtedly the original fortress, perhaps two thousand years old. Here, if anywhere on the Wakhan, was the mecca of an archeologist. Under the two older forts, he might profitably dig for evidence of the ancient caravans and conquering armies that had passed this way before and after Marco Polo.

Mahbob Khan, the commandant, had disturbing news. Af-

Franc and Rahman Qul discuss our future in the latter's spacious *yurt* in Bozai Gumbaz. We were about out of writing paper, and an old air-mail envelope had to serve as the receipt for our two bodies.

This is our guide, Tilah Walduh, who led us to the Wakhjir Pass, and then up the mountains toward the Delhi Sang. Here he sits in the isolated *yurt* on the Pamir Plateau rim, where we slept for the night, with a terrible old woman for our hostess.

One of our pack yaks jumps a crevass on the glacier below the Delhi Sang. Two Kirghiz push while one pulls. The altitude is above 17,000 feet, and wind has swept the south slopes clean of snow.

Franc and a pack yak, both very tired, stand on the crest of the 20,000-foot Delhi Sang Pass looking over into Pakistan. A steep slide down the cliff just behind them brought us into Pakistan.

ghan Kirghiz tribesmen were engaged in fighting with tribes on
the Chinese Turkestan frontier of the upper Wakhan. It was
possible that the border might be closed. We pressed him for details, but his replies, as interpreted by Koshan, were vague. Knowing that Koshan colored the statements of others to make them fit
his own wishes, we suspected that our intrepid translator was
making quite a war out of a minor frontier skirmish.

That night, Koshan announced that he was going to sleep in
Rashid's room in the commandant's quarters. Franc and I sensed
something was up, and discovered what it was in the morning.
Koshan and Cadet Rashid, behind a united front, demanded that
we turn back.

Franc didn't react excitedly, as I expected he would. He took
care of the situation with a quiet efficiency. "I wonder what
the King will say?" he mused.

"The King will say to what?" asked Koshan. When anyone
said "King," Koshan always jumped slightly, as if shocked.

"What the King will say when I tell him that the men he
trusted to guide us through the Wakhan became afraid and
turned back because of a rumor."

Koshan winced, and reported Franc's words to Rashid. They
held a short, excited conference. Franc and Rashid indulged
in pantomime conflict. Rashid glared. Franc turned his back in
contempt. Then Koshan approached us and said, "On second
thought, after further consideration of the military situation,
we have decided to go on."

But we never felt secure with Rashid and Koshan again. It
seemed clear that on any excuse which would sound valid in
Kabul they would abandon us. There seemed no way in which
we could go on alone. Without Rashid we could not commandeer
the horses and packers, and without Koshan the language problem was insurmountable.

In four days of travel from Zebak to Qala Panja we had
climbed only 500 feet, the road dipping and rising from 8,500
to 9,000 feet. From Qala Panja on, the climb was precipitous, and
the thinning oxygen added to our difficulties. Any undue exertion caused us to breathe rapidly, and we tired so quickly it

was frightening. For hours we toiled up the side of a rocky cliff, our horses picking their way with probing steps along a narrow ledge. Both Koshan and I were riding mares with foals, and the mares almost had nervous breakdowns trying to guard their young from disaster. The nervousness of the mares infected Koshan. He rode in tense and silent misery.

At the 12,000-foot level wild roses bloomed in profusion. Yet only a few gnarled and twisted trees leaned close to the cliff, cringing from the constant gale. On the mountainside above us dozens of springs gushed from solid rock, and were guided to tiny terraced fields on the bleak slope far below.

The few silent people we passed appeared healthy, but their garments, as Marco Polo had related, were mostly skin—their own and the skins of animals ("The men . . . generally clothing themselves with the skins of wild animals; other materials for the purpose being scarce.") Some of the men were covered with shaggy patchwork cloaks of antelope hide and sheepskin. Their barren fields were fenced with the bones and the horns of mountain goat and ibex. When Marco Polo passed this way, he also noted, "In this particular plain there are wild animals in great numbers, particularly sheep of a large size, having horns, three, four, and even six palms in length. Of these the shepherds form ladles and vessels for holding their victuals; and with the same materials they construct fences for enclosing their cattle, and securing them against the wolves, with which, they say, the country is infested . . ."

It was wild country, and eerily beautiful.

I was immersed in admiration of the grandeur of the Hindu Kush, brooding over us like giants shoulder to shoulder, when I heard a wild scream. Koshan, entangled in his padded saddle, fell heavily to the narrow trail. His saddle girth had broken. Fortunately, he tumbled off on the side close to the mountain. Had he fallen on the far side, he would not have stopped for 2,000 feet.

We dismounted, and Franc fixed another girth on Koshan's skittish mare. Rashid laughed like an idiot until Franc told him sharply to shut up. This needed no interpretation, and

Rashid cooperated. Koshan was so immobile with fear that we had to help him up on his horse again. He had fallen before, but this time truly he had come close to death. He was badly frightened and, to be frank, so was I.

Thereafter, a subtle change took place in Koshan.

He had brought his prayer rug from Kabul, but at first had had but little time for his God. He had only prayed in the mornings, or when it was convenient and there seemed little else to do. Now, he began to pray more frequently, and carried his prayer rug beside him in the saddle. By the time we reached the Pamir plateau, he was praying regularly five times a day.

And we went on, with the valley ever narrowing and the water of the Oxus becoming more turbulent in the steepness of its fall.

Several times we asked Rashid how much farther we had to go before we reached the next village, called Kharat. He haughtily disdained to reply, more sullen than usual, which was very sullen indeed. All Koshan could do was shrug his shoulders and hang on desperately to the pommel of his saddle. We rode hard all afternoon.

The trail dropped down to the river bed, and there, in a rocky valley, all trace of it disappeared. I shivered in the evening's chill as the sun dropped from sight. Two hours after dark, with the horses balking and whinnying their protest, it was obvious that we were lost. I suspected that Rashid had led us in a circle, and said so. "The flood," Rashid told Koshan, "must have washed away this trail."

At that, Franc called a halt. Our horses were lurching and stumbling among enormous rocks, bigger than upright pianos. It was better that we wait for morning rather than wander farther in the gloom.

Our pack animals and Rashid's soldiers had left before us that morning. Now they were somewhere far ahead, with, among other necessities, our bedrolls. We prepared to sleep in our *chapons.*

Dismounting, we slipped on wet and treacherous stones. All over the valley, great boulders had been scattered as if by a giant's careless hand. Around us swift mountain rivulets crisscrossed in a silvery network that we knew could swiftly envelop us in flood if it rained. And the valley walls echoed dismally to the night cries of birds and animals.

Rashid and Koshan held their millionth conference. For once Rashid did not seem arrogant. "He says he has been told that there are wolves hereabouts," Koshan told us. "We will have to stand a watch during the night."

I had read of the wolves of the Wakhan. Marco Polo mentioned them and Sven Hedin's expedition to the Pamirs had been repeatedly attacked by the fierce packs. We had wolves and coyotes in Texas. I cannot say that I was frightened.

Koshan was limping and sore from his fall. When he complained that he was exhausted and could not stand a watch, I felt sorry for him and offered to take his turn.

"You'll do nothing of the kind," Franc said. "I'll stand watch until midnight. Rashid can relieve me until four in the morning, and then I'll take it again until dawn."

Koshan, with relief, interpreted this for Rashid, and then found a sheltered spot, wrapped himself in his *chapon,* and promptly fell asleep.

Franc tucked me in between two boulders, and sat down beside me. Though the rocks were rough and cold and I was terribly hungry and tired, nevertheless I was soon sound asleep too. At midnight I heard Franc awake Rashid, and Rashid took the watch. Franc curled up beside me.

It was three in the morning when Franc and I suddenly sat up, both startled awake, although what sound had roused us I do not know. The horses were uneasy and nickering. Rashid had fallen asleep at his post, and was snoring. Franc repicketed the horses closer to our boulders, and I stroked their noses to quiet them. Franc was groggy, while I was wide awake, so I insisted on standing watch for an hour or two. We did not bother to arouse Rashid.

It would have been easy for me to fall asleep on watch. The wind moaned a low song through the crevices between the rocks, a half moon had risen to dilute the darkness, and the night cries of the birds and animals had ceased. But the horses were still nervous, and their skittish movements kept me awake.

The horses whinnied, and their ears lay back in fear as they bunched close together. I knew that something strange was near.

We carried no gun on this trip, on the theory that it might get us into more trouble than it could get us out of. Rashid had a pistol in his Sam Browne belt, but I hesitated to awaken him unless I was sure there was real danger. I didn't want to stir up an alarm because of a goat, and then get laughed at.

When I saw eyes in the darkness, I told myself it was probably imagination. The eyes vanished, and then reappeared, much closer. I felt around for a weapon, or a rock—anything that I could throw. My hand found the camera flash gun. I raised it quietly, pointed the reflector at the yellow eyes, and let go.

In the brilliant flash of the bulb, immobile for the fraction of a second, stood a lean-ribbed, shaggy wolf with a nasty smile on his face. He let out a wild yelp, leaped sideways, scrambled madly on loose stones, and then got out of there, yipping. He was undoubtedly the most frightened beast in the Wakhan.

The three men awoke. Rashid fumbled for his gun, Koshan hid behind a rock, and Franc sat on the ground and laughed.

Then Rashid and Koshan had an argument. Rashid claimed that he had never been asleep.

"Tell him," Franc said to Koshan, "that he wasn't lost, either."

Just after dawn, the soldiers found us. They had safely reached the village of Kharat with the pack horses. When we failed to arrive by midnight they had turned back, with villagers as guides, and spent the night in search of us. They had been worried, they explained, for there were many wolves in the area.

Franc told how I had routed the wolf, and the soldiers and villagers were astonished. It was necessary for me to illustrate the workings of the flash gun. To the Wakhis this was an awesome secret weapon. "Tell them," Franc said to Koshan, "that it was really nothing. In America all women are trained to protect themselves from wolves."

An hour's ride brought us to Kharat, a village of friendly people, none of whom had ever seen a foreigner. After tea and a nap,

I noticed pots of hot water steaming in every hut, and suddenly was aware of my need for a bath. I had slept in my clothes for a week, and there were dark rings of dirt around my wrists.

In sign language, and with Koshan's help, I explained my wish, not an easy thing to do, as the people of Kharat did not understand about baths. It is doubtful that anyone there had ever voluntarily taken one. Since I desired a private bath, and since the doors of most of the huts had been removed for the summer, it was first necessary to find a house with a door. Then women fetched hot water from the other houses, as Koshan suggested, and emptied it into the largest earthenware pot in Kharat. But my hopes of bathing in private were in vain. A half dozen women, overwhelmed with curiosity, simply would not be shooed away. All right, I thought, this would be a semiprivate bath. I started to undress.

I took off my windproof jacket, and the women watched the workings of the zipper in amazement. One dashed outside to spread the news of this miracle, and within five minutes the hut was so crowded I hardly had room to stand. Doggedly I kept on undressing. All right, I thought, this will be a public bath.

I was wearing a cashmere sweater, slacks, long red underwear, and several pairs of socks. As I peeled off each garment, it was passed around the circle, and the women felt of its texture. What really astonished them were the nylon panties and bra. They caressed them with their brown, coarse fingers, exclaiming at their transparency, but doubtful of their practicality, and regarding me with wonder and envy.

My cake of Lux soap further delighted the women, not so much for its cleansing effect, but because of its smell. They passed it around, sniffing it appreciatively. The matriarch of the village indicated that she wanted a piece. I smiled, yes. She cut a chunk off the cake and slipped it down the front of her rags. Before I could protest, my bar of soap was torn to bits, and every woman had a portion in her clothing. Instantly, I was soapless. I had to borrow back a piece to wash my socks.

I tried, by example, to persuade the women to use their bits of soap to wash their hands and faces, thinking it would be a useful community project, but I had no luck. So far as they were concerned, soap was much too precious to be used for bathing.

That day we pushed on, over terrifying trails, to Nurss. At some points the path was literally tacked to the cliff by branches and sticks jammed into cracks in the rock wall, and covered by brush and rocks piled on top. This is a type of construction that would give an American engineer apoplexy, but it is common in the Wakhan, and elsewhere in the Pamirs. There are accidents, of course, on these crude trails, but I told myself that there were also accidents on eight-lane superhighways. Still, it was disconcerting to look down *through* the road, and see daylight. Koshan closed his eyes, prayed, and allowed his horse to worry. I tried to concentrate on the scenery.

Three huts and a horse compound composed the village of Nurss, and the houses were so filthy that Franc and I scrambled down into the valley with our sleeping bags. Even in the valley our altimeter read 10,500 feet, and a freezing wind blew straight off the glaciers. But I remember Nurss for another reason. There we were introduced to yaks, which replaced horses as our pack animals. We also rode them on occasion.

The yak is a wonderful beast. He lives comfortably above 10,000 feet, and seems to enjoy the rarefied atmosphere and intense cold. Like a dog, he has no sweat glands. At the 10,500-foot altitude of Nurss, the yaks panted in great, frightening gasps.

Yaks are powerful animals, tall as horses and heavier than steers, with beautiful shining coats varying from black and gray to brindle that are so long they sometimes trail the ground. Their feet are huge cloven hoofs, and they are easy-gaited and sure-footed. It is not necessary for a yak to follow the cleared trails. If he desires, he can climb straight up a mountain. He will so desire if he sees some edible grass on a short cut.

But the yak is much more than a beast of burden. To the Kirghiz, and indeed all the tribes of the Pamir Knot, he is a one-animal social-security program. He carries heavy loads, and can be ridden like a horse. His coarse hair is woven into stout cloth for outer garments and small tents. His thick hide makes sturdy boots and thongs for tying tents. The cows give milk so rich that a few shakes turn it into butter. But its milk is scanty and it is not unusual for a Kirghiz tribeswoman to milk forty yaks in a morning. Yak milk, butter, and ghee are mainstays of the tribal diet. The meat makes *warkh,* a tough but nourishing sausage. The horns are carved into utensils and knife handles. And the animal furnishes the only export which enables the Kirghiz to trade with the outside world—yak tails.

The tail is really the most valuable part of the animal. In India it is prized as a fly whisk. Every proper public official keeps one on his desk. And we found, to our surprise, that great numbers are exported every year to the United States. It seems that there is nothing quite like their long, silky strands for making realistic whiskers for department store Santa Clauses.

Useful a yak may be, but comfortable he is not. His back is as broad as a dining-room table, and to straddle him you must do the split, and remain in that position. Although yaks don't tire easily, when they do, heaven help the rider. A tired yak is one of God's most unmanageable creatures. If he thinks he can get away with it, he will brush you off against the side of a cliff or the trunk of a tree. Or he may leave the trail entirely and set out upon a tack of his own choosing, oblivious to your cries, kicks, and jerks on the rope in his nostrils. Or he will start walking in small circles, preferably around a thorny bush or tree that tears your clothes and rips your skin at every revolution. As for retaliation by kicking or spurring him, you might as well dig your heels into a steel barrel. I have never won an argument with a yak, and that shows how stubborn they are.

Finally, a yak doesn't mind swimming in ice water, which was fortunate, as we spent four hours that morning fording the Oxus, crossing eight separate glacier-fed streams in the mile-wide, stony river bed. It was grueling, and it was dangerous. Our pack yaks struggled and staggered to keep their feet in the racing torrents. The water was frequently over my stirrups, and I balanced atop the saddle with my feet on the horse's neck. Franc's long legs were soaked to the knees. Koshan's mountain of bedding, for once, came in handy. He perched unsteadily atop this pile, cross-legged, like a nervous Buddha.

Wakhi guides rode ahead of us at each crossing. The only moment of comic relief came when Cadet Rashid contemptuously refused to follow the guides' directions, picked his own spot for a crossing, waved for us to follow, and promptly plunged in over his head, horse and all. The icy chastening of his arrogance was a lovely sight. We preferred to follow the natives.

Daily Franc badgered me to eat more mutton and ghee, because I was growing quite thin. Franc, too, had lost at least twenty pounds since Kabul. But Franc was hard and fit, while my loss of weight was more costly. My endurance seemed to disappear at the end of each day. Yet I found it almost impossible to force the greasy mutton down my throat, and I had visions of crisp green salads and rare roast beef, followed by strawberry shortcake. I pleasured my mind with tasty thoughts all the way to Baroghil, also called Sarhad, the last army post in the Wakhan.

At Baroghil I was so exhausted I couldn't eat at all. The commandant, a tall, wide-shouldered man of considerable dignity and quiet strength, led us to a pleasant mountainside grove, from where we could look down upon the pastoral settlement. Small children tended herds in the lower valley, and ponderous, shaggy yaks ambled along the trails between the small cluster of low stone houses. I unfolded my sleeping bag and fell atop it, asleep in an instant.

I awoke with a definite hallucination. I could have sworn I smelled fried chicken. I looked up, and there *was* fried chicken, a real fried-chicken dinner, with peas and buttered bread, on a wooden platter. Franc stood over me, smiling. In the Bible no angel appears bearing a fried-chicken dinner; I had gone the Bible one better. When my worst hunger pangs had disappeared, I asked Franc how he did it.

While I was sleeping he had taken a walk and had noticed green peas growing in a nearby field. Then, in the village, he had seen a hen, and promptly bought it. He had sent children on easy missions to find bread, goat's milk, and yak butter, after which he built a fire and prepared this feast. It was in every way superior to our last dinner at the Ritz. I used my spoon, forgotten in our luggage for days, so as not to lose a pea or drop of gravy. There were hairs in the yak butter, but I didn't mind a bit. There are *always* hairs in yak butter.

The children were horrified when they saw me devouring the green peas, ravenously, for I had not seen a fresh green vegetable since Kabul. They made graphic signs that we would be sick, and jabbered at us in Persian. As for the peas, it was the custom of these people to dry them and grind them for bread, Koshan explained later. They never ate fresh peas.

We had just finished eating when the commandant climbed up to our camp site with Koshan. He brought alarming news. Earlier reports of warfare along the Chinese frontier were not exaggerations. There had been ambushes and shooting. The political situation in China was unpredictable. No one knew exactly what was happening, because no travelers had come through in recent weeks. He was concerned for our safety.

Franc asked why he was so concerned.

While we were in territory under his command, the commandant answered, we were his responsibility. If anything happened to us, he would have to answer to Kabul. And a number of things, including death, could quite possibly happen. He dispassionately sketched the situation.

From here at Baroghil to the Chinese border post, the trail led across the Pamir plateau at an average elevation of 15,000 feet. On the way we would find no villages, but only the *yurts* of wild, nomadic Kirghiz. The Kirghiz nominally owed allegiance to Afghanistan, but they crossed at will into China, Russia, and Pakistan, and were contemptuous of all authority. They were fierce and unpredictable people who even in the most peaceful times looted caravans. What they might do to foreigners laden with such valuable equipment as cameras and camping supplies no one could say, for no such party as ours had ever penetrated so far into the Wakhan. Even the commandant himself had never ventured out onto the great plateau, although he had been stationed at Baroghil for two years.

It was the commandant's judgment that we should turn south, across the Baroghil Pass into Pakistan, and then make our way to Chinese Turkestan via the Hunza Valley and the Mintaka

Pass, thus avoiding the Pamir plateau entirely. However, he had seen the prime minister's letter. It was an order, and he was a soldier. If we insisted, he would help us take any trail we desired, even if the lives of all of us were in jeopardy. The commandant looked at me, and then he looked at Franc. He said not a word, but I knew his serious glance held this question for Franc: "Do you want to risk her life?"

As I sat there, bundled in my ungainly *chapon*, my hair in neglected pigtails, my nose blistered by the sun, lips and hands chapped, ghee on my chin, and badly in need of a bath, I didn't feel that Franc would be risking the flower of American womanhood. He turned to me and said, "Well, how about it, Jean? You know the danger, and you know your own strength."

So the decision was up to me. We hadn't come thousands of miles, and spent months in cutting red tape, and endured Koshan and Rashid, and penetrated the Wakhan thus far, just to be stopped by a border war. Whatever happened, I wanted to go on. And I knew Franc felt the same way. All I said was, "With that fried chicken under my belt, I can go anywhere." And with a false bit of bravado I added, "Why are we sitting around talking when we should be packing? We've got to get an early start in the morning."

Koshan translated my answer, I believe accurately for a change. The commandant smiled, and grasped my hand in both of his and made a little speech.

"The commandant says he is proud to know you," Koshan interpreted. "He says he will come with us himself as far as the last Kirghiz encampments, and that tonight he will pray our journey be a safe one."

When the commandant left for his quarters, Koshan spread his carpet, faced Mecca, knelt, and also prayed—fervently.

No one offered us shelter that night. Fortunately the weather was clear, although bitterly cold. We spread our tarpaulin, the King's rug, and then our sleeping bags, and climbed in. We assumed that Koshan, like Rashid and the soldiers, would sleep in the barracks. Not so. Soon Koshan appeared with his bundle of bedding, and without a word spread its mass crossways against our feet. He crawled between the fourth and fifth layers and was soon asleep.

The tall poplars rustled overhead, the stars burned cold and bright, and we chatted quietly about the day ahead—and the days after that. Before dozing off, Franc murmured: "Now I know why medieval knights always had their faithful servants sleep at their feet. Nice and warm, isn't he?"

We were up at dawn the next day, and it was immediately apparent that the commandant would be a definite asset. Where Rashid had dallied over his hookah and tea in the morning hours, the commandant gave orders with quiet efficiency. Our yaks were securely packed and on the trail at sunrise, and we were fifteen minutes behind them. Our new riding horses were stout animals with comfortable saddles.

The trail east from Baroghil rose almost straight up, over paths of treacherous shifting shale and around sheer rock chimneys. We crossed our first pass at 13,400 feet, and thereafter were rarely below that level, often far above it. Until then, we had not been overly troubled by anoxemia, for our climb had been comparatively gradual. But after we left Baroghil, and approached the Pamir plateau, every unusual exertion—even mounting into the saddle—left me gasping.

The trail clung to the cliffs by rock fingertips, and here again we could often look down through the rocks to slender rivers twisting far below. In many places we were forced to dismount and lead our horses across steeply pitched, sliding rubble, or around hairpin curves where one misstep would be the last. At times the trail was so narrow that had I extended my elbows one would have bumped the rock wall while the tip of the other would have been over airy space.

The Pamir (Daliz) Pass over which we labored is a series of 14,000-foot crests interspersed with 10,000-foot valleys. That day we crossed six ridges higher than Pikes Peak. When I looked ahead and behind at the procession of yaks, horses, and men, all gasping and straining, I wondered how Marco Polo fared during his journey so long ago. Then I remembered that the road was no worse then, the tribes no fiercer, and his provisions and pack animals certainly more plentiful and sturdier than ours. And in his day this trail, now so neglected, had been a highway to Cathay.

The commandant pushed us relentlessly all morning. Even the Wakhis were worn out by noon, when we stopped for tea and bread, and stretched gasping on the rocks like landed fish. The commandant, as we rested, explained that there was a bridge well ahead of us, a most dangerous bridge, that must be crossed before nightfall.

With his constant urging, we reached the bridge at five o'clock. It was about sixty feet long, with a drop of fifty feet to the raging rapids below. Four slender tree trunks, interlaced with branches, formed the longitudinal skeleton, and this was covered with flat rocks, unsecured. The whole structure creaked and swayed when the commandant stepped out on it.

He ordered us to cross one at a time, leading our animals. An argument broke out among the six yak pullers as to which one should try it first. They weren't vying for the honor. I became exasperated, slipped off my horse, grabbed the bridle firmly, and led him out onto the bridge. I could feel it shift and heave under our weight, and I don't recall breathing until I reached the far side.

That ended the arguments, and one of the yak pullers hauled his bellowing animal over. The others followed. Each yak strained the bridge to its limit. Franc, on the other side, was busy taking pictures. Yak and man tumbling from a collapsed bridge would make a very spectacular shot, even if it would mean the end of our expedition. That was what I fully expected. But one by one, the yaks safely crossed until the last yak, revolting against the ring, rope, and man straining at his nose, put a hoof between two rocks, and his leg slipped down through the branches. The whole structure lurched frighteningly while the yak puller, abandoning his charge, skipped in terror to my side.

Certainly the bridge was going to collapse. I imagined myself stranded on one side with six yak pullers, with Franc on the other side—forever. But a yak is smarter than one would think, sometimes smarter than a yak puller. This yak regained his balance and with careful, muscle-straining effort, pulled his leg from the hole. He then trotted over to our side. The others of our party followed, leading their horses. Except for Koshan, who refused. He wobbled over alone. So Franc came last, leading two horses, which was certainly an overload and unnecessarily dangerous.

When the commandant ordered a brief, welcome rest on the east bank, Franc scrambled down to the river for a drink. Just as he leaned over, a rock turned beneath his feet, and he tumbled flat on his stomach, arms outstretched, into the freezing water. Much annoyed and thoroughly drenched, he dragged himself up the bank and stripped off the wet clothes. Blue with cold, wrapped in a *chapon*, Franc huddled beside a yak-dung fire.

While we waited for him to thaw, and his clothes to dry, I dug out our map case, so Franc could mark the bridge. After studying the map for a minute he began to laugh hilariously. He had traveled 11,000 miles into the Pamirs just to fall into the River Shor! I thought the coincidence incredible, and showed the map to Koshan. He was not impressed, nor did he think the name unusual. "Shor in Persian means salty," he said. "By any chance did the stream taste salty?"

We started again—straight up! The trail zigzagged up a shale chimney at a pitch close to the perpendicular, the steepest ascent I had ever seen. Less than halfway up, we dismounted as it was obvious the horses could make it only without riders. The horses would climb a few steps, then pause while their knees shook and their heads drooped. The yaks panted and wheezed like ancient freight engines. All of us struggled for ourselves—all but Koshan.

Our interpreter closed his eyes, wrapped his arms around the neck of his laboring mare, and let her stagger along under his weight. I had been amused by Koshan's weakness before. Now it was not funny. I began to regard him with what can be described as intense loathing.

At the top of the chimney, we sighted our first *Ovis poli*, the giant mountain sheep whose existence was first recorded by Marco Polo. Our predecessor up the Wakhan, Lt. John Wood, had taken the first horns to Europe only a hundred years before and there the enormous sheep was named in compliment to the Venetian. The great-horned sheep gazed down on us, without fear, from safe heights, then bounced away over a ridge.

The mountainsides were masses of wildflowers—wild pink roses, nodding daisies, yellow buttercups, purple morning-glories, lavender thistles, dandelions and wide patches of edelweiss. Within a few weeks they would be under a blanket of snow. Fat marmots popped into holes as we passed.

My horse gave out, so I switched to a yak. I rode this wide-backed beast until I was almost torn in half, and then got back on the horse. The sun dropped behind the mountains and was replaced by a full moon that bathed the trail in an eerie, silvery light. Our shadows stretched long against the cliff, grotesque and unreal.

One by one, men and animals reached the point of exhaustion, gasping and sobbing. I was riding a contrary and very tired white pony that belatedly developed the habit of bucking whenever I smacked her with the quirt. And it was necessary to use the quirt often or else she would have stopped entirely and gone to sleep standing on the trail. It was terrifying, riding a bucking horse on the edge of a 3,000-foot precipice. Finally I dismounted and led the mare, although my legs too trembled with fatigue.

Gradually the other horses reached the stage where it was impossible to goad them further, and ultimately we were all on foot. Except Koshan, of course. He found a well-padded yak and added himself to that poor animal's already heavy burden. All our yaks were carrying about 160 pounds, considered the maximum load.

At nine o'clock Franc noticed that I was crying. These were the tears of absolute fatigue. I simply couldn't help it. I had never wanted anything so much as to lie down on a rock and sleep. Franc comforted me, much concerned, but all I could do was sob. Then he asked the commandant when we could stop.

"There is a Kirghiz band," the commandant said, "at a place called Langar. We should reach it by midnight."

This was my own doing, or undoing. I had made a foolish speech, back at Baroghil, and now I was paying for my bravado.

I had to go on, now, if it killed me. I dried my tears on Franc's handkerchief, and we trudged ahead. Every rock under my feet became a boulder, every step a mile.

The commandant was a shrewd psychologist. We reached Langar, at an altitude of 12,400 feet, in one hour—not three. Since I had steeled myself for the longer haul, that hour was comparatively painless.

On our large-scale maps of the Wakhan, Langar looked like a sizable village. It was a dot somewhat larger than the other dots, that is. Actually, it consisted of two uninhabited, ruined stone huts and two densely populated Kirghiz *yurts*. Just as we reached the first *yurt*, the commandant's horse dropped dead. We had been on the trail sixteen hours.

The Kirghiz, the first we had seen, received us hospitably. Here were the hardy, independent, nomadic people who lived in the Russian Pamirs, Chinese Turkestan, or the Wakhan, with little regard for national boundaries. They offered us food, and though Franc and the Afghans ate large chunks of mutton, I was too exhausted to eat. Instead, I sat in a corner of the *yurt* and studied the Kirghiz. After our days among the sickly, undersized, backward Wakhis, these nomads were an amazing contrast.

The Kirghiz were alert-looking, friendly, and intelligent. Nearly all the men were more than six feet tall, deep-chested, and powerful. The women were clean and not unattractive, and the inside of the *yurt* was spotless. It was perhaps twenty feet in diameter, constructed of felts lashed over a willow frame about four feet high and held in place by wide bands of bright woven wool. Arched poles crisscrossed above to form the dome-shaped roof. A reed door, with a felt overcovering, was the only entrance, admitting a little light and breeze. A vent in the roof drew the smoke from the yak-dung fire. Kirghiz women can tear a *yurt* apart and load it on yaks within an hour, and it can be reconstructed almost as quickly. *Yurts* are cool in summer and warm in winter, as easy to move as an automobile trailer, and easier to keep clean.

One section of the big, round room was partitioned off by a woven mat of reed and wool. Behind this the women kept their household supplies—yak milk, yogurt (or *mast*), heavy clotted yak cream, and a soft, mild cheese made from yak milk, which is the consistency of wet cement. Their favorite drink is a concoction of tea, yak butter and milk, flavored with prized and expensive salt, and served boiling hot. The Kirghiz are richer than the pitiful Wakhis and can afford to import salt from China— when they can't loot it from the infrequent caravans. Bread is eaten during the two winter months, and meat is served only at feasts. Otherwise the Kirghiz live on a milk-products diet.

While the Wakhis are tied by inertia and ignorance to an area that apparently lacks essential ingredients for healthy living, the Kirghiz roam wherever the grazing is best. As a result of their dairy diet, rich in protein and probably containing all the necessary vitamins and minerals, these nomads are among the finest physical specimens in the world, capable of remarkable endurance even at the great heights at which they live. But Franc suggested that—like the yaks—they might not thrive at sea level.

We slept that night as if dead, and indeed we must have resembled corpses lined up side by side after a disaster. One *yurt* accommodated not only our entire party, including the six yak pullers and four soldiers but also twelve members of two Kirghiz families. The yak-dung fire, tended by the women through the night, kept us warm and comfortable.

In the morning Franc checked our pulses, as Lt. Wood had done a century earlier, to see how we were reacting to altitude. While we lay prone, our hearts were beating at 110 a minute, a rate Franc did not consider dangerous.

We struck out straight across the Pamir plateau for Bozai Gumbaz, the largest Kirghiz settlement. Our path led through a lush green bowl-shaped valley, 13,000 feet high, rimmed by 20,000-foot peaks. Occasionally we passed isolated *yurts* surrounded by grazing herds. While the Kirghiz are by nature a migratory people, a number of families had settled permanently in this valley—although not permanently enough to construct stone houses. They had found the rich grass adequate the year around, and this season they were busy erecting haystacks that looked like giant mushrooms.

Before the sun was at its height we were intercepted by a tall young Kirghiz on a white horse. His enormous fur hat made him look a head taller than Franc, and he wore a Russian overblouse, corduroy britches, and high boots of fine black leather. He introduced himself as Quolan Larh, chief of the valley Kirghiz, and asked us to be his guests at the noon meal.

He led us to a nearby collection of *yurts,* of which his was the largest. It needed to be. When he dismounted, Quolan Larh proved unquestionably to be one of the biggest men I have ever seen. There were three or four women in his *yurt,* and when their curiosity compelled them to examine my clothing, he cuffed them about and ordered them outside. They obeyed, although not without grumbling. He doubled a massive fist and uttered one word. The women kept quiet after that, and hurried to bring us food. This exhibition of male supremacy kept Franc chuckling happily all day long.

We were served a delicious meal of yogurt with clotted yak cream in wooden bowls, and hot yak-butter tea. I was glad to be out of the ghee area at last. Quolan Larh was in every way a perfect host until we asked permission to photograph his family. For an hour he balked and shook his head, no, but at last gave in, only because he was fascinated by our cameras. I showed him, in sign language, and by example, how to make a picture. He grabbed the camera and insisted on making a color photograph of us. It didn't turn out badly, either, just tilted a bit. When we were ready to leave, he decided to guide us as far as Bozai Gumbaz. "There," he said, "you will meet our leader."

The commandant seemed surprised. He didn't know that the fiercely individualistic Kirghiz acknowledged one leader. They did, the towering Larh insisted, and the name of this leader was Rahman Qul. Perhaps the commandant had heard of him?

The commandant looked unhappy. Yes, he said, he had heard of Rahman Qul. He did not elaborate.

All afternoon, across that fertile valley, Franc rode side by side with Quolan Larh, and feeling companionable, they began to sing. Over and over the Kirghiz chanted a deep dirge with a martial beat. When Franc finally mastered a verse the Kirghiz was so delighted that he smacked him between the shoulders, and

almost knocked him off his horse. Then Franc taught Larh "Oh!
Susanna," which Larh caught on to quickly. This time, at least,
Franc wasn't spreading American culture in the shape of a sing-
ing commercial, as he had with the Tungan bakers at the Lake of
Heaven.

It was on this valley trail that we saw, imprinted in the soft
earth, the incongruous tread of large rubber tires. We all reined
up, and Franc got down on his knees and studied them like a
frontier trapper. "This is impossible!" he said. "But there it is.
Some vehicle has come through here just ahead of us. Only one
track, can't be a car, must be a motorcycle. But no motorcycle
has ever crossed the mountains into this valley, unless—"

"Unless what?" I asked.

"Unless it was brought in on a yak," Franc said.

I pictured a motorcycle tied on the broad back of a yak, and
said the whole idea was ridiculous.

Franc glared at me. "Look for yourself," he said. "Did, or
did not, a motorcycle come through here? And very recently.
See how wet the prints are!"

I took a good look. The diamond-shaped track was undoubtedly that of a tire. But it seemed to bump along the ground, with
spaces between the prints.

Koshan interpreted our conversation but as Quolan Larh had
never seen a motorcycle, it was a tedious session. Finally he said
he not only had never seen a motorcycle but doubted that such
a monster existed.

As we went on, the irregular tire trail grew fresher. "That
motorcycle," Franc said, "must be in low gear. Very, very low."

Thirty minutes later we overtook a wizened, white-bearded
Afghan trader, his skin brown and weathered, leading a sturdy
pony. He was on the way to Kashgar, in Chinese Turkestan.
While we chatted Franc kept looking at the ancient's feet and
suddenly said, "Koshan, ask him to let me see his shoes."

The old man lifted his boots warily. They were soled with
tire rubber. The mystery of the motorcycle on the Pamirs had
been solved.

An hour before sundown we reached Bozai Gumbaz where

twenty *yurts* were dotted along a clear stream, and women were busy milking a large herd of yaks tethered nearby. Quolan Larh spoke to guards at the doorway of the largest *yurt* we had ever seen, bade us good-by, and rode off. Impassively, the guards bowed us inside.

The diameter of this *yurt* was at least forty feet. It was carpeted with brilliant Yarkand felts and fine Khotan rugs. Brightly painted metal trunks and chests, some brass-bound and apparently very old, lined the walls. In just such a tent had Genghis Khan lived, ruled, and stored his loot. Displayed in one corner were a dozen large brass samovars of Russian design. The inevitable fire in the center of the *yurt* was topped by a giant tripod, and water was boiling in a kettle.

A half dozen tribesmen, the elders of Bozai Gumbaz, joined us, smiled and bowed in welcome, and we were soon warming ourselves close to the fire, and noisily (therefore politely) sipping bowls of yak-butter tea. Then a man taller than all the rest entered. This was obviously Rahman Qul, the Kirghiz Khan. We all stood up.

Rahman Qul unslung an Enfield rifle from his shoulder and unbuckled a cartridge belt, from which hung a pistol holster. He pushed back his karakul hat, exposing a broad, balding head, and greeted us in Persian. The commandant introduced himself. While they were extremely polite to each other, one sensed a tension, a bristling between two strong men. Then the commandant nodded in our direction, identifying us as Americans. Rahman Qul smiled, stepped forward, and shook hands.

The Kirghiz Khan, obviously an intelligent and quick-witted man, was elegantly dressed. His knee-high black boots were of the finest leather, and carefully polished. His overblouse was belted and fur-lined, and I had the disturbing thought that it must once have belonged to a Russian officer. Around his neck, under the collar of an American GI shirt, was a lavender scarf of fine Chinese silk. His flat Mongol face, in repose, seemed a bit sinister with its almond eyes and thin mustache drooping around the corners of his mouth. He looked like the Hollywood

version of an Oriental villain, though his manner was straight-
forward and almost friendly.

Koshan explained our presence in Bozai Gumbaz, and em-
phasized that our journey had the blessing of the King. There
was much head-shaking and frowning, with frequent glances in
our direction, especially when Koshan mentioned that we were
en route to China. Koshan refrained from interpreting what
must have been Rahman Qul's objections. Then Qul spoke to
two young men seated, silent and cross-legged, in the shadows
behind the elders. They went outside, mounted horses, and rode
off across the plain at a long lope.

The chief led us to a smaller *yurt* near his own, explaining
through Koshan, that "there had been bad feeling at the border."
He had sent out scouts to make a reconnaissance. We would remain his guests until he thought it advisable for us to go on.
If he did. We felt that Koshan wasn't telling us the whole story.

The Kirghiz pointed to piles of satin-covered quilts along the
walls of this guest *yurt*. Would these be suitable as beds during
our stay? We smiled our pleasure. Perhaps we should rest for
a few hours, he suggested. That night there would be a feast in
our honor.

After he left, I prowled around the encampment. The broad-
faced Kirghiz women regarded me in awe, no doubt because I
was dressed like a man. At first they appeared shy, as I watched
them weaving, and at their continual household chores of making butter and cheese from yak milk. But quickly they grew
bolder, and began to poke at my ribs and rear, making comments
that required no interpreter. By their standards, I was woefully
skinny. These women, who wore long quilted cloth coats and
multitudinous skirts over soft boots, obviously did not approve
of my trousers. Again I found myself wishing for a fancier outfit. Had I worn a sequined gown I would have been discussed
for years to come. Dressed as I was, I was a curiosity but by no
means an alluring one.

Apparently these women preferred red, for most of their
clothes were fashioned from prints of that color. Like their

kinsmen, the Turkestan Kazaks, whom we had met near Urumchi, they wore the traditional white head scarf of the Turkic
tribes. Their jewelry consisted of strings of silver coins. I gave
them a few United States, French, and British coins to add to
these necklaces. After that, they became very friendly, and shared
with me all the gossip of the tribe. I regretted that I could not
understand a single word.

So that all the tribesmen could be present, the feast started
out of doors, around a smoldering campfire in front of Rahman
Qul's tent. A wild-looking Kirghiz in a shaggy fox-fur hat slit a
sheep's throat. He fed the blood to a pack of snarling dogs,
and expertly pulled off the skin as one might peel off a sweater.
The liver and kidneys were skewered, grilled, chopped into
small pieces, and passed around on a wooden platter. It was a
bit unnerving to see a live sheep reduced to hors d'oeuvres in
such a few minutes, but it was a tasty appetizer. Between courses
Franc and I retired to our *yurt* and toasted our uncertain future with the last drop of bourbon. At 13,000 feet a small jigger
was as stimulating as a shakerful of cocktails.

When the sheep was thoroughly roasted, it was laid on a
rough plank, whole, and carried into the big *yurt*. The men
drew their knives and attacked it. Every Kirghiz carries a knife
at his thigh, as natural a part of him as his hand. Rahman Qul,
seeing that we had none, loaned us two of his, long and razor-
sharp. To make certain that his guests of honor got their share,
he shouldered his followers aside, neatly severed a leg and handed
it to Franc. We were on our own for the rest of the meal.

It was a scene out of the Dark Ages. The Kirghiz were ravenously stuffing handfuls of meat into their mouths, their knives
glinting in the firelight. The only sounds were the scrape of steel
on bone and the crunch of teeth on flesh. At this time of year,
a whole sheep was a special treat. The skeleton was torn apart,
and the bones gnawed. One old man, who had captured the
sheep's head, held my attention. In one hand he clutched his
long knife and dug out hidden morsels. Then with both hands
he would raise the skull to his mouth and gnaw. Since he still
held his knife, the blade grazed an eyebrow with each bite. It

was a gruesome, but fascinating, spectacle for a "formal" banquet. Momentarily I wondered what an informal meal with the
Kirghiz would be like.

None of the women ate with us. They entered the *yurt* as
unobtrusively as possible, only to bring bowls of yogurt topped
with clotted yak cream, and to replenish the fire. No portion
of the meat was saved for the women, nor did they appear to
expect any.

In the middle of the meal the two scouts returned, followed
by five more armed men, to report to the Kirghiz Khan. We
asked Koshan, who had overheard, what news they brought.
Koshan hesitated. He, Rashid, and even the commandant looked
troubled. When Koshan did reply, he gave us the old lie. "It
was about some yak tails."

It was obvious that the news was grave, and that Koshan did
not care to discuss it with us. Something had gone very wrong.
Koshan, Rashid, and the commandant shared a secret—a dangerous secret—which they dared not confide to us.

Rahman Qul was unperturbed. The faces of his men showed
no emotion whatsoever. Their attitude toward us was as opaque
as their expressionless eyes. They just kept on devouring the
sheep.

After dinner the women brought delicate jasmine tea. I offered
Rahman Qul an American cigarette. He refused, produced a gold
case from an inner pocket, and offered me one of his—Abdul-
lah Imperial Preference. I had seen the brand only in the better
tobacco shops of London and Paris, but once they had been the
favorite smoke of Russian grand dukes. They certainly weren't
the kind of cigarettes one would expect to find on the Pamir
plateau. Then Qul pulled out a thin Swiss watch with a beautiful gold case, another item not exactly indigenous to the scene.
Where had he gotten the cigarettes and watch? It would have
been indiscreet, if not dangerous, to ask. Unlike GI jackets and
Enfield rifles, such items were not normally procured by trade in
Central Asia.

The party broke up at ten. Rahman Qul summoned the commandant, Rashid, and Koshan to a parley with the elders. We

went to our *yurt,* aware that the conference could only be about us. We lay down on the thick quilts. But we worried instead of slept. It was probable that Rahman Qul was a smuggler, fortuitously based at the juncture of Afghanistan, Pakistan, Russia, and China, in an area so forbidding and remote it could not be patrolled. It was possible that he was a highwayman preying on lonely pilgrims and caravans. What else he might be we did not wish to guess.

We feared the worst, and the worst happened. In the morning Rashid, Koshan, and the Baroghil commandant solemnly entered our *yurt.* Kirghiz women brought tea, and we sipped politely, waiting. Koshan dropped the bombshell. The Kirghiz, he reported, had been fighting for two weeks with the Chinese at the border. Everything east of our encampment was a no man's land. Several men had been killed in the past few days. He concluded forcefully: "There is nothing for you to do but turn back. The Kirghiz will not guarantee your safety beyond here."

My instinctive reaction was a blunt, "No!"

"You can go back to Baroghil," Koshan wheedled, "and cross the pass there into Pakistan, and enter China another way."

"What kind of Chinese are at the border—Nationalists or Communists?" Trust Franc to ask the important question. In Kabul we had heard rumors that the Communists were advancing everywhere, and even menaced Shanghai, which to us seemed incredible. (Actually, at that moment, although we did not know it, they had already taken Shanghai, and much of Central China.) If the Communists held Sinkiang Province and the Chinese Turkestan frontier which was our goal, it would mean imprisonment, at least, to try the border.

"Nationalists," Koshan replied. I sighed with relief.

Franc and I held a serious conference in that comical American dialect, pig Latin. There could be no doubt that if we went on it might be at the risk of our lives. We talked of the half a world we had already traveled, and of our depleted bank balance. We spoke of Koshan's unwillingness to help us further. Both the Kirghiz and the Afghans seemed to want to get rid of us as quickly as possible. Furthermore, there was a mysterious undercurrent to these discussions that we didn't understand. Certainly Koshan wasn't telling us the whole truth. We both agreed that it would be wiser to turn back. We both agreed to try to go on.

Franc stated our decision flatly to Koshan: "Nothing doing. If we are forced to return to Baroghil, we will go all the way back to Kabul and report that you failed in your duty to guide us to the border."

Koshan was shaken once again by this threat to report his cowardice to the King. He whispered our decision to the commandant and Rashid. The commandant was impassive. It was apparent that he would not try to influence our decision. Rashid was indignant, and spluttered in anger.

Koshan tried again. "There is great danger," he said. "These tribesmen have no respect for life—not even the lives of soldiers or government officials. Even if you and Mrs. Shor are willing to take the chance, you must think of others. Remember that you have an escort of Afghan soldiers, and that I am an official of the government. Certainly, it would never do to expose an Afghan soldier to an area where there might be shooting! Why, it could provoke an international incident!"

"Nobody's keeping you here," Franc said. "We'll go on alone."

"The Kirghiz," Koshan said, "will not let you."

"I'll believe that," said Franc, "when I hear it from the Kirghiz themselves. I want to talk to Rahman Qul!"

Koshan and Rashid and the commandant left the *yurt*, and we could hear a great deal of what in China is called *wallah-wallah*. Franc looked at me, and I looked back at him. What Evert Barger had called "your great enterprise" had now, it seemed, come to an ignominious end.

Koshan returned and tried another argument. "What about your wife?" he told Franc. "Do you think you should risk her life at the border?"

"My wife has made her decision," Franc said.

"Well," said Koshan, "if we turn back, what will you use for pack animals, and who will guide you to the Wakhjir? Or if you take our pack animals, how will we get them back again?"

This was a more difficult problem. Franc and I held another conference, at which it was decided that I would play the part of a reluctant hostage. Franc told Koshan of our plan. "I'll take one soldier and one yak and go alone to the Chinese border post. There I'll get pack animals from the Chinese, and return for Mrs. Shor. I will leave her as guarantee that I will bring back the animals and the soldier."

Koshan assured us, with a sudden display of chivalry, that it was not necessary to leave me as a hostage. All Afghans were gentlemen. He would not hear of it.

"Well," Franc said, "how about sending a message to the Chinese border post, asking them to send animals?"

This was impossible, Koshan replied. At this critical time, the Kirghiz dared not even approach the border. There might be trouble. There had already been trouble—grave trouble—although we were not to learn the details until later.

As each of our suggestions was rejected, we became more and more determined. Finally Franc tired of the debate. "Koshan, take us to Rahman Qul. We're going on."

Koshan sighed, shrugged, and walked with us to the chieftain's *yurt*. Rahman Qul was seated cross-legged before the fire, smoking. He had been expecting us, he said.

Franc made a little speech, earnestly and in a low voice. He spoke very slowly, in the hope that Rahman Qul could not mistake his meaning, should Koshan distort the words. But, to his credit, Koshan interpreted exactly, for once.

"We have traveled more than eleven thousand miles to reach your encampment," Franc said. "We have crossed oceans and deserts and continents. We have spent much money, and months out of our lives. And here, only two days' travel from our goal, we are told we must turn back. I put our lives entirely in your hands. If you can help us reach the Chinese border, we can make our own way from there. From here to the border, we must beg you for animals and a guide. We will pay whatever you ask."

The Kirghiz Khan smiled. He rose and placed both hands on Franc's. "I accept your trust," he said. "I will be responsible for your lives. I can accept no pay. You are my guests. I am only ashamed of the cowardice of your escort, for while I am a Kirghiz, I am also an Afghan."

Rashid looked very unhappy. "I am responsible for the bodies of these people," he said.

"If you are responsible," Rahman Qul told him, "maintain your responsibility and go with them to the frontier."

"That I cannot do," said Rashid, "because of the many involvements we spoke of."

"So now I have taken the responsibility," said Rahman Qul.

Rashid started to argue further, but thought better of it. Instead he began thinking of ways to cover his retreat. "I cannot let them go unless I have something in writing."

Rahman Qul considered this demand, and then nodded in agreement. Koshan sat down and wrote half a page of Persian script. Rashid approved it, and it was passed to Qul. The Kirghiz Khan read it carefully, and then signed it. "There is your receipt for the two Americans," he said. Koshan studied the signature, and handed it to Rashid, who tucked it into his wallet. The whole procedure had an air of serious business, conducted in legal fashion. "You are now out of our hands," said Koshan.

I suppressed a small cheer.

It was a strange feeling, being passed on like a chattel. It made us feel helpless and a bit foolish. Yet we felt overwhelmingly grateful to Rahman Qul. Of a sudden he didn't look like an Oriental villain but like a protector.

We wished we had something to give Qul to express our gratitude. That would be hard, for he was a man who had everything. He had more money than we did, he had hundreds of yaks, and probably at least four wives. Nevertheless, Franc rummaged around in the barracks bag and found something he thought might be acceptable. Holding it in his hand, he approached Qul and handed it to him, saying, "Please accept this as a token of our respect. It is for your wife."

Wife? I wondered. What manner of gift would that be? Qul smiled with pleasure and dangled a lovely gold-and-enamel lapel watch in his fingers.

No wonder he looked pleased. Franc, the louse, had given him *my watch!*

Qul told us we could leave the following morning. He would supply two good horses, two yaks with their pullers, and a guide. It was everything we needed.

I went out to do my laundry in the stream's freezing water that afternoon, and half the children in the encampment came to watch. The current was so strong that the pieces that were soaking had to be weighted down with large stones. Our laundry soap was gone, so I tried the local system of pounding our socks with a flat rock. Each piece that I laid on the tall grass to dry was instantly snatched by the children, who ran off to show it to their mothers, and then returned it to its exact place.

The children, to whom I gave the last of my fruit drops, were fat and merry, and chased each other in interminable warlike games around the *yurts.* Big dogs, which looked like a cross between a Husky and a German shepherd, were their companions.

A few of the Kirghiz men, from whom I also attracted considerable attention, wore the Afghan karakul hat, like Qul, but most of them preferred caps of black or gray fox fur. Their clothes reflected their position at a crossroads of Asia. Some preferred padded coats, Chinese style, others wore Afghan *chapons,* and a few had Russian greatcoats.

Two young Kirghiz, sharp dressers of the High Pamirs, sported huge red fox-fur caps, tightly fitted GI jackets nipped in at the waist by wide cartridge belts, and black trousers tucked loosely into high boots. One of them took a fancy to my Paisley printed wool scarf and, grinning, snatched it off my head. I smiled in a most friendly fashion and grabbed it right back. At this stage, I felt just as rough and primitive as any tribesman, a feeling my would-be tormentor sensed and thereafter kept at a respectful distance.

That night we carefully counted and packed the last of our emergency rations: two small tins of cheese, two quarter-pound bars of Swiss chocolate, and a small bottle of Bovril, my favorite British beef tea. We thought these would last us for two days. In addition, the Kirghiz had baked for us twelve flat loaves of bread, and left them in a sack at the door of our *yurt*.

In the evening Koshan, suspiciously affable, came to pay us a final visit. He was afraid Mr. Rishtya would not be pleased if he returned and admitted he had left us at Bozai Gumbaz. He wondered whether Franc would write a letter absolving him of blame in case anything happened to us. "Perhaps it would be well," Koshan suggested casually, "If you gave me a note saying you had been delivered safely at the frontier. Just a formality, of course. Do you understand?"

Franc said he understood perfectly. Koshan, after all, was not a very difficult person to understand. He typed a note to Rishtya.

"There is one other thing," said Koshan, as he carefully buttoned the note in a pocket. "The matter of the altimeter. If I do not bring the altimeter back, the air force will ask questions, and no doubt I will have to pay for it."

"Why can't I send it back from the border?" Franc asked. In such mountainous country, largely unmapped, an altimeter is often as important as a compass. Also, the altitudes on our maps were based on old and sometimes faulty surveys. We were anxious to check the maps, as we had all through the corridor, right into China. Without an altimeter, our records would be incomplete. We begged him not to insist on taking the altimeter, but insist he did.

"The altimeter will not be necessary," he said, using Oriental reasoning, "because Rahman Qul will furnish a competent guide."

Franc tried once again. "Koshan," he said, "it was the original intention of the minister of war, when he loaned it to us, that we take it to the border. As you say, the Kirghiz guide is certainly trustworthy, and he will return it to you here in less than four days."

Koshan hesitated. Intuition prompted me to ask, "Or hadn't you and Rashid intended to wait here to see whether we arrived safely in China?"

Koshan fidgeted and hedged. It was painfully apparent that he was going to leave as quickly as possible. "As a matter of fact," he reluctantly admitted, "we plan to leave before dawn tomorrow. I am sure Qul's man will see you to the border safely."

There seemed nothing more to discuss. Koshan got the altimeter.

We had a last meal that night with Koshan, Rashid, and the commandant. We five had covered some rough ground together, and ordinarily past frictions would have been forgotten at such a time. But we were not sorry to part from them. The commandant I liked best of the three, for he was at least efficient and considerate, although choosing to remain aloof from discussion or involvements. He had carried out his responsibilities as a soldier. Rashid was a mean and insufferable minor-league martinet, and I was glad to see the last of him.

As for Koshan, he had been more exasperating than offensive. He would be overjoyed to get back to the civilization of Kabul—and he would stay there. He agreed to take back our letters, notebooks, and film, and mail them from Kabul. Despite our misgivings, this part of his mission he fulfilled without error.

As he left our *yurt* he shook hands, smiled weakly, and assured us that we would have no further trouble, that Rahman Qul would take care of everything. (Two years later we received a letter from Koshan in which he spoke with feeling of how much he worried over our fate after he left us "with that terrible man.")

Later that night, while Franc was packaging the notebooks and film, I started a long letter to my parents. I was sitting with the typewriter on my lap when Rahman Qul entered the *yurt* and sat beside me. I smiled at him and continued typing. He leaned over my shoulder and, distinctly and without accent, began to read aloud: "Three September, Kirghiz encampment, Bozai Gumbaz. Dear Mother and Dad. We are about ready to leave on the last stage of our trip to the Chinese border. It may be quite some time before you hear from me again. This letter . . ."

I was astounded, and for a moment terrified. What was going on? Had Rahman Qul understood everything we had been saying? Where had he learned his English? I called Koshan in to translate. If Koshan's translation was no more garbled than usual, we learned that while Qul could read and pronounce English, he could speak and understand very little. He had learned to read it many years before from a British archeologist in western Sinkiang. He also spoke Urdu, Persian, Pashto, some Russian, and some Chinese, in addition to his native Turki. He knew enough English to worry me, so I smiled politely and moved to another side of the room to finish my letter. He complimented my caution with a wide grin.

We rode out of Bozai Gumbaz on the morning of Sunday, September 4, with Tiluh Walduh, a dour Kirghiz guide, and two yak pullers. It was cold enough for the ground to hold frost but except for white cumulus powder puffs, the sky was unmarred. Rahman Qul took us to the edge of his camp and held a whispered conference with Walduh. Then he shook our hands, said a Moslem prayer for travelers, calling upon Allah to protect us. He bowed, turned and strode back toward his tent. We kicked our horses, and soon were strung out across the grassy plain, with the peaks ahead barring our way like white-helmeted giants, shoulder to shoulder. One of those shoulders was the Wakhjir Pass, but which one we did not know.

The two yak pullers prodded their lumbering beasts until, like heavy locomotives, they picked up speed. Just out of sight of the Kirghiz camp, we passed a row of tombs, called *gumbas*, with domed roofs, the graves of forgotten warriors. They were well tended, with bits of white cloth fluttering above them from poles.

I studied the yak pullers. One was a short, stocky, middle-aged Kirghiz with a round, pleasant face. The other was a teen-ager with vacant expression, prone to giggles. Fine, I thought. They've unloaded the village idiot on us. But his I.Q. didn't really matter much, because he possessed the two skills necessary for this particular assignment. He could pull a yak, and he could push a yak.

As for our guide—if Rahman Qul looked like an Oriental villain, Tiluh Walduh was Hollywood's version of a Mexican desperado, tall and slender, with smoldering black eyes and a thin drooping handlebar mustache. He was the silent type, and so were the yak pullers, except for their monotonous curses as they prodded, pushed, and pulled. We were not long on the trail when I realized that this part of the tour was going to be without benefit of lively chatter. We could not understand more than five words of Tiluh Walduh's language, and he could not understand one of ours.

An hour's ride out of Bozai Gumbaz, Tiluh Walduh left us. In sign language he pointed out the path we should take, and then indicated with a wide sweep of his arm that he would go out on the flank, and watch for danger from the hill summits. He loped off across the plain, climbed a ridge, and vanished.

All that day, we had an uncanny feeling of being remarkably little, and alone. The vast emptiness of the Pamirs spread around us. The peaks seemed always in the same place, so distant that we could never leave those behind, or reach those ahead. It was as if our horses walked on a slow, silent treadmill against a painted backdrop of forbidding scenery. There was no sound except for the steady clop of their hoofs and the deep, rumbling breathing of the yaks.

Franc and I drew close together, and silently rode boot to boot. The Kirghiz pasture land grew sparse, and the plain gave way to rocky waste. At noon we stopped in the shade of an overhanging rock for lunch of bread and cheese, and made a disturbing discovery. Our sack of bread had shrunk from twelve to three loaves. During the previous night, someone had "borrowed" nine loaves—the bulk of our provisions. Since the tribesmen of Rahman Qul had all the bread they needed, it was easy to guess that Rashid and his men had "requisitioned" our bread when they left the encampment before dawn, while we still slept.

The simple arithmetic of our food supply was not encouraging. Five people must exist for two days on an arduous trail with three flat loaves and a goatskin bag of pasty Kirghiz cheese, plus our skimpy emergency rations. The yak pullers carried the cheese, made from leftover yogurt rolled into balls and dried in the sun. It was called *karut* and tasted like cheese-flavored putty. It was necessary that they share our bread, just as it was necessary that we share their cheese, although nothing complimentar·

Between Gulmit and Atabad
in Hunza, one of our escorts
adjusts the load on a pack
horse. I waited in foreground,
wisely leaning away from the
precipice.

Near the Mintaka Pass, I served tea to Franc in the shelter of a cliff. This camp
site turned out to be a poor choice, for a heavy snow fell during the night,
covering us and our equipment.

H. H. Mohammed Jamal Khan, the Mir of Hunza, sits in Durbar dress on the roof of the 600-year-old ancestral castle in Baltit. Rakaposhi, the unclimbed "Queen of the Snows," rises over 25,000 feet in the background.

The Mir of Hunza holds court every morning. With the members of his Council (dressed in chogas and wearing the distinctive Hunza cap) he listens while a farmer pleads his case on water rights. This man, to the apparent amusement of the audience, accused his neighbor of using too much water.

could be said about it except that it was better than having an empty stomach. Nor could we turn back for more provisions, even had we wished, for somewhere ahead Tiluh Walduh patrolled our route.

We rode all afternoon through the incredible silence with no sign of our guide. As we reached each crest we scanned the whole sweep of desolate terrain ahead, watching for a single silhouette. Not once did he appear. The yaks and their pullers plodded along far behind us. The empty distances stretched ahead. Somehow the feeling grew on me that we were the only people left in the world, that the civilization of skyscrapers and automobiles and aircraft and supermarkets was just a dream. There was no one else—just the two of us. As if in answer to my thoughts, Franc reached out and took my hand. It was comforting. At least there were two of us.

When evening approached and the shadows galloped down the slopes, it grew cold very quickly. We had been climbing slowly but steadily. September is a month of swift change in the Pamir Knot. Winter is eager to reconquer its domain after the short months of summer.

Twice in that afternoon we forded the upper reaches of the Oxus. Once one of our yaks slipped and almost was rolled under in the racing current. After regaining its feet, the yak stood stubbornly in midstream and would not budge. Franc had to ride back into the water and help the yak puller. He pushed while the puller pulled.

At dusk Walduh appeared out of nowhere, signaling silently that all was well. We camped on the bank of a stream, brewed tea, and shared the second flat wheel of bread. While we slept, the Kirghiz took turns standing watch.

The next day passed in the same fashion—hours of silent progress through a silent land. We paused at noon to divide our last loaf. Then, at sundown, one of the yak pullers urged his animal into a trot, drew up with us, and pointed to a notch in the mountain wall two miles ahead. "Wakhjir," he said. "Wakhjir!" Franc put an arm around me and squeezed my shoulders. I must have cheered. The Wakhjir Pass—end of the Wakhan.

Through that pass, 16,000 feet above sea level, lay China. We had made it—the first foreigners in modern times to reach China on the ancient route of Marco Polo! We kicked our tired horses until they trotted.

Suddenly, less than a mile from the pass, a low, clear whistle sounded through the still evening air. We stopped, expecting to see Walduh materialize. Our yak pullers dragged their animals toward us, signaling for us to dismount. Puzzled, we swung out of the saddle.

The Kirghiz led all the animals into a little gully, and we followed, mystified. In a few minutes Tiluh Walduh joined us. He seemed tense and strained. At his direction we crept around a rock at the mouth of the gully and he pointed upward to the crest between us and the pass. Silhouetted against the darkening sky were three Chinese soldiers. That, we knew, would be the vanguard of a patrol.

We looked questioningly at our guide. He shook his head, no, his mouth taut and grim. We tried to explain that the soldiers would be friendly. Franc pointed to the patrol, then clasped his hands and shook them vigorously. I embraced an imaginary Chinese friend. Walduh pointed at the soldiers, and then at himself and us. He drew his forefinger across his throat. I have never seen sign language so expressive.

We squatted there, discussing our predicament. All the whispered conferences at Bozai Gumbaz, and Koshan's evasions and equivocations, took on fresh meaning. It looked as if this "border dispute" was a small war. Tiluh Walduh was not going to take another step toward China. Yet our credentials were in order. There was no reason for the Chinese to harm us.

"Suppose we walk on alone?" I suggested.

"You're not going to look like an American girl from up there," Franc said. "You're just going to look like a target."

I said something intelligent, like "Oh!"

On the Central Asian borders, it is quite customary to shoot first and identify the bodies later. Even when there isn't a feud, or border dispute, or war, or whatever was going on here.

The Chinese were beyond shouting distance, and yet we

found ourselves whispering. Our lives were in danger because of our escorts, and yet we could not leave them. We dared not go ahead alone; in fact we couldn't go anywhere alone. We were helpless, we were stopped dead in our tracks. There was nothing to do but obey Walduh.

We sat quietly beneath the bank until dark. It was bitterly cold as we remounted and turned our backs on the Wakhjir. My heart was cold, also. I was stunned and bitter.

After a mile we left the trail by which we had come, and struck out toward the south. I told Franc, hopefully, that at least we weren't headed back for Bozai Gumbaz. Perhaps Walduh knew a detour and would sneak us past the patrol and through the pass.

"Maybe," Franc said. "I don't know where we're headed."

For ten hours our horses shuffled across the Pamirs, halting for a few minutes' rest and grazing only when they shuddered and would go no farther. The bright moonlight made travel easy, but in its cold glow the mountains looked bleak and desolate and endless. I began to feel hunger pains, cramps that ebbed and flowed and refused to go away. I tried unsuccessfully to banish fearful thoughts from my mind. Suppose these cramps were not hunger but the onslaught of illness? Suppose a horse, or man, stumbled and broke a leg? Suppose the Chinese were following us, or we blundered into another patrol farther on? Then my muscles grew so sore and the cold stabbed me so incessantly that I forgot my hunger, and my imagination was stilled by the pain of the present.

At dawn Walduh let us stop for a few hours' rest. I slid off my horse and collapsed on the spot. When I awoke, Franc was studying our maps.

They showed streams where no streams existed, and the mountains were woefully misplaced. There was one large section over which was imprinted one word: UNSURVEYED. We were in the middle of that area.

Franc thought we were possibly fifteen miles south and a little west of the Wakhjir, but it was just a guess. So much of our progress was up, down, or around mountains that it was im-

possible to estimate straight-line distances. For the first time
since leaving Venice I wanted to go back. I tried to tell Walduh
that I wanted to go back. I repeated again and again, pointing
in the direction I thought was Bozai Gumbaz, "Rahman Qul!
Rahman Qul!"

My pleas had the reverse effect. Perhaps Walduh had orders
to get us out of the Kirghiz territory at any cost, and my repeating of his leader's name only reminded him of these orders.
Perhaps he was afraid to bring us back. In any case, he simply
shook his head and pointed toward a wall of mountains, an
enormous massif where no break was visible.

Walduh got on his horse. There was no way to argue with
him. We mounted and followed. Before noon we reached what
must have been a source stream of the Oxus, confined in a valley
so narrow that we had to ford it half a dozen times as we progressed upward. The perverse yaks had to be goaded across. Our
barracks bags were thoroughly soaked in the deepest crossings.
Not only were we higher now, but the snow line was lower. It
had crept down toward us each night since we arrived at Bozai
Gumbaz.

That afternoon we toiled endlessly up a mountainside, dismounting often to lead our horses over steep shale inclines.
Sometimes the shale gave way beneath our feet, and as we slid
backward, a shower of stones crashed into the canyons below. On
that day there were no paths or level ground. The scenery may
have been glorious. I don't know. All my concentration was on
moving ahead, and I seldom took my eyes from my feet.

Just before dark we began to climb an even steeper ridge.
About two thousand feet above, the trail dipped into a grassy
hollow. In the center of this remote and tiny valley stood a single
small *yurt,* two horses, and the biggest yak we had ever seen.
Three children, one an eight-year-old girl in a red dress, one a
nude boy of four, were playing tag around the yak. This, I
thought, is truly the end of the earth. Here are people living in a
valley with no name, set in a range of uncharted mountains.
Yet I was glad to be there.

A fierce, tattered Kirghiz, an ancient rifle resting in his arms and a long knife hanging bare at his side, stood beside the low door. Tiluh Walduh shouted to him, and several times we heard the name "Rahman Qul." The man nodded as if accepting orders, and finally lowered his gun. He signaled to us to dismount, and led us inside.

The interior of the *yurt* reflected the solitude and poverty of its owner. It was the only dirty Kirghiz habitation I have ever seen. A naked baby grubbed in the filth near the fire. As we entered, a wrinkled hag came from behind the reed partition, bent like a witch, with a face evil and twisted and filthy. The old harridan, either the man's mother or mother-in-law, controlled the household by sheer venom and viciousness. Trailing after her was an apathetic younger woman, mother of the children.

The old woman greeted our reluctant host with a blast of abuse. Even the magic name "Rahman Qul" failed to stem her flow of invective. Perhaps she was too old and miserable for fear. There was no question about our being welcome—we weren't. But there was no other place to go, except to a rocky bed on frozen ground, so we sat on the floor and warmed ourselves, trying to smile and appear at ease. Welcome or not, that lonely *yurt* looked inviting.

We tried to be friendly. Franc offered everyone cigarettes. The old lady grabbed one and demanded the rest of the pack. I lit her cigarette, and she snatched the box of matches out of my hands, complaining because it wasn't full. I rubbed some vaseline on my face, cracked and swollen from exposure. Our hostess demanded the rest of the jar. As a desperate peace offering, Franc gave her some French aluminum coins, all we had left. She hefted them disdainfully, bit one or two, and furiously threw them into the fire. We kept waiting for food. Even mutton and ghee would have been acceptable. A few days earlier I had gagged at the thought of this greasy dish. Now I craved it. But there was no mutton and ghee, nothing was offered. We broke out our unfinished tin of cheese. We shared it with the Kirghiz family, and grandmother demanded more. She didn't get it.

Avarice sometimes brings its own reward. Franc took a flash

picture of the chubby children and ejected the still hot bulb on the floor. The witch snatched it out of the dirt, despite Franc's warning gesture. She dropped it with a yowl, and screamed in rage, shaking her finger in Franc's face.

Even her son (or son-in-law) laughed. I still wanted to placate her, for we must spend the night there, so I treated her hand with ointment. She demanded the remainder of the tube. She didn't get that, either, for I had made a fascinating discovery. On the label of the tube was reading matter!

Something to read, like salt, you don't miss until you have none. Since Kabul, we had had nothing at all to read. Not only had we been deprived of newspapers, magazines, and books, but there was not so much as a road sign, a pamphlet, or an old calendar on a wall. We did know what day of the month it was, but that was only because each night one of us jotted down the day's events in our notebook. If, in exhaustion, we skipped a whole day and night, we tried to make it up the following morning. But we were starved for something to read—and all the time we had been carrying reading matter in our packs, without realizing it!

That label was wonderful. After reading it, I passed it on to Franc. He read it, then reread it aloud, and asked, "What else do you have in the library?"

There was the label on the Kraft cheese can we had just discarded. We read all about how healthful it was, and how many ounces it weighed, and how it had been made in Australia. It was a very romantic and interesting tin. The menthol tube was nearly finished, but I unrolled it like a precious scroll, and we perused it lovingly.

The bottle of Bovril read like an exciting novel. The label said, "Delicious when added to any soup. Excellent for gravies and sauces, delightful in sandwiches with cream cheese and countless other fillings." Tears came to my eyes at the thought of a long procession of sandwiches, each with a different filling. I read on: "Tasty canape spread, stimulating drink in hot water or milk. Adds zest and flavor to a variety of other dishes."

"Anything else?" asked Franc.

We had the label on a bar of Tobler's chocolate, but I insisted on saving that for the next day.

Although there was no mutton and ghee for supper, the Kirghiz family did brew a pot of yak-butter tea. The *yurt* was warm and relaxing, and we spread our sleeping bags and crawled in. Everyone else lay down to sleep, heads against the outside felt wall, feet toward the fire, like spokes of a huge wheel. It was very cold, and we spread our *chapons* on top of us. Our silent, harassed, henpecked host was the last to retire. Before he lay down, he lifted my feet and carefully tucked the *chapon* under and around them. He did the same for Franc. Even in an atmosphere poisoned by the old woman there still existed a spark of kindness. When I murmured my thanks, the hag unloosed another stream of obviously vile remarks.

After the others slept, we talked quietly. Now, for the first time, we admitted fear. We didn't know where we were, or where we were going. Our hosts were unfriendly, and the next ones might be worse—or there might not be any "next ones." We were entirely unable to communicate with our companions. Franc soon dozed off, but I remained awake. I had been badly shaken by the events at the Sinkiang border, and now I realized it wasn't only my nerves that bothered me. For the first time, I was suffering from the altitude—17,000 feet of altitude.

My heart beat at a frightful pace, as if it were trying to burst through my ribs. I was breathing in such short, shallow gasps that I was in fear of choking to death. In the stillness, the hammering of my heart was like a drum stirring me to panic. I tried to fight down my fear, knowing how useless it was; every extra exertion—even the exertion of being afraid—only increased my distress. Franc stirred, heard my gasps, and awoke. "Sit up," he advised, "and see if that helps."

It did help. Soon my heart slowed down. The rest of the night I dozed propped against the side of the *yurt*.

We had discussed the danger of anoxemia before leaving Kabul, and both of us predicted that Franc would feel it first. But between Kabul and this lonely *yurt* in an unmapped valley he had lost twenty pounds, and was down to a lean, hard 180. I

had lost ten and was just plain skinny. Both of us were perceptibly weaker than when we rode out of Zebak. The cruel mountain trek had drained our strength.

At dawn we broke an inch of ice crusting a small spring near
the *yurt,* washed, and then hurried back to the fire. When I
looked at my face in a battered pocket mirror, I was shocked.
My nose and lips were swollen by sunburn; my face was weathered and cracked. The sun, at this altitude, beat down with un-
merciful intensity, reflected by the snow fields on the surrounding
mountains. My hair, unwashed, hung in untidy braids. I had
aged ten years since Faizabad. As for Franc, the beard he had
been growing since Tehran, which at first he kept clipped in a
neat goatee, now straggled over his cheeks. He looked unkempt,
hard, and mean—definitely not the kind of man a girl would
care to meet in a dark *yurt.* But then I wasn't a girl you would
care to whistle at, even in the bazaars of Kabul. But we had to
admit that we were perfect companions for one another.

We breakfasted on hot yak milk and a bowl of yogurt. I ate
ravenously. While we were eating, the crone snatched Franc's
last bar of soap, no doubt thinking it a delicacy we were re-
serving, and took a bite. She munched it violently, began to
froth at the mouth, and spat it out, screaming.

Franc brought out his precious box of cigars after breakfast.
There were eight left. He lit one for himself and gave another
to the Kirghiz. They passed it around like a peace pipe.

The yaks were packed, and then we received a final blow.
Tiluh Walduh approached Franc, bowed low, took both his
hands, and said a polite "Salaam." In Afghanistan "salaam" can
mean either hello or good-by. In this case there could be no
doubt—it meant good-by.

We were stunned.

Walduh pointed to the man of the *yurt,* and in sign language
indicated that he would be the one to guide us on. Then, with
no further explanation, he mounted his horse and rode away
toward the north, where lay the domain of Rahman Qul. He
turned once and waved farewell.

I can't describe our dismay at seeing him depart. He was our last link with anyone we knew, or who knew anything about us —our whereabouts, our purpose, our destination. Up to now, we had been passed on from one protector to another, starting with the King, in Kabul, extending through the commandant at Baroghil to Rahman Qul, and finally to Tiluh Walduh. But the chain of responsibility had broken. If anything happened to us now, if we simply disappeared, it would be months before the news filtered back to Kabul—if it ever did. And we had lost all power of decision. We had no alternative but to follow help-lessly him who led us. We could not possibly get back to Bozai Gumbaz by ourselves, nor could we go ahead alone. We were in the hands of our silent, unwilling host who had instructions to take us somewhere—we knew not where. This time no receipt had changed hands for "our bodies," as Koshan had put it.

In hopes of starting off on a friendly footing with our re-luctant sponsors, I gave the old woman a silk scarf. She pulled at it savagely, as if hoping it would tear. Franc presented his black-and-red checked cap to the young girl.

We waited until our guide finished sewing new soles to his *chamooses,* a chore he had begun the previous evening. Then we mounted and started off. As he passed his daughter, the Kirghiz snatched Franc's cap from her head and slapped it on his own. We rode away serenaded by the daughter's wails and the curses of the old crone.

The Kirghiz, on foot, led our little procession. Franc and I rode immediately behind, on the horses loaned by Rahman Qul. To our rear the two yak pullers urged on their animals.

For an hour we climbed a gentle gradient of grassy turf, crisp with frost, wet and springy underfoot. The next hour took us over a massive mountain shoulder, still climbing, but now and again over shale, shifting and dangerous. Our horses actually trembled with fear. Franc rode a stubborn, dirty gray stallion nicknamed "Backfire" because of his rude personal habits. My horse we called "Nipper," as he would bite any flesh, animal or human, that came within range of his long, yellowing teeth.

240 AFTER YOU, MARCO POLO

They were not lovable animals, but they were strong and willing. Qul had promised us good mounts, and he was as good as his word.

Our guide carried a goatskin packed with yak cheese, and a wheel of bread. We were down to one tin of cheese, the Bovril, and two bars of chocolate. As the horses climbed at their methodical pace, I felt giddy and lightheaded. I laughed without reason. The mountain pinnacles wavered and reeled. I may have needed oxygen. Certainly I needed food. The first agony of real hunger perhaps resembles an addict's craving for opium. I couldn't tear my mind away from food.

"Franc, I've got to eat. When do we stop?"

"Whenever Junior lets us. Think of something else."

A good part of the morning we were off our horses, leading them and encouraging them over heaps of rocks where a slip would have broken their legs or our necks. The guide led us ever upward on nothing that resembled a trail. We crawled over moraine pushed down by glaciers and heaped into haphazard piles. Springs burst from the mountainside everywhere. Often we were kicking our way, boot-deep, through water and gravel. Several times, in their blind scrambles upward, our yaks wedged themselves between boulders.

Once, when I felt I had reached the limit of my endurance, I shouted for a halt. My horse, equally exhausted, stood behind me with spraddled legs and lowered head. He didn't even try to bite me. But the Kirghiz, refusing to halt even for an instant, continued his steady climb, ignoring me. We had to keep up with him, or fall behind and get hopelessly lost. We kept up.

We came at last to a miniature plateau where patches of stunted grass grew, fit for grazing the famished horses. Here the guide called a halt, and shared his loaf of bread and mushy cheese with us. For dessert we split a bar of chocolate five ways, and then we reclined against a stony bank to contemplate what lay ahead.

Above us stretched a mile-wide snow field. At its pinnacle was a sheer and forbidding wall of white, perhaps two hundred yards high. Beyond that we concluded there must be a summit, although the summit of what we did not know. We spread out our maps, and Franc tried to pinpoint our location. Nothing like this little plateau, snow field, or knifelike ridge appeared on the map. We couldn't even decide what country we were in. Still, the guide seemed to know where he was going. Ahead there must be a pass, but where it might lead we had not the remotest idea.

The old snow field ahead—the snows of previous winters which would gradually spread downward—was wrinkled with crevasses. Without any climbing aids, it looked impassable. The guide pointed at the sun, made part of an arc with his arm, and showed with further gestures that later in the afternoon we would attempt the field. At midday, he pantomimed, the snow and ice were soft, and we would sink through. As the sun sank, it would crust and freeze hard.

Every half hour, as the sun dipped and the air grew colder, the Kirghiz tested the texture of the snow with his *chamooses.* Finally he nodded, and we moved slowly out on the treacherous white surface.

For four hours we fought our way up that slippery, frozen field. Beneath six inches of snow was a layer of ice, and from somewhere far below we could hear the gurgle of running water. Time after time the burdened, straining yaks, despite their broad hoofs, broke through the icy crust and floundered helplessly until we pulled and shoved them out. Our dainty-footed horses avoided the soft spots as if by instinct.

Once, Nipper, having stepped carefully across a two-foot gap, slipped on the uphill side, his rear legs slipping slowly back into the hole. I threw myself forward, head first, diving over his shoulder into the snow. Regaining my feet I tugged at the bridle, while he scrambled to get a footing. Franc was occupied with his own precarious progress and missed the show until Nipper was safe on four feet. Then he turned for the first time, saw me off my horse, and shouted, "Can't you stay in the saddle any better than that?" I lacked breath and strength for explanation or protest. I remained on foot for the next half hour.

Four times we were halted by crevasses—jagged, bottomless cracks, one nearly five feet wide—which we and the animals had to jump across from our wet and treacherous springboards of snow. At the first one, the worst, the yaks didn't think they could make it, and wouldn't try. Both of the yak pullers concentrated on one yak. They beat him and screamed at him, while he bunched himself on the edge, bellowing in fear. Franc got off his horse and swung his big boot against the animal's rump. Miraculously he soared across. I had unslung my camera, figuring that the yak would go across, or he would go in, and either way it would make a remarkable picture The yak, triggered by Franc's desperate place kick, surprised me. I got a good photograph of the tip of his tail.

The second yak balked as well, but the yak pullers practiced indignities upon him that would have brought screams of protest from the SPCA. It was obviously no time for me to interfere with local customs, but I was relieved when he finally jumped. This time, Franc used the camera, and got a fine shot of a pain-crazed yak in mid-leap.

After the yaks, the guide jumped across and without turning his head plodded up the slope. We kicked our horses, and they sailed over easily. Next the two pullers, and then Franc. Suddenly I was alone on the down side of the crevasse, with no one to encourage me, offer me a hand, or even kick my rear. I took a short run, shut my eyes, and leaped. I landed on the other side on my knees, in an appropriately prayerful position. No one noticed my bravery except me.

We came finally to the last few hundred feet, steep and slick as a ski jump. We had gained two thousand feet in altitude since we started across the snow field. The others, like myself, were taking in air in deep sobs. It was an effort to speak, except in grunting monosyllables. Our lungs were too busy keeping us alive. Up this last stretch we clawed our way on our hands and knees, dragging the floundering animals behind us. Once my horse slipped back twenty feet. To me it was utter disaster. Every nerve and muscle in my body cried out for me to leave him there.

But I was driven on by the knowledge that we must cross the ridge and reach a lower altitude before dark. A night on the glacial ridge, exhausted as we were, could end only in death. This was a certainty, absolute. Go on, or die. Even our Kirghiz companions, who had spent their whole lives on this towering plateau, conditioned to this existence, were gasping for breath and falling in the snow.

We were numbed by exhaustion, but crawled on. I don't know where the strength came from. There truly are hidden reservoirs in the human body that can be tapped only in the most desperate emergency. Even when the mind is ready to give up, the body insists on living.

We were progressing only a few yards at a time, then lying with our faces in the snow, recovering from the effort of the brief advance, and waiting for another bit of strength so we could crawl a few yards farther. Finally, as I scratched my way upward, it seemed easier. I tried to rise to my feet, and was startled to find that I could. Franc rose at my side. We stood together on the roof of the world.

We stood on the crest of a great mountain range, on a stony ridge swept clear of snow by constant wind. All around us, as far as the eye could see, soared endless mountain chains. Ahead was the Karakoram Range; beyond, the Himalayas. On either side, and behind us, lay the Hindu Kush. Magnificent peaks punctuated the endless distance. We looked, in silence and in awe. Though exhausted and gasping, we could not take our eyes from the majestic panorama.

Finally, I asked Franc, "Where do you think we are?"

"At the top of something," he answered helpfully. "That's all I know. We're very high. How I wish I had that altimeter!" Tired as we were, it was just as well, at that moment, that we didn't know how high we were.

We rested at the crest for thirty minutes. The visibility was incredible. Surely I shall never see such an evening again. The sun's dying rays coated the summits with gold, and purple shadows were falling in the valleys. Our guide beckoned to us and pointed to a waist-high cairn. Here he placed a stone, as had those other unfortunates who had crossed before us. Franc and I followed suit, feeling the strangeness of performing this little ritual on an unknown pass.

One of our yak pullers placed his stone on the cairn, but the other—the village idiot—hesitated, and then suddenly threw his aside. Without a word, he turned and fled down the snow field, back in the direction we had come. The grade was so steep that his steps were enormous, and as he gathered speed and leaped crevasses his footprints came ever farther apart.

"There," said Franc, "goes the Abominable Snowman."

We yelled at him, but of course he paid no heed. Our guide made no attempt to stop him, and thereafter pulled the second yak himself. Now we had one less mouth to feed, but the boy's desertion made us uneasy about the guide and the remaining yak puller. If they too deserted before we reached some habitation or encountered another human, starvation would be inevitable in this high and icy waste.

The dying sun reddened, and it suddenly got much colder. With signs we asked the guide to show us the path onward. To our horror he pointed straight down the snowy mountainside directly in front of us. We would have to slide for about two thousand feet before the ground leveled. There was no possibility of riding or walking. The angle looked to be about sixty-five degrees.

For us to go over this precipice, bone-weary and starved, at the end of three days of cruel travel, seemed like madness. We hung back, looking around for an alternate route, but could see none. Our guide chose to wait no longer. He shrugged, grabbed the nose rope of the nearest yak, and leaped off into space.

The yak bellowed, braced his front legs, and slid off into the void after the Kirghiz. The heavy animal, sliding on its haunches and breaking through the heavy snow, acted like a sea anchor, slowing the descent of the guide. A plume of snow followed them down. Immediately, the remaining yak puller followed with the second pack animal in tow.

Franc and I stood speechless—and alone—on the crest. I had never seen anything like that slide. The thought of doing it myself was as frightening as being told to make a parachute jump from a jet plane, or walk a tightrope across a canyon.

I had fussed earlier about being left behind, on the down side of the big crevasse. Now I got my reward. "Ladies first," said Franc. "Over you go!"

I will not say that he pushed me. But over I went, hanging to Nipper's reins, and digging my heels through the stiff crust into the snow beneath. It was like being the center stone in a small avalanche. With a heavy horse sliding at my shoulder, I dared not brake too sharply with my heels, and yet I dared not slide too fast lest I lose the reins and plunge unchecked to the bottom. A spray of snow filled my eyes and mouth. Franc, who took off right behind me, was having similar troubles. It was a wild and dangerous way to descend a mountain. Any well-organized expedition would have found a way to traverse the slope with safety and decorum. But at that point we were not exactly well organized. In fact we weren't even an expedition.

We did not slide the full two thousand feet at once, as I had feared. Small ledges, unseen from the top, stopped us every few hundred feet, so that we had time to stand up, wipe the snow from our eyes, and feel for broken bones before taking off again. All the downhill progress was on our rears, and it took almost an hour to reach a fairly level stretch of ground.

When we could stop and catch our breath for a moment, before following our guide in a zigzag path downward, my shaky knees simply collapsed under me. Only my hold on Nipper's bridle kept me from pitching headfirst down the rock-strewn slope. Franc, who had nearly lost a wife, turned and called, "Better stand up. We've got a long way to go." He knew better than to soften me up with too much sympathy, but I could have used a little.

We worked our way down a rubble wall pushed up by a long glacier that filled the valley in front of us. Long after dark we paused beside a glacial stream. The Kirghiz pointed to the frozen ground—our bed for the night. We gouged a shelf out of the shale, as protection against the wind, and tethered the horses and yaks. There was nothing on which these weary and pitiful animals could graze, and we had nothing to feed them.

The Kirghiz sat on their heels, moody and silent, while Franc and I collected ancient chips of yak dung and built a fire. The

flame burned blue in the thin air, just as Marco Polo had noted
in the High Pamirs. An accurate observer, that Polo.

We divided our last tin of cheese, a half bar of chocolate,
and brewed some tea. The Kirghiz ate our food, but offered none
of their *karut* in return. Their attitude had begun to change in
an ominous manner. The yak puller was sure we were hiding
bread from him. He looked into the empty bag, and muttered at
us. The guide demanded one of Franc's last cigars. He didn't get
a whole cigar, but Franc let him have alternate puffs.

I sought the last crumbs of cheese in the edges of the can, wondering how long it would be before we had another meal. Except
for a half bar of chocolate, the Bovril, and a handful of *karut* in
the yak-puller's goatskin, our food supply was exhausted. The
loss of those nine loaves of bread in Bozai Gumbaz now loomed
as a major catastrophe. We had no idea how far we would have
to go before securing fresh provisions. We had eaten only when
necessary, and then sparingly, but now almost all the food was
gone.

As the fire dwindled, black clouds slid across the moon. We
crawled into our sleeping bags. I closed my eyes and was drifting
into sleep when something like a cold, wet feather brushed across
my face. Winter had caught up with us. It was snowing. Since the
Kirghiz had no protection, we huddled more tightly into our
sleeping bags and gave them our *chapons* to sleep in.

Around midnight I heard Franc stirring and mumbling in
what I thought was a nightmare. He had wakened very thirsty,
with a terrific headache and pains that shot through his chest. He
had not wanted to awaken me, and so had stayed in his bag,
reaching a hand out through the opening, and quietly quenching
his thirst with snow.

None of this did I know until morning. All I knew was that he
had stirred in his sleep and mumbled.

We awoke before dawn, cold and wet and miserable. Two
inches of wet snow covered everything. Our boots were full of it,
the Kirghiz were soaked, the horses shivered, the saddles were
clammy. When Franc said, "I feel lousy," and told me what had
occurred in the night, I felt his head. It was very hot. We had

a few aspirin left, and I popped two into his mouth, praying that it was just a cold. We didn't eat anything, or try to light a fire. We just wanted to get out of that place.

It was a miserable morning. We rode through swirling gusts of big wet flakes. I tried to follow the Kirghiz closely, but several times lost him in the snow squalls. Again and again I called and asked him to slow his pace, but he ignored me. I was terribly worried about Franc, slumped silent and uncomplaining in his saddle.

Many times we were forced to dismount to lead our horses down steep ravines, through streams, or over piles of rock. By nine o'clock the wind faltered and the blizzard stopped. Soon afterward we rode out onto a plain of bare rock. We were still above the timber line, and it was a desolate scene, the brooding mountains under a gray overcast. The magic vista of our mountaintop was gone.

Though he refused to admit it, Franc looked really ill. His face was flushed, his head very hot, and he stopped at every rivulet to drink.

At ten the sun finally broke through and I insisted that we take a rest. When Franc got off his horse, he was weaving on his feet. I built a fire there on the rock barrens, brewed tea, and we ate the last of our chocolate. Franc couldn't choke down a mouthful.

Despite the protests of the Kirghiz I took time to dry out our wet bedrolls and our extra clothing, taking advantage of the fire and the only sunlight we were to see that day. It was not conscious planning but for some intuitive reason I felt that it was most important that our bedding be dry, and I refused to leave until it was.

At noon we stopped for an hour beside a clear brook, at a spot where there was grass for the horses. They had not eaten for a day and a half, and were growing weak. When Franc dismounted, his face was deathly pale, and he was having a chill. He wobbled over to a tree and leaned against it, as if afraid to sit down for fear he could not rise. The guide and yak puller observed his condition, and drew their own ugly conclusions. Where they had been only surly and grumbling before, now they became arrogant and deliberately rude. Suddenly they were stronger than we. Rahman Qul and Tiluh Walduh were on the other side of the mountain, and there was no authority here to restrain them. I felt myself growing panicky, and fought grimly to keep control. We must push on—somewhere.

Franc slowly sagged to the ground. I insisted he drink a little hot tea, and wrapped his *chapon* around his shoulders. When he shakily lit a cigar the guide demanded one for himself. Franc found another, but it was slightly damaged, as they all were. The guide took it contemptuously, rolled it in his fingers, and demanded a better one. Franc got to his feet, swaying like a tree in the wind, but still looking impressively tall. In a few phrases which needed no translation, he told the guide what he thought of him. The Kirghiz lowered his eyes sullenly. While conscious and on his feet, Franc was still boss.

I got him into the saddle quickly after that, and rode at his side whenever possible. We were finally on a trail of sorts. It was narrow and dangerous, but people had passed this way before. Often there yawned a thousand-foot drop straight down the cliff, but I wasn't afraid for Franc so long as he could stick on his horse. The horses instinctively knew mountains better than we.

In mid-afternoon Franc raised his hand for a halt. His voice was a hoarse whisper, "I've got to stop, Jean. I can't hang on another minute."

I made the guide stop, although he didn't want to. He seemed utterly indifferent to our troubles. Franc slid off the horse, rested for a few minutes leaning against the saddle, and drank water trickling down a rock. Then, seemingly refreshed, he mounted without help. But as we rode on I realized he was growing weaker. His chin often bobbed on his chest, his eyes were sunken and glazed, and sometimes he swayed dangerously in the saddle. But he kept doggedly to the trail. I had ceased to wonder where we were headed, but I yearned ardently for that unknown destination.

About four o'clock we came upon a low stone hut, twelve feet square and less than five feet high. It was not a human habitation but an abandoned sheepfold. Here I called a halt, although the guide grumbled and pointed ahead, even threatening to go without us. Franc needed shelter quickly, for a cold wind was rising. I still had no idea what was wrong with him, but I knew that if we stayed on the trail any longer, whatever it was might be complicated by pneumonia, if it wasn't pneumonia already.

Franc slid from his horse and sank to the ground, his teeth chattering uncontrollably. I could not lift him and the guide and the yak puller offered no help. They just watched, mildly interested. Mercy and kindness were emotions unknown to them. Fear they understood. Only the fear of Rahman Qul had propelled them across the pass, and kept them with us this long. While Franc leaned against the hut, I unpacked the yaks by the simple method of untying the ropes and letting everything fall to the ground. I unsaddled the horses, then rolled the barracks bags inside. Another blizzard seemed to be brewing.

The dirt floor of the sheepfold was littered with dried dung. Lighting one of the candles from the bazaar in Faizabad, and working rapidly, I swept out a dry corner with a cedar branch. There I spread Franc's sleeping bag and helped him crawl in. He was pitifully grateful and apologetic for his weakness. I took his temperature. It was 102.6. At that altitude—it must have been at least 15,000 feet—any temperature is bad, and 102.6 in an adult could be dangerous indeed. I searched through our medicine kit, and found two bottles—sulfaguanidine and Chloromycetin. The sulfa was chiefly for dysentery, but I wasn't sure about the Chloromycetin. It was supposed to cure all sorts of virulent diseases, so I gave him two of those tablets and the last two aspirin, hoping I was doing the right thing.

He washed the pills down with snow water and immediately had a violent chill. I laid the wonderful Afghan rug across his sleeping bag, but he continued to shake. I added my own sleeping bag on top, but he murmured that he was still freezing. Whatever his malady, it would have to run its course before we could go further. While I worked, the Kirghiz sat cross-legged at the far side of the fold and watched in stony-faced silence.

We had to have a fire. I had noticed chips of wood and sticks outside, and while bringing in an armful, motioned to the Kirghiz that they should do the same. They sat immovable, except that the guide turned his head away, as if to emphasize his lack of interest. The need for a fire was too urgent for me to argue. I kindled one with sheets from our notebook, and then went outside in the gathering storm to collect as much fuel as I could find. I stacked it inside the hut.

The sheepfold had no vent in the roof, and only one foot-square window in the wall near the door. With no draft, the room quickly filled with heavy smoke, and Franc began to cough. I had to warm the place and fix him something hot to drink, but without suffocating him. I tried to fan the smoke toward the door, but it only billowed up against the low, flat roof. I worked hunched over, unable to stand straight, and coughed and gagged until my eyes watered. Desperate, I kicked the fire over under the window, where a draft from the door sent most of the smoke out through the window. However, I still found breathing easier if I stayed on my knees.

By then the guide and the yak puller were eating lumps of their crude cheese. I started to ask for some, but thinking that they might refuse, and not wanting to lose face or antagonize them, I kept silent. All they had to do was walk out, saddle the horses, and ride away. That would have settled things.

A dozen times in the past few days I had been tempted to open the Bovril, but always something had stopped me. Now, that blessed little bottle was worth more to me than a bucket of rubies from the Shah of Persia's treasure. I heated water and made strong beef tea, lowering it gently to Franc's mouth. He gagged and turned his head, protesting that he didn't want anything. But he managed to drink half a cupful.

The Kirghiz, who had been watching and sniffing, now demanded what was left of the Bovril. The guide reached arrogantly for the pot. I drew back my arm as if prepared to throw the steaming liquid in his face. He lowered his hand. I drank it myself.

Franc saw what was going on and struggled to get out of his

sleeping bag. I made him lie down, not a very difficult feat as he was so weak. I could handle the Kirghiz, I told him.

"Are you sure?" he whispered hoarsely.

"I am sure." It was not bravado. I *was* sure.

Then Franc spoke clearly, but slowly, as if putting the words in their proper sequence was a difficult matter, and of great importance. "You know best. I am very dizzy, but there are certain things that I must do. Get my checkbook out of musette bag."

I was astonished. I thought he was delirious. "Why in the world do you want your checkbook?"

He raised himself on one elbow. "Let's face it, Jean. I may not get out of here. You don't have enough money to get back home, and when my bank hears that I am dead they'll tie up my account." He paused to get his breath. I could hear the phlegm rattling in his throat. "So I'll write checks, and you can cash them when you get out."

I had been fighting to keep out of my mind the thought that Franc might die. Now he had deliberately dragged the idea of death inside the hut so that it could not be ignored.

"That's silly," I protested. "You're going to be all right."

"I hope so," Franc said calmly, "but get my checkbook."

As he wrote, I touched his head. His fever was rising. His hand moving in shaky, slow motion, he wrote five or six $500 checks. The writing was like that of an enfeebled old man. "You won't have any trouble cashing these," he said. I didn't tell him that his signature was illegible. Then he insisted on writing a codicil to his will on a page of our notebook. The letters were big and round at first, but then they grew smaller and finally trailed off the paper. No court would have said it was his handwriting, or, for that matter, that the writer was of sound mind.

Franc lay back in the bag, shivering. "This fever is crawling into my brain. If I get delirious, make those bastards sit on me and hold me down. Whatever you do, don't let me get out and wander around in the snow."

It all sounded so final and hopeless that I became slightly hysterical. More than slightly, in fact. I cried, and kissed him, and told him he mustn't die. Our two goons watched this dramatic performance impassively. One of them was smoking a cigar, obviously taken from Franc's pack. He smoked insolently, daring me to do something about it.

When it grew dark I lit another candle; the first one was almost gone. I gave Franc two more Chloromycetin tablets, and made him drink more Bovril.

Each half hour I took his temperature until it reached 104.6. I had read that no one could survive a fever of more than 104 at such a height. With a fever, the metabolism rate is increased, and oxygen is burned at a faster rate. In this rarefied atmosphere, Franc couldn't absorb enough oxygen to appease the fever. In addition, he was rapidly becoming dehydrated. The combination could kill him. His skin was dry, his lips swollen and cracked. He grew so hot that he threw off the rug and untied the lacing of his sleeping bag.

I tried to think of something, anything that might help. I shook our empty canteens, pleading with the Kirghiz to find water. They ignored me. Reluctantly I left Franc for a few minutes to find a stream murmuring in the darkness. Luckily it was nearby.

I bathed his head and wrists with this glacial water, and then tried to move him as far from the fire as possible. I tugged at him, submerged under the mountain of sleeping bags, but didn't have the strength. I couldn't budge him. I appealed to the two men for help. Their eyes were expressionless, but they were almost smiling. They made no move. Then it struck me: certainly they were hoping Franc would die! They were waiting like vultures. And I recalled again what Marco Polo had said of certain men of the High Pamirs: "Amidst the highest of these mountains there live a tribe of savage, ill-disposed, and idolatrous people, who subsist upon the animals they can destroy, and clothe themselves with the skins."

The Kirghiz were figuratively waiting for our skins. Our sleeping bags, our clothing, the prized rug, the cameras, the Chinese silver taels and British gold, these comprised a treasure hoard be-

yond the wildest dreams of these primitive nomads. And it would
not be murder, exactly. They had only to wait for Franc to die.
Then they could easily pack the yaks, saddle the horses, and ride
away with their loot. While there were two of us, we might es-
cape, but a woman alone, stunned by death, would be helpless.
At Bozai Gumbaz they could claim that I had died also. This
most certainly would be true, in due time.

I tried to tell myself that my imagination was running wild,
but I had only to look across the room to know it was no nightmare, but the hard, cold reality of savage men in a savage place.
They opposed every move I made to save Franc. They begrudged
every drop of broth I forced down his throat. Now they watched
in scorn, hoping my woman's strength could not move him. But
somehow I did, although the effort left me panting and spent,
and I had to sit down and hold my head in my hands and wait
for my heart to stop its mad pounding. For a long time there was
no sound in the sheepfold except the outcry of my heart.

Franc began to moan and stir. He sat up, his eyes bright and
staring. He tried to fight his way out of the sleeping sack, but
I forced his hands away and tied it shut. Then I sat on him. I
took his wrists in my hands and shouted at him. I don't know
what words I used. I was pleading for him to lie still. He only
struggled the harder, and he is a powerful man. I found myself
tossed about as if on a bucking horse. I held on. Finally he gasped
and became quiet, and I sobbed and collapsed against the wall.
My hope and spirit were all but gone.

The Kirghiz watched me. The guide dipped into the goatskin
bag and brought out the last ball of that loathsome cheese. He
held it in his hand for a few seconds and then crammed it into
his mouth. If the performance was for my benefit, it was wasted.
I was beyond hunger.

I went back to work on Franc, busying myself with cold packs
on his wrists and forehead, changing them constantly. After the
first hour, he seemed no cooler. He talked crazily, mostly complaining that his chest ached terribly. Then he told me that an
Englishman was making him a new chest out of the finest English
yew. He spoke of it for some time, and I assured him that it

would certainly be a fine chest. It was a terrifying conversation. I made some more Bovril and drank it, ignoring the Kirghiz. Afterward, I felt a bit stronger. By this time I was giving Franc two Chloromycetin tablets every two hours, instead of two every four hours as our doctor had recommended. My home nursing course had never prepared me to face a night like this.

Again he began to moan and toss, raving of strange things and uttering names I had never heard. But when I held his hands he would grow quiet, although I am not sure he recognized me. Once, he thought I was an army nurse. Another time, he thought I was a professor in a language school, and repeated Chinese phrases over and over. Occasionally consciousness broke through, and in those moments he grew calm. Once he inquired whether I had eaten, at another time how the Kirghiz were behaving. He insisted that I take his picture as a matter of record, should he die. I winced at this ghoulish idea and changed the subject.

It was after midnight that he began to writhe beneath the sleeping bag. I stroked his head and found it wet. He was perspiring!

Suddenly the fever broke, and minute by minute thereafter I could see life and reason and strength returning to my husband. He relaxed and dozed, breathing more easily. I fought against sleep, for the Kirghiz were still awake, still waiting. I covered Franc carefully. He was so wet that I dreaded another chill. I built up the fire. I wiped his face. But my mind began to wander, and finally I slept. After perhaps twenty minutes I awoke suddenly. I was relieved to find the Kirghiz asleep at last, and Franc too. I moved the surviving candle so that it would light up the Kirghiz, slumped in the opposite corner. Then I slept, leaning against the jamb of the door. If I lay down, I would sleep too soundly, but in this position I could only cat-nap, and neither Franc nor the Kirghiz could get out without waking me.

I was awake at first light, refreshed. It would be a clear, cold day. Franc was swimming in perspiration, and awake. While his face appeared pale under the beard, his eyes were alert, and he was back with me. He even managed a smile. His temperature read only 102.2.

I nudged the Kirghiz awake with my boot. They sat up,

startled, and looked over at Franc, confidently expecting he would be unconscious. Instead, Franc greeted them with a few terse words and a cold and steady stare. Their attitude took another, almost visible, change. Their coveted treasure, and my nightmare, had vanished with the sun. They were no longer emboldened vultures, but a sullen guide and a shambling yak puller. Franc was boss again, and he was eager to be off.

It was dangerous for Franc to travel while he still had fever and was terribly weakened, but we had no choice. No food remained except our half jar of Bovril. The shrunken goatskin of the Kirghiz lay on the floor, limp and empty.

It took all Franc's strength and mine to get him up on his horse, but when he steadied in the saddle he looked quite fit. He was a welcome sight for my tired eyes. At 7:30 we started down again I knew not where—Afghanistan, Pakistan, or China—but I was determined to stop at the first inhabited place and send for help. For that mission, the gold sovereigns would certainly suffice.

The trail led downhill, and soon we were below the snow line. My spirits soared optimistically: this was our lucky day! Then, as we forded a shallow stream, I saw Franc lurch and tumble broadside into the water, dragging with him the saddle, *chapon*, our medical kit, and the photo bag.

The girth on his saddle had broken.

He was up before I could get off my horse. He retrieved his gear and scrambled to the far bank, shivering and water-soaked. The temperature was still below freezing, and his *chapon* stiffened with ice. I pulled him, unwilling and protesting, into the lee of a boulder. The guide, under duress, gathered wood for a fire. Franc undressed and changed his clothes, ranting all the while over the delay. But since he hadn't died of fever during the night, I didn't intend that he should die of pneumonia now. I was furious at everyone over this minor incident—just when I was so sure that we had weathered the storm.

The guide and yak puller, grumbling, mended the girth. Fortunately, our film was not soaked, and we lost only an hour. But the unfortunate incident, following our awful night, unnerved me so that I wept, off and on, all morning.

We followed the stream into which Franc had fallen down to

a wide river bed which we crisscrossed many times. It was comforting to go downhill without having to slide, or leap, or stare over the edge of a precipice. As we descended I began to feel better. For the first time in days I literally breathed easier. We leveled off at perhaps 11,000 feet, and I realized what a relief it was to have all the oxygen one needed.

The river widened and we found ourselves following a trail along an abrupt cliff. Soon I could look down a thousand feet simply by glancing over my horse's shoulder. The guide signaled to us to dismount and lead our horses. I wondered whether Franc could walk very far, and how I could help him, for the trail was too narrow to walk by his side, so narrow, in fact, that in some places we had to unload the yaks before they could negotiate a corner.

But Franc could walk steadily enough, and he said he believed his fever was gone entirely. He wasn't positive enough, however, to let me take his temperature. He was troubled by only one thing. He had lost so much weight that his trousers kept slipping. He had to call a halt in order to drill a new hole in his belt to uphold his pants and his dignity.

At one point the trail was so narrow that it could be spanned by Franc's two outstretched hands, thumb to thumb. For the record, we stopped while I photographed this remarkable section of highway.

We didn't take a lunch stop, because there was no lunch.

The Kirghiz had suddenly become quite helpful and I wondered whether the guide's more cordial attitude coincided with our nearing some place where we would find authority.

We came upon it without warning, rounding a hazardous hairpin turn. A half mile below, a square stone fort, complete with battlements, towers, and embrasures, stood in a green valley. It looked, from our height, like a child's castle. Farther on, stone houses lined the river.

In high excitement, we urged our horses down the steep grade, ignoring the danger of the precipice. We crossed the river on a stout log bridge, so exuberant over finding an inhabited place that for the moment we forgot the hard days past, Franc's illness, our weariness, and our hunger.

Five minutes later we reined up beside a canvas tent. Soldiers stepped out—tall, slender, well-uniformed men. I looked up at the fort and recognized the green-and-white flag of Pakistan.

Pakistan!

I was bewildered and disappointed. I had thought it would be China! Certainly our guide had been instructed to take us to the Chinese frontier. After our trouble at the border, we expected to be led over an encircling route that would eventually bring us out in the vicinity of the Wakhjir.

These Pakistani soldiers, while courteous and friendly, spoke little English. They couldn't enlighten us as to where we were, exactly, or how we had gotten there. I learned only that the name of the fort was Kalam Darchi.

The soldiers inspected our passports and found them in order. Suddenly I was thankful that we had secured Pakistan visas in Kabul—just in case. The Kirghiz had no passports, and I found myself worrying about their status. At that moment, I couldn't bear anyone ill will. The soldiers, in their few words, said that since the men were with their own pack animals they could continue with us as far as the first village. They motioned down the road. "Bungalow," the corporal said. "In bungalow men speak English."

I felt as if I were on the corner of 42d Street and Broadway!

We rode on, past a green meadow to an apricot orchard. We were looking up hungrily at the ripe fruit when children playing under the trees saw us. They shook the limbs and apricots cascaded to the ground. I rather expected them to pelt us with the ripe fruit. Instead, they gathered the apricots in their hands and ran to offer them to us. What strange and wonderful place was this?

A bit farther along the trail we encountered a caravan that had just come down from Kashgar, in Chinese Turkestan. Franc hailed the leader, a Moslem Chinese, and they held a long conversation. The trader asked where we were bound and Franc told him Urumchi. He smiled and said, "You are Americans, are you not?"

Franc admitted as much.

"If you're going to Urumchi," the caravan leader said, "you'd better hurry. The Communists hold all of Eastern China and the western provinces will certainly fall soon. Mao Tze-tung has been proclaimed premier, and Peiping is the new Communist capital."

We were stunned. It did not seem possible that the Nationalists could have crumpled so fast. Still, we might be able to reach Urumchi and then head south into India, thus avoiding Communist-held territory.

We asked more immediate questions. Where were we? What was the name of the village?

"It is a place called Misgar," the trader said, obviously surprised. "Do you not know that you are in Hunza?"

I gasped in amazement. The fabulous Hunza Valley!

In China and in England and in Afghanistan we had heard incredible stories of the principality of Hunza, said to be the true Shangri-La. In a single day, and by lucky accident, we had dropped from the lonely, barren, cruel land of rock and ice into an earthly paradise.

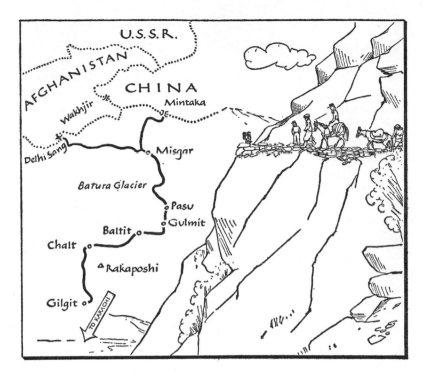

# 8

# HUNZA

THE PRINCIPALITY of Hunza is a state of mind, induced by matchless scenery paired with proud and friendly people. It is more than a hundred miles long and often less than half a mile wide. Its river is a twisting silver ribbon hung with gold-and-emerald fields and orchards of flecked jade, the whole encased against intruders between some of Asia's highest mountains. When we slid into the western tip of this valley from Afghanistan, we knew little about Hunza, except that it was ruled by a man bearing the improbable title of Mir, that Pakistan took care of its foreign affairs and defense, and that it was not only odd in shape but

259

odd in character. Or it may be that the rest of the world is odd, and the 25,000 happy Hunzukuts normal. The rest of the world has more than its share of troubles, the Hunzukuts almost none.

The land is incomparably beautiful. The arable soil of the valley slopes is terraced and watered, while all around rise the peaks of the Karakoram, twice as tall as the Alps. From the fort of Kalam Darchi to Misgar we rode for two hours through carefully tended fields of millet and orchards of apricots and apples. The riverbank was so lush with flowers that the air was heavy with scent. Everyone we met smiled a "salaam."

For a time the Hunza River parallels the Chinese border before swinging south to empty finally into the broad Indus. Just north of us an ancient caravan route, little used, vaulted into Chinese Turkestan. In spite of what the trader had told us, we still hoped to reach Urumchi, but not until Franc regained his strength.

Misgar's fifty clean stone houses were clustered on both sides of a tributary stream. At the first building, a combination telegraph and telephone office, a tall, slender, handsome man greeted us in English as warmly as if he were an innkeeper and we were old friends with reservations. His name was Nabi Khan, and he was Misgar's chief of communications. He led us across the bridge connecting the two halves of the village, and to a two-room bungalow perched jauntily on the edge of a chasm. We would find such a guest house in every village in Hunza, he said. They had been built by the present ruler's grandfather. While very few foreigners had come to Hunza in recent years, the bungalows were always kept ready.

The village elders, with henna-dyed beards, and groups of chattering children inspected us while we inspected the bungalow. The Kirghiz did not seem to be included in the welcome. Silent and strangely subdued, they carried the luggage inside.

The bungalow consisted of two scrubbed, whitewashed rooms, each with a corner fireplace, and a bathroom with a large, square stone to sit on while sponging from buckets. Adjoining the bathroom, and extending out over the chasm, was a tiny room with a two-hole toilet. Through the holes one looked down 1,400 feet into space. Perhaps it was not the most modern toilet in the world, but it was undoubtedly the deepest, and the draftiest. A German climber, visiting Misgar some forty years before, had decorated the walls of the bungalow with charming sketches of fruits and flowers. Across the front of the bungalow ran a veranda from which we could admire the incomparable view. Hunzukuts, we were to learn, were justly proud of their spectacular country and a porch was their substitute for a picture window.

The two Kirghiz evidently were anxious to leave. In sign language we suggested that they rest overnight, but they vehemently refused. While the horses and yaks grazed hungrily, the men went into the village and returned with cheese and bread. Franc paid them generously, something they obviously did not expect. Then Franc brought out his last two cigars, mashed and cracked, which I repaired with band-aids and handed over as a parting gift.

Now that we were safe, the memory of our ordeal faded like a nightmare, and it was difficult to hold a grudge. Puffing their Havanas, riding the tired but still willing horses, and leading the unburdened yaks, the Kirghiz departed for their High Pamir homeland. We waved and shouted a farewell, but the Hunzukuts watched them leave in silence and suspicion.

A young man entered the bungalow and in good English introduced himself as Sholam, Misgar's schoolteacher and postal inspector. He wore the distinctive stocking cap of white wool which is standard attire for the Hunza male. Sholam had come to help us. How could he be of assistance?

"First we need food," said Franc, "and then we need a long rest."

"Food is already being brought," replied Sholam, and as he spoke a little girl entered with a platter of apricots, followed by a woman bringing ten eggs wrapped in a bright scarf. Next in the procession was a man with a live chicken, then another carrying a basket filled with rice, onions, and turnips.

We had been munching apricots ever since leaving the fort, but we were still starved. Franc, sitting cross-legged on the floor, said, "I'm going to eat that chicken raw. I'm too tired to go out and chop wood for a fire."

"You can't eat it raw," I said, "or at least not alive."

Franc looked so determined, and Sholam and Nabi Khan so astonished, that I was about to go in search of fuel when two men entered, one carrying a bundle of wood. Thus we met Khodiar and Barokha who, self-appointed, became our cook and helper. Both wore Hunza caps, white homespun shirts, baggy wool pants tucked into high boots, and loose, hand-knit sweaters. Khodiar was a smiling eager worker. Barokha had a thin, sharp, eagle's face decorated with a drooping mustache. He was a Dakh runner, but at the moment there were no messages to be carried so he had come along with his friend.

We spread our rug in the second room, kindled a fire, and lighted the lamp of ancient design filled with sheep tallow. Khodiar and Barokha brought the stewed chicken and vegetables, and everyone thoughtfully withdrew. After the rigors of the Wakhan, the terror of the pass, and Franc's brush with death, the hospitality of the Hunzukuts was almost too much for me. I might have had a good cry over it all if I had not been distracted by the aroma from the stew.

But we couldn't quite finish the chicken. Five days of near starvation had diminished our capacity. Khodiar banked the fire, bid us, "Salaam aleikum," and we bedded down for the night. Franc still had a slight fever, but it would be gone by morning. The thought of awakening in Hunza instead of in a savage land was wonderfully soothing.

In the three previous days and nights of terror and exertion we had slept only a few hours, and yet that night, in comfort, warmth, and safety, we slept only fitfully. Toward dawn, however, I fell into deep slumber. By the time Franc woke me, the sun was high. My watch said nine o'clock. I looked around me, then, and gasped. Ten henna-bearded old men were sitting leaning against the walls of the room, intently watching us.

Our visitors had come early, politely, and silently, waiting until we awoke. It didn't seem quite adequate, but I said, "Good morning."

They nodded their heads sagely, and replied in the Hunza tongue, which few but Hunzukuts can understand.

"Do you mind if I get up?" I inquired.

They held a short conference, and all nodded.

Apparently they did not mind, so I crawled out of my sleeping bag just as I had crawled in—fully dressed, minus boots. At this point the elders, with great wisdom, decided that their presence was unnecessary. They bowed and left. Undoubtedly they reported to their wives that "American memsahibs wear wool shirts and sweaters, wool trousers and even socks when they go to bed."

I bathed and changed my clothes—how world-shaking these acts seemed then! Franc shaved for the first time in weeks, and trimmed his beard to an inquisitive point. With his lean cheeks, the beard made him look considerably older and quite distinguished—rather like an explorer, to be exact.

Sholam, our schoolteacher and postal inspector friend, arrived after breakfast. I asked whether all foreigners received such hospitable treatment. "Of course," he said. "We Hunzukuts take no payment for food and lodging. Our country is our home, so a traveler come to Hunza is a guest in our house."

When Sholam helped orient us on our maps, we made two surprising discoveries. Running my finger from Fort Kalam Darchi to the west and north, I found that the pass we had crossed was the Delhi Sang—more than 20,000 feet high! No wonder we suffered as we clawed our way up that snow field!

When we showed the route to Sholam he said, "Very difficult and very high. It is only used by a few Kirghis who know the best way across. You are very fortunate to be here."

The second discovery was even more disturbing.

The village mayor, or *arbab,* joined us on the veranda. He was a handsome man in his sixties—the prime of life in Hunza —erect and strong, with a fine henna beard. Sholam, translating, told of our crossing the Delhi Sang. The *arbab* nodded, surprised, and said: "Those Kirghiz you came with belong to the tribe of Rahman Qul?"

"Yes," Franc said. "Rahman Qul is a good friend of ours—a remarkable man."

The mayor shook his head. "Rahman Qul is a very bad man," he declared. "He robs caravans. He kills many people. Very bad, very cruel."

We stared in disbelief. And then he told us a few tales about
our benefactor. Two years before, Rahman Qul and his tribe had
crossed into the Russian Pamirs. There they had looted a caravan
and murdered everyone in it. Pursued by the Russians, they had
fled into Chinese Turkestan and taken up residence near the border post of Mintaka.

Qul had become a close friend of the commander of the Chinese border garrison. Life is dull in such an isolated post, and the
Chinese must have enjoyed the companionship of the intelligent
Kirghiz Khan. Less than a month before we met him, Qul had
invited the commander and his garrison of eight to dine at the
Kirghiz encampment on the Mohammedan feast of Id, an occasion
of banqueting and friendship. While the Chinese were seated in
the big *yurt,* eating roast sheep with the tribesmen (just as we
had), the Kirghiz had suddenly turned on their guests and
slaughtered them all.

"But why?" I wanted to know.

"For the gold," answered the mayor. The Chinese commander,
as is customary in the Orient, had been collecting "squeeze" from
caravan traders, and from Tungan pilgrims passing through
Mintaka en route to Mecca. It was known that the commander
had two boots filled with gold pieces. This, plus the guns, ammu-
nition, horses, and supplies stripped from the garrison made a
valuable haul for the Kirghiz. After the massacre, Qul and his
men retired to Bozai Gumbaz, across the border in Afghanistan.

We now understood much that had been hazy and mysterious.
Koshan's reference to "bad feeling at the border." The wariness
of the Afghan commandant who had conducted us to Bozai Gumbaz. The frantic desire of Rashid and Koshan to get out of the
area. The hostility of the Chinese patrol at the Wakhjir, and
Tiluh Walduh leading us away in flight from the border.

"For many years this Rahman Qul murders and robs people,"
the *arbab* continued. "Why he no murder you?"

I remembered the night we had pleaded with Qul for help. How
strange that must have seemed to him! We, ignorant of his reputation, were in need of aid. The novelty of the situation may

have amused him. Franc had said, "We put our lives entirely in your hands," and Qul had answered: "I accept your trust."

"Why he no murder you?" the *arbab* repeated.

We looked at Sholam and the mayor and could only shake our heads. We had no idea why Rahman Qul had treated us so honorably. Now, after much thought, we have a theory. Had Rahman Qul harmed us, his position in Afghanistan would have been as untenable as it already was in China and Russia. He would have had no place of sanctuary. So he sent us off to the border, and the outnumbered Afghans back to Faizabad. But perhaps it was something less practical. Perhaps there is a touch of Robin Hood in every highwayman.

That day our Dakh runner dashed off to the telegraph office with our passports, and returned with a note. It was painstakingly addressed to "Mr. G. D. Bowie, Camp, Misgar."

The design of an American passport leaves a great deal to be desired, particularly in areas where little or no English is spoken, and again there had been confusion.

Occasionally border officials tried to read our passports upside down. Many times, particularly in China, they read them from back to front. Invariably there was confusion over the front page, where the local official confidently expected to find the traveler's name, but instead was faced with the name of some relative who was to be notified "in case of death or accident." Often it proved very misleading.

My father's name, G. D. Bowie, and Franc's mother's name, Mrs. R. G. Klein, thus confronted the telegraph operator in Misgar as he penned his note.

Addressed to Mr. G. D. Bowie, it read: "Would you take tea with me at my residence at four o'clock? Please bring your lady companion, Mrs. R. G. Klein. (signed) A. N. Khan." The delicacy of that "lady companion" delighted us. We sent Barokha back with an acceptance, and an explanation that we were legally wed.

Barokha returned with a second note from Nabi Khan, enclosing the most touching gift I had ever received. "I know that your food has been bad for so long. Please accept this meager offering and use it in your cooking. Your friend, Nabi."

I unwrapped a bit of tissue paper, and held in my hand Nabi's gift—three cloves, four peppercorns, two cardamon seeds, a sliver of cinnamon bark, and a lump of sugar. This was no small gift. In a village like Misgar such spices are priceless and rarely seen. Sugar is virtually unknown. That afternoon, when we met for tea, Nabi Khan explained that he brought these condiments to Hunza when he was assigned to the Misgar post two years before.

Nabi, who had worked as a telegrapher for the British in India, had moved to Pakistan for religious reasons, after the partition of Pakistan and India. He had served, he said, in other remote posts, but none so remote as the present one. "As a matter of fact," he added flatly, "there is no post so remote as Misgar." Yet in Misgar he was a man of importance, for he was the connecting link with the outside world, and with the Mir, seventy miles down the valley at the capital, Baltit. Also, Nabi owned the only three chairs and table in Misgar. The Hunzukuts, like the Afghans, customarily use no furniture.

Nabi told us much of the valley. First, about the people. They are fairer than any of their neighbors, and even taller than the Afghans. Their features are Caucasian rather than Mongolian; their noses straight and prominent; their deep-set, dark eyes not slanted. They could be southern Europeans of exceptional physique—and perhaps their ancestors were.

There is a legend, Nabi told us, that all Hunzukuts are descended from three soldiers of Alexander the Great who found beautiful wives in Persia. The women accompanied them while Alexander campaigned along the Oxus. When the Greek conqueror turned south, the three couples went on through the Wakhan, discovered this wondrous valley, and settled there. Scholars, while attempting to dismiss the tale as mere folklore, admit that the people of Hunza are different, and can offer no better explanation for their presence in this mid-Asian paradise.

Once the Hunzukuts were mighty mountain warriors, feared by the surrounding countries, Nabi continued. But now they live in serene peace with each other and their nervous neighbors. There is no poverty in Hunza, and yet money is not considered a necessity. Education is free to all. Longevity is a national characteristic. While the *arbab* of Misgar was in his sixties, some of his advisers were pressing a hundred. Many of the diseases of civilization, including cancer, are unknown. It seemed as if hardly anyone dies in Hunza unless he falls off the incredibly narrow trail that links the villages down the valley and is dashed to death on the rocks below.

"Tell us about the Mir," Franc asked. "How does he govern? Does he visit each village regularly? And by the way, where are the soldiers and police?"

Nabi Khan laughed. "There are no police," he said, "because there is no crime. Therefore there are no jails. Nor does Hunza have an army. The soldiers you saw in Kalam Darchi are all Pakistanis, and they are the only soldiers in Hunza, here only because Kalam Darchi is a strategic frontier stronghold. A few years ago the Mir had a small bodyguard, but he disbanded it. Why should he have a bodyguard? He has no enemies."

Each village elects its own *arbab*, Nabi Khan explained, who governs with a council of elders. The *arbab* arbitrates all community disputes, mostly over water rights. But when a dispute arises that cannot be settled locally, the *arbab* telephones the Mir. In a matter of great moment, such as a dispute over an inheritance, the interested parties can petition the Mir in person. All they have to do is walk to Baltit.

"Actually," said Nabi, "the Mir governs by telephone. There is a telephone in every village. Once a day the *arbab* must call the Mir and tell him what's going on. You should have heard our *arbab* report on your arrival yesterday. He hasn't had news like that in years.

"As I said, they all call the Mir—all but one. One *arbab* is so long-winded and so dull that his phone has been fixed so he cannot make outgoing calls. On occasion, the Mir calls him."

The much discussed telephone rang at that moment. Nabi answered, listened for a moment, and then handed it to Franc. "For you, Mr. Shor."

I wasn't surprised. By then I could not have been surprised at anything that happened in Hunza.

Franc picked up the old-fashioned instrument and a voice greeted him in cultivated English: "Welcome to our country, Mr. Shor. If we had known you were coming, your bungalow would have been better prepared. Is there anything we can do for you?"

Assuming that the voice belonged to a British official in the Hunza service, Franc asked whether there was any late news from central and western China, and explained that Urumchi was still our destination.

The English-speaking voice said that Turkestan was gradually falling to the Communists, and that he had received word in a recent communiqué from Kashgar that the American consul, his wife, and staff were preparing to flee Urumchi. Franc relayed this disturbing news to me. I thought of what faced Hall and Vincoe Paxton, whom we had not seen since our honeymoon trip to Sinkiang.

Franc explained our trip, and said we still hoped to cross the Mintaka Pass and again pick up the trail of Marco Polo. Perhaps we could only get as far as Kashgar. In that case, we might meet the Paxtons and come out with them.

The voice warned that it might be dangerous to attempt it, but of course he would not interfere.

I heard Franc say, "Well, we'll give it a try anyway. If we find we can't get through there are a couple of good stories in Hunza. I'd like to do an article on the Mir. I hear he's a very colorful character, and quite democratic and friendly. A picture story, maybe. Think he'd mind?"

"Certainly not," said the voice on the phone. "You can take all the pictures you wish. We'll be glad to help."

"Sounds wonderful," Franc said. "But can you speak for the Mir?"

"Yes," was the reply. "You see, I am the Mir."

That evening a procession entered the bungalow. First came Khodiar carrying a very vocal sheep; then Barokha holding aloft a plate piled with nine pounds of butter; then two villagers bearing platters of potatoes, turnips, carrots, apricots, and apples; and finally the *arbab* of Misgar.

"A gift from His Highness, the Mir," announced the *arbab,* with a sweeping gesture.

"How did it get here?" I asked.

"By telephone," explained Sholam, who had come along as interpreter.

"In our country," I said, "it is possible to telegraph flowers. But this is something new."

I think the schoolteacher misunderstood. That evening, while Franc was cooking a leg of lamb, flavored with Nabi's spices and wrapped in aluminum foil that we usually reserved to protect exposed film, a villager arrived with a bouquet of wild roses. From the Mir!

AT TEN the next morning, when we phoned the Mir to thank him for the banquet, he had exciting news for us. "I have just talked to the commander of the Pakistan garrison in Gilgit. He has heard from Kashgar that all is quiet there, although the Communists have crossed the eastern boundary of Sinkiang. It may be safe for you to cross the Mintaka, but I cannot advise you to go beyond Kashgar. It is true, by the way, that the American consul has fled Urumchi."

That afternoon I washed all our clothes and started to pack. Nothing was said about it, but I knew we would try the pass. We had come so far on Polo's trail that it was unthinkable that we should give up now. We were still tired and weakened from the Wakhan and the Delhi Sang. My memories of captivity by the Chinese Communists grew vivid again, along with the nightmare of Franc's illness. And if our consular officials were leaving Sinkiang, how could we hope to travel safely to Urumchi—and get out again? To this last question there was no answer, except that we must try.

Our travel north would be over the famous Hunza road, in more peaceful times the route of the Kashgari traders and pil-

grims bound for Mecca. Most of the famous explorers of Central
Asia—Stein, Sven Hedin, LeCoq, and Pelliot—had used that
road. Now, however, political tension had all but eliminated
travel over it. Though there was as yet no snow in the Hunza
Valley, the nights were bitterly cold, and the snow line on the
mountains crept lower each morning. Still, we were fairly certain
we could cross the 15,500-foot pass into China before it was
blocked by the snows.

We left on September 13, a party of five until we got beyond
Misgar's last stone fence. Then we discovered we were six. A
silent Hunzukut with no pack, carrying only an old copper teapot, had joined our retinue. No interpreter was with us, and it
was impossible to discover why he had come. When I indicated
that he should tie the teapot to a donkey's load, and then return
to Misgar, he objected violently and trailed along.

Franc entered him in our account book as "tea caddy."

We were two days' travel from the Chinese border post across
the Mintaka Pass from Hunza. We quickly retraced the five miles
to Kalam Darchi and passed the tents of the Pakistani soldiers,
who shook their heads in foreboding. Where a branch of the
Hunza River became the Mintaka, we headed straight north.
Here a herd of shaggy Bactrian camels were grazing on the slopes.
"Belong Mir Sahib," said Khodiar. The thought of riding camels
on the narrow Hunza trails gave me the shudders. We learned,
later, that they were a gift to the Mir from a Kashgari official.
Since the camels made the Hunzukuts shudder also, they were
seldom used, became unmanageable, and were allowed to run
wild.

All that afternoon we rode in silence, plodding up a rising wall
of shale. Down the valley soared eight peaks of more than
24,000 feet like super-Dolomites. Fifty years ago Lord Curzon
wrote, "The little state of Hunza contains more summits of over
20,000 feet than there are of over 10,000 feet in the entire Alps."

Several times we forded streams. Khodiar rode the tea caddy's
shoulders, piggyback, across the first one, and at the next the tea
caddy was carried across. It was a nice, democratic arrangement,
I decided, everyone ended up with wet feet.

While we were resting at lunch, a lean Dakh runner, laden with mail and messages from Tashkurgan, in China, trotted down the trail toward us. For centuries Dakh runners have been the message-bearers of this Central Asian area. They can, and do, run from dawn until dark, possessing an amazing stamina. This one talked excitedly to our men, and tried to tell us something which we couldn't understand. The runner declined a cup of tea and ran on toward Misgar, apparently alarmed at finding us on the trail. Our Hunzukuts were reluctant to go on. While we urged them forward, we had a very definite premonition that all was not well.

At nightfall we came to a tiny settlement called Boihill, that on our map appeared to be the last inhabited place on the Hunza side of the border. Two families lived there in stone huts, and tended a large flock of sheep already penned for the night against a high bluff. After our recent experiences with hunger, it would have been foolish not to take an extra supply of meat. We would buy a sheep, and Khodiar could skin it and hang it until morning. In sign-language bargaining, we settled on the price, the equivalent of $1.20, and the shepherd indicated that we could pick out any sheep.

Franc asked for a rope, knotted it into a lasso, and twirled it tentatively around his head. The Hunzukuts looked on curiously; this was an entirely new shepherding technique to them. Here was a race of people who had never seen a ten-gallon hat, Hopalong Cassidy, or a movie of any kind. Franc, as Hunza's first cowboy, gave them a professional exhibition of roping and tying one small, fat, bleating lamb after chasing it up and down the valley. We all shouted encouragement, and shrieked with laughter.

Our shelter that night was a wide crack in the granite cliff. Our feet to a fire, we watched the stars and listened to the soft bleating noises of the sheep below and to the wind whining in the rocks. We talked briefly of our prospects. "One more hurdle," said Franc, thinking of the pass ahead, "and we're in China. But I wonder what that Dakh runner was so excited about?"

I kept silent. In spite of my fears, I could not bring myself to suggest going back.

That night I dreamed I was lying on the middle shelf of an icebox. I awoke at one A.M., to find it snowing. First it came down in flurries, and then the wind rose and the sky was filled with fat, scudding flakes. We moved our sleeping sacks deeper into the cleft under a sharp overhang, and dragged our boots and luggage behind us, piling our barracks bags as a wall against the freezing wind. We had reached Boihill just in time for the season's first blizzard.

However, at dawn the skies had cleared. We dusted the snow from our gear, helped load the donkeys, and washed down a breakfast of cold lamb and turnips with cups of our tea caddy's best brew. We were the only ones anxious to be off. Franc thought our companions were probably wary of climbing the Mintaka in the new loose snow. I was scared, too, but nobody asked me.

We approached the pass on a gradually rising trail, which the deep snow made treacherous. The animals slowed their pace, cautiously seeking safe footing. The height of the Mintaka, a recorded 15,500 feet, didn't worry us. Compared to the Delhi Sang, it was not such a barrier. But what would we find beyond?

A few hundred feet from the crest, the trail rose sharply; and concentrating on climbing, we did not notice a Dakh runner overtaking us until we heard his sharp shouts to stop. Below us, he was waving a paper in his hand.

"Now what?" said Franc, leaning against a boulder while we waited for him to catch up.

The runner was exhausted. He had run from Misgar all through the night, through the snow. His message was from Nabi Khan, written on an old telegraph form.

"The border is closed," it said. "There is much trouble in Turkestan. The Mir insists that on no account do you cross the frontier and leave the protection of Hunza. Word has been received that the American consul and his party have left Kashgar and are on their way to India. Turn back immediately. The Mir will welcome you in Baltit."

"That does it," said Franc. "This is as far as we go." His voice was flat and final.

I sat down in the snow, too tired and deflated to express my disappointment. Neither of us reacted with much surprise. But this was the end of the Marco Polo trail. All our months of effort, our planning, our struggles, our good fortune, all the help from old friends and friends newly met, all in an instant vanished like a snowflake in the fire. No Shah or King or Kirghiz bandit could help us now. We had run up against the inexorable and ruthless force rolling across half of Asia. There was no argument now. We had to turn back.

I felt empty and cheated. But there was one thing we could still do. We were only a few minutes' climb from the crest of the Mintaka Pass and the border. The Chinese post, we knew, was several hours' travel beyond.

"I want to put my feet in China again," I begged. "It won't take long. I want to look down into the Taghdumbash Pamir."

Franc smiled in agreement. It was a pathetic "second best," but still a vague symbol of accomplishment. We left our companions and climbed alone to the ridge, back to Chinese soil. The sun on the other side seemed warmer, the path easier. Far ahead we could imagine the desert, and across the desert snaked the Marco Polo trail. We could not quite tie the two ends together, but still we had followed Marco Polo step by step from Venice to China, the first time it had ever been done.

I made a small cairn there while Franc waited patiently, not speaking. Then we turned again, away from China.

As we threaded our way back down the valleys to Misgar, I realized that the emptiness I felt—the feeling of having nothing further to do—would have plagued me had we reached Hami and completed Polo's circuit. The exhilaration was in the try, not the accomplishment. And I could not help feeling some accomplishment. We had successfully followed the footsteps of Marco Polo across much of the ancient world. We had seen things that no American had ever seen before, crossed territories barred to foreigners for more than a century. Finally we had been turned aside not by physical difficulties, but by a political cataclysm.

*     *     *

Now WE WERE to be privileged to see Hunza, which already fascinated us, and which Marco Polo had not seen.

When we reached Misgar, we found that the Mir had given orders that horses and guides were to be provided for the journey to Baltit. Khodiar, who had become indispensable as a cook and companion and was rapidly learning English, could accompany us halfway.

On the trip up the Mintaka, Khodiar had acquired a useful vocabulary of words such as "egg," "meat," "sleep," and "water," and a few of the amenities such as "thank you," and "please." But he invariably said "Yes, sir," to me although I repeated "Yes, ma'am," over and over. He should have been able to distinguish between the two genders, particularly since Sholam told me their own language had eight.

The Hunza language, Burushaski, is not related to any other known tongue. Its origin, like that of the Hunzas themselves, remains for scholars a fascinating mystery. It is not a written language, and yet it is fantastically complicated by, among other things, sixteen plural forms. It has a curious ring to it, and I was not able to catch the meaning of even a single word.

While we rested for a day, preparing for our trip to Baltit, two schoolboys visited the bungalow and presented us with a bouquet—of turnips—with the compliments of their classmates. Franc put his hand into his pocket and brought out a rupee, but the children shook their heads, no. One of them turned to Sholam, and he translated. "They would rather have pencils, which are very scarce here. They need them at school."

Franc found two still new pencils in the typewriter case and gave them to the delighted boys.

Then Sholam proudly introduced us to his domain, the school. The stone-and-mud building had only two rooms, a wide porch, and an enclosed courtyard. Since the weather in Hunza, barricaded against winter blizzards by its guardian ranges, is almost always fine, the pupils usually study outdoors. They were seated in circles in the courtyard, cross-legged, intent on their reading. Sholam explained that all education is free, financed by the Aga Khan, spiritual leader of the Ismaili, the Moslem sect to which Hunzukuts belong.

Since the Aga Khan was one of the richest men in the world, I wondered aloud why he permitted the Misgar school to lack for pencils. It was an unfortunate accident, said Sholam. Some weeks before he had sent a Dakh runner to Baltit with a requisition for pencils, but the man had vanished, and it was feared that he had fallen from the road. Sholam took occasion to warn us of the Hunza Road. It was five days' travel to Baltit, and hardly a yard of the way was wholly safe. It was, he said with grave pride, the most dangerous trail in the world.

After what we had seen before reaching Hunza, I was inclined to doubt him. Later I agreed completely.

We were well mounted, thanks to the Mir, when we said good-by to Sholam, Nabi, and our other friends in Misgar, and headed south. The Hunza Road, stretching from Chinese Turkestan to Gilgit in northern Pakistan, for a thousand years has been known for its beauty—and its danger. It is the very terror of this road that has allowed Hunza to exist in serene isolation, safe from more powerful neighbors and untouched by modern civilization. No man could penetrate very far into the Hunza valley unless he were welcome.

For centuries it was the chief highway between Kashgar and Kashmir. Intrepid Chinese traders led pack trains laden with silks, tea, and porcelain into India along its frightening and incredible galleries. Returning to Cathay, they brought spices, jewels, gold, and ivory. A successful round trip could make a trader rich for life, but many lost their caravans—and life itself —in sudden landslides or the collapse of the galleries, called *rafiks*.

By the *rafik,* the Hunzukuts have created foot room where nature had no such intention. They have often been referred to as "triumphs of engineering," but I prefer to think of them as triumphs of faith. The principle of the *rafik* is very simple. The road builders are moving along a natural ledge on the face of the cliff, 2,000 feet above the valley. The ledge grows more and more narrow, and then disappears entirely, to reappear, as a rock fault often does, many feet ahead. How to bridge the gap? Usually there is a crack in the sheer cliff following the fault line. Into this crack the Hunzas drive a line of flat rocks. On these they lay other rocks, each successive layer protruding a bit farther over the abyss. More layers are added, interspersed with branches, until a ledge perhaps thirty inches wide, and sometimes only eighteen, projects from the cliff.

Occasionally where there was no crack, long poles were hung across the gaps to form a shaky bridge against the wall. These creaked and sagged as we crossed. The trail was not designed for two-way traffic, or for corpulent travelers. We passed only one trader, fortunately at the river level. Nor did we ever see a fat man in Hunza, which may account for their longevity.

An overloaded pack horse or a violent wind or an unpropitiated god can tumble a *rafik*. They are always under repair, as they have been for a thousand years.

From one gallery I looked down and saw horses splashed like overripe grapes on the rocks 500 feet below. When Franc mentioned this in Baltit days later, the Mir replied, "Oh, yes. That gallery blew off in a high wind. I worried while you were coming. We've had such windy weather."

I am not troubled with acrophobia, but on our first day's travel down the trail to Khaibar, I dismounted and walked more than I rode. It was not that I distrusted my alert and sure-footed horse. It was simply that I trusted my own feet more. My horse did have one dangerous habit. He shied every time he saw his own shadow. Since his shadow was always on the cliff face, he invariably shied toward the void.

Once he shied abruptly, and feeling that this time he was going into the abyss for sure, I threw myself out of the saddle— on the inside, of course. Hearing the commotion, Franc turned in his saddle and called, "I think it's safer to stay *on* your horse just here." Naturally he would side with the horse!

Once those ahead slowed almost to a halt, and Franc waved for me to be quiet as I drew up with the others. A large snake slithered nonchalantly up the trail ahead of our procession. It was obviously no place for a horse to shy, rear, or buck, so we proceeded at the snake's pace for the next twenty minutes until he found a hole and disappeared.

Several times the trail descended to the thundering river, and we crossed swaying rope suspension bridges. The broken bridge floors were covered with large flat stones which prevented the cautious animals from seeing swirling patches of white water below. Once, wading a ford, Franc's horse slipped into quicksand and in an instant was down to his shoulders. Franc scrambled up on the saddle and successfully made a flying leap to a nearby rock. At the next ford, a pack donkey fell into the water and refused to rise. It took all of us to lift him out bodily.

Khaibar was not so large as Misgar, but its guest bungalow was much the same. Since theft is unknown in Hunza, there are no locks—and neither is there any privacy. So long as they saw a lamp burning, people entered the bungalow without bothering to knock. When we awoke the next morning we were not surprised to see a ring of quiet visitors who had been contemplating us as we slept.

We breakfasted in Khaibar on a fluffy omelet of partridge eggs and set out for Pasu. Between us and Pasu lay the Batura Glacier, twenty-five miles long and the largest in the entire region, a mass of crumpled old ice covered with grit, dirt, and large rocks. My experience with glaciers was rather limited, but I preferred the nice white ones. The trail, which cut directly across the Batura, changed with the season and the vagaries of the flowing ice. Our route lay across the widest part, which we estimated to be about four miles. It took us three hours to make the crossing.

Walking across any glacier is a hazardous undertaking, and this one was particularly trying. We led our horses down a steep moraine incline, and stepped out on the detritus-covered ice where we could get a foothold on the rubble. We moved cautiously, for under the coating of earth and pebbles lay slick ice. When I dislodged a ten-pound stone, it slid away like a hockey puck and disappeared into a thin crevasse below. I waited for it to hit bottom, and counted the seconds before I heard a dull *plunk* from the subglacial waters. In the center of the glacier was a wide crevasse which we were forced to by-pass. Khodiar told us in gleeful detail how a Hunzukut had lost two mules in the gap a month earlier.

The village of Pasu, at 8,ooo feet, sits with its back against the mountain wall and its feet in the river. Villagers came out to greet us, carrying bunches of white grapes, tight on the stem and elongated in shape, called "ladyfingers." You nibble them like corn off the cob.

We approached the houses over a flat stretch of river sand. Our Hunzukuts had walked thirteen miles that day, and crossed a difficult glacier. Yet they spontaneously broke into a run when their feet touched the sand, and raced at top speed for the first house.

The longer we stayed in Hunza the more we were impressed with the stamina of the people. It is not unheard of for a Hunzukut to hike sixty miles over the mountain trail in a single day. They climb mountains higher than any in the United States with greater nonchalance than I show walking up four flights of stairs in an apartment building. As mountain porters they are rivaled only by the Sherpa of Nepal, who made the conquest of Everest possible.

Sir Robert McCarrison, once surgeon-general of India, describes the Hunzukuts as "unsurpassed in perfection of physique . . . capable of great physical endurance, and enjoying a remarkable freedom from disease in general." Most authorities attribute their unusual vitality and longevity to their simple, healthful diet, and their system of agriculture under which every scrap of vegetable matter is added to animal fertilizer and returned to the soil as compost.

Trotting across a plateau outside Pasu, headed for the next town, Gulmit, we passed four laughing Hunzukuts, well mounted, and carrying—polo mallets. Although we had read that polo was Hunza's national sport, it seemed as incongruous as encountering skiers on a desert island. The only flat ground in Hunza villages were the polo fields, often odd in size and shape, but always carefully groomed. The Mir had promised to arrange a game of Hunza polo when we reached Baltit.

Gulmit was the summer residence of the Mir, where he lives also during the October duck and partridge season. At Gulmit we parted from Khodiar, our merry companion, who returned to Misgar. We paid Khodiar exactly what we thought his services as cook and attendant were worth, according to Middle Eastern standards. He was overwhelmed. We did not realize at the time that we had given him more rupees than the average Hunzukut sees in a whole year.

Money in Hunza is the least important of commodities. The silver Pakistani rupee, worth about twenty cents, is the favorite currency. The Hunzukut prefers the single rupee piece to the five- and ten-rupee notes, for silver keeps better than paper, and the Hunzukut rarely has occasion to spend more than one rupee at a time. Half the people in the country could not change a ten-rupee note.

In Hunza, only the Mir has real need for money. He conducts all import and export on behalf of his subjects. Local trade is by barter, and the Hunzukut who during a lifetime accumulates the equivalent of $50 is considered a hoarder, even a miser. Seldom does a man handle more than $5 a year in cash.

Of what use is money in Hunza? There are no taxes, no license fees, no duties. He cannot buy or sell land, for the land is very limited, and by law must remain in the family. The only large landowner is the Mir, with 320 acres. On occasion he gives a parcel to a deserving subject who has failed to inherit any. Or the Mir may lease an acre or two to a promising young couple at a tiny annual rental which may be paid in apricots, apples, meat, ibex horns, or services.

No Hunzukut covets a cash surplus, even for purposes of emergency. If a flood should sweep away his house, the neighbors will help him build another. Should his horse tumble into the gorge, a neighbor will lend him a horse until he can obtain a replacement. There are no banks, no moneylenders, no interest.

For centuries the Hunzukuts obtained their outside necessities

—cotton cloth, kitchen utensils, salt, silk, and knives—from the caravans traveling the Hunza Road. The traders bartered these goods for the dried fruits and produce of the valley, and for lodging and meals. In addition, the Hunzukuts made a little cash by renting horses and serving as porters.

We came to Hunza at a critical period. The day the border closed in our faces at Mintaka, all traffic to China ceased.

Waiting for us just outside Atabad, eleven rugged miles down the Hunza gorge from Gulmit, stood a man who looked like Snow White's seven dwarfs all rolled into one. Mirzah Hussan greeted us in English, and added: "Mir Sahib sent me to serve you. Your supper is ready in the bungalow."

Mirzah Hussan had a long white mustache, a happy smile, and agility that belied his seventy-five years. He had served the Mirs of Hunza for half a century and as a young man had assisted in the household of a British consul in Kashgar. His English was rusty through disuse, but it was rapidly recalled during his days as our companion. From there on throughout our stay, Mirzah took charge, and our way was easier.

One morning we reached the 500-year-old fort of Altit, perched casually on the edge of a precipice, and were at last within sight of the capital. Ahead we saw a castle, ancient and impressive, set high upon a mountain shoulder, while below in the valley sprawled the town of Baltit. Over this scene towered Rakapushi, the unclimbed 25,550-foot "Queen of the Snows."

The trail zigzagged downward until we reached the level of the old castle, its battlements crumbling and apparently uninhabited. We turned into a cobbled street, and found ourselves in front of a new castle, a modest palace of Western architecture built of hand-hewn Hunza granite. Mirzah proudly led us into the grounds where the Mir himself waited to receive us.

The Mir, short by Hunza standards, and squarely built, was dressed in riding britches and a tweed coat. His dark hair and thick mustache shone in the sunlight, his complexion was ruddy, his dark eyes twinkled with good will and good health. He looked like a Scottish laird welcoming guests to his hearth and heather. The Mir at thirty-five, a mere youth by Hunza stand-ards, had already ruled eight years.

"I hope the trail was not too arduous," he said. "You are welcome here, and we hope that you will remain for some time. We think you will like it." He had been educated at a British school in Gilgit, and his English was excellent.

The Mir escorted us to the palace guest house, overlooking the incomparable view of the Hunza Valley with its terraced fields rising steplike from the river. We had a living room with fireplace, a sunny dining room, a bedroom spread with Persian carpets and hung with Chinese scrolls, and a bathroom where hot water steamed in giant earthenware pitchers. Everything there was solid and comfortable—but I stopped entranced in front of a huge upright piano. Other than delivery by helicopter, I could not imagine how it had reached Baltit.

"My grandfather had the piano brought from Kashmir," the Mir explained. "Twenty men carried it over the mountains. It took ten days on the trail from Gilgit." Later that evening, I tried a few notes. They should have carried a piano tuner to Hunza, too.

Sitting opposite the Mir and his cultivated brother Ayash, at a five-course lunch, I was uncomfortably conscious of my cracked nails, weathered complexion, rumpled and dusty clothes, and worn boots. The long table was set with damask cloth, crested china, cut glass, and old English silver. But the Mir and Ayash treated me as if I had just walked out of a beauty salon, and my embarrassment vanished. After the sweet and coffee, I was languid from overeating.

Several hours and two hot baths later, we strolled over to the palace for tea, and began to know a remarkable man, ruler of a remarkable state which by the accident of geography, and his wisdom, had remained an island of peace in a maelstrom of hatred, suspicion, and violence. Technically a part of Pakistan, bordering an aggressive China and an uneasy Afghanistan, only a few miles from the frontiers of Russia, Hunza managed to re-main aloof from the fears and troubles of all.

"We are the happiest people in the world," the Mir said with a quiet sureness which precluded any boastfulness, "and I will tell you why. We have just enough of everything, but not enough to make anyone else want to take it away. You might call this the Happy Land of Just Enough."

Besides Burushaski and English, the Mir speaks fluent Persian, Urdu, Arabic, and the dialects of half a dozen neighboring princely states. He has a fine collection of guns and mounted heads, and was proud of his Yarkand carpets and sets of Russian chinaware which belonged to his ancestors. He had a radio, stacks of good books, and maintained a communications system of runners to bring the news up from Gilgit. He divided his day, the mornings for business, the afternoons for leisure and sports. His Highness Mohammed Jamal Khan was a happy man.

His beautiful Rani had her own wing of the palace, as she lived in purdah (seclusion). But the Mir promised that before I left, the Rani would receive me, although Franc could not meet her, nor could she be photographed.

The Mir works hard at his job of ruling a happy land. Each morning he meets with his council of elders, none under sixty-five, and his grand vizier, who is ninety-eight, to decide the problems of the day.

One of the Hunza customs we showed particular interest in was the spring planting festival and the Mir graciously offered to duplicate it for us, gold dust and all. The villagers, ever ready to attend a fete even in the off season, entered into the occasion with high spirits and this "dry run" was readied for the following afternoon.

The Mir dressed for his performance in a magnificent gown of gold brocade, belted at the waist. At his side hung a gold-hilted sword in a scabbard of carved ivory. A jeweled pin held a plume of egret feathers in place on his black karakul cap. Ayash and the little crown prince were in similar costumes.

"The spring planting festival rites are hundreds of years old," explained the Mir as we walked to a field where hundreds of villagers had gathered, "and some writers say it resembles that performed by the ancient Greeks."

Two black oxen, scarcely larger than six-months-old Angus calves, were hitched to a wooden plow. The Mir's grand vizier was waiting. With him was a teen-age lad, who looked as if he were made up for Halloween. Flour covered the boy's face, hands, and the U.S. Army jacket he was wearing. On his back a bag held a bundle of green branches. Another sack contained barley.

The people cheered as the Mir grasped the handle of the plow. The grand vizier made a brief speech. The Mir responded, then drove the oxen down the field and back, plowing a shallow furrow. The grand vizier next took a handful of seed from the youth's pouch and placed it in the Mir's cupped hands. From a purse he drew a pinch of gold dust, which he mixed with the seed. Then the Mir broadcast the mixture over the new furrows, while the crowd shouted. Three times the ceremony was repeated. Finally the Mir threw a few handfuls of grain over the crowd. The villagers scrambled for the ceremonial seeds, and the celebration was over.

"In the spring when I do this ceremony in seriousness," said the Mir, "I repeat it in three villages, so that every Hunza farmer, by walking only ten to thirty miles, has a chance for a golden seed. For they believe that if they catch a few of the grains I throw, and mix them with their own seed, they'll have a fine harvest."

"Do you believe it?" asked Franc.

The Mir laughed. "Yes—if the weather is good, with plenty of water, and they till the fields well, they will have a good crop."

"But that boy with flour on his head?" I wondered who he was.

"He with the flour, seeds, and green shoots, is a Hunza symbol of fertility," Ayash explained. "His position, one of great honor, is hereditary."


THE MIR FIXES and collects the road tolls charged the caravans, using the money to buy basic medical supplies. There are no doctors in Hunza—except an occasional foreign medical man who visits to marvel at their phenomenal freedom from disease. McCarrison, who spent some time in Hunza, noted the complete absence of ulcers and dyspepsia, as well as the nonexistence of cancer.

At least once a year the Mir travels the whole length of his land on a polo pony, accompanied by his wife on a mule, for a tour of inspection. While the Mir consults with local elders, the Rani, a princess of Nagar in her own right, visits the women to hear their needs.

And each year, in the cold and bleak months of December and January, when the passes are closed and no work is possible, the Mir presides at the famous Hunza sword dances, celebrating their fierce past, and there is much merrymaking. Since the Ismaili are the only Moslem sect to countenance wine drinking, a little wine is made during the summer for these celebrations.

Each winter the Mir is called upon to perform a mass wedding ceremony. A Hunzukut is unlikely to forget his anniversary, for all weddings take place on the same day, a December Thursday chosen by the village diviners in consultation with the Mir. Hunza parents still select marriage partners for their children, but the young people can refuse their parents' choice.

"We have one custom which Westerners find unusual," said the Mir. "The groom's mother spends the honeymoon with the newlyweds, acting as guide and teacher. Marriage, we believe, is too important to be left to chance."

It must be a successful system, because no one can remember a divorce in Hunza.

While marriage is important, so is birth control. There are only a limited number of arable acres in Hunza, and if the Hunzukuts had as many children as other Asiatic or Oriental peoples, there would soon be serious overpopulation. Centuries ago they solved the problem. When a wife becomes pregnant she leaves her husband's bed, not to return again until the baby is weaned, two years for a girl, three for a boy.

Families, therefore, are small, usually three or four children, and the population does not vary appreciably. The land is inherited by the most capable son, not necessarily the oldest. The other sons become laborers, mountain porters, trail runners, guides, or serve in the Gilgit Scouts, a regiment of the Pakistani army.

Women cannot inherit land, since it is felt that they cannot till the fields. They can own other property, however, and have an equal voice in family matters. The Mir's wife is the only woman in the land who lives in seclusion, called purdah, her face never seen by men other than her immediate family. The other women of the country move about freely, unveiled. Though shy, they smiled and salaamed as we met them on our walks around Baltit. Occasionally one would squeal and run when Franc pointed a camera at her, but I put this down as coquetry, not real fear.

Occasionally, from the guest house, I would see a flurry of scarfs or glimpse a veil on an upstairs balcony of the palace. I knew it was the Rani, and that she must be as curious about me, as I was about her. One evening the Mir said that the Rani expected me for tea the next afternoon. Ayash would interpret for me, since the Rani spoke no English. The day of our meeting, word came from a professional hunter, called *shikari*, that some Marco Polo sheep, the rare *Ovis poli*, had been sighted. Franc borrowed a gun and, guided by Mirzah, was off to join the hunt.

I dressed in my pitiful best—faded blue slacks and a freshly pressed plaid shirt—and joined Ayash for my interview with the Rani. She received us in her suite, where embroidered Chinese fairies skipped gaily around the silken wall hangings, and layers of brilliant carpets covered every inch of floor. We sat on piles of yielding cushions beside great brass trays with short legs, which served as tea tables.

The Rani was dressed in ballooning silk pantaloons, a black lace jacket, and a tiny cap of petit-point embroidery with a long chiffon scarf draped across it. Her black hair was wound into a large knot. Her lovely serene face had a cameo profile. Her fingernails and toenails were bright pink. She looked just as attractive and voluptuous as an Oriental Rani in her boudoir should look.

We were joined by several of her aunts and female cousins, and her oldest children, girls of eight and ten.

Since it is recognized that the Mir must provide a strong line of succession and, as he has plenty of land for his male offspring, the Hunza system of birth control does not apply to the ruler. The Mir and Rani have had nine children, seven of them alive.

She spoke of her children as "this year's baby," "last year's baby," or "the baby of five years ago." She explained that soon after birth the children were given into the care of a wet nurse, who then remained in the household as a servant. There was certainly no lack of women about the palace that afternoon.

I soon discovered that instead of interviewing the Rani, she was interviewing me. She possessed endless curiosity about America. Without the flicker of a smile, Ayash translated all her questions. The Rani had never been farther from the Hunza Valley than Peshawar in the Northwest Frontier Province, but she regularly looked through American fashion magazines and Ayash translated the ads and the stories for her. This caused considerable confusion as to the morals and mores of Americans.

"I am puzzled," she said. "In these magazines I see the most beautiful dresses, yet you wear trousers. I have been visited by several other foreign ladies, and *all* of them have worn trousers. Why is this?"

I explained that all foreign women who visited Hunza must come by horseback, that American dresses are not adapted to horseback riding, and that trousers were more modest and comfortable. The Rani found this hard to believe, pointing out that her pantaloons were suitable either for the boudoir, or for riding a mule. Obviously, all American women should wear pantaloons instead of dresses. It was necessary to explain, then, that while most Hunzukut women had never ridden in an automobile, most American women had never ridden a horse. The problem of *haute couture* on horseback was not a pressing one in America.

The Rani accepted this, and then asked: "Must all American men hunt big game and drink whisky if they wish to be distinguished?"

I was astonished. "Of course not!"

She produced a dozen full-page whisky ads, in color, every one showing a Man of Distinction, glass in hand, and if there weren't lion or deer heads on the wall, there were rifles or shotguns or hunting dogs somewhere about.

"There you are," she said, with an expressive and graceful gesture of her hand.

This required elaborate explanation of our advertising methods, concluding with the flat assurance that it was unnecessary to drink whisky and hunt big game to be distinguished.

"Do you not consider your husband a distinguished man?" the Rani parried. "And is it not true that at this moment he hunts the great horned sheep? And does he not drink whisky soda?"

Her logic was so sound I had to admit that the description fit perfectly.

Then came inevitable questions about American men, and the curious custom known as dating. I countered with a question for the Rani—had she ever seen the Mir before their wedding day? She admitted she had stolen a surreptitious peek from the balcony when the Mir came to call on her father, but added, "*He* never saw *me*. . . . But your American courtship and marriage— I cannot understand these customs at all. Tell me," she continued, "what part does cold cream play in your betrothal ceremony?"

I thought this over for some time. "I give up," I said. "I can't think of the slightest connection."

Triumphantly she produced a copy of the *Ladies' Home Journal* and confronted me with a full-page photograph of a ravishing debutante, with the caption:

"She's Lovely—She's Engaged—She Uses Pond's."

I went briefly into the fields of cosmetics and matrimony as big business, explaining how American women were lured into beauty by the bait of matrimony, and American men lured into matrimony by the bait of beauty.

There followed a long inquisition on engagement rings, courtship customs, and the wedding ceremony. I was dizzy when the ladies-in-waiting brought tea and cakes, and was just about to ask some questions of my own when Ayash cleared his throat.

"Her Highness wants you to tell her," he said, "what is a twoway stretch?"

It was obvious from the Rani's generous figure that she didn't wear a girdle, and the word would mean nothing to her. I tried pantomime. Whether the ladies thought I was describing a garment or an American mating dance I am not certain. Ayash finally lost his poise, became hysterical, and the party dissolved into gales of laughter.

On parting, the Rani presented me with a duplicate of her little hat, telling me that the petit point was her own work, and promising that we should meet again before I left.

Two days later when my bedraggled man of distinction returned from his hunting trip, tired and thinner by several more pounds, I tried to tell him all about the Rani. But he was in a pink haze, having tracked down the Marco Polo sheep and, what is more, collected a fine head. That night he added the story of the hunt to our journal:

"Met *shikari* and trackers. They presented steel-pointed six-foot pole for climbing. We set off.

"Mir an honest man, and when he said *Ovis poli* only 'few miles up the trail' he probably meant just that. Forgot to mention miles all straight up!

"Guides found my progress slow. *Shikari* stayed with me but trackers ranged ahead like hunting dogs, traveling at least three times as far as I did, yet showing no fatigue. At dusk reached 16,000. Paused for a half hour. Ate handful of dried apricots and walnuts.

"Made another 1,500 feet in next three hours. Hunzukuts ready to go on all night. I was through. Feet leaden, lungs bursting, heart pounding rumba rhythm. Scooped a hole for sleeping bag, turned in. Friends slept in their *chapons*.

"Tair Shah, the *shikari*, roused me at dawn. So stiff and sore could scarcely unzip the bag. More apricots and walnuts. Started off up mountain, of course.

"An hour of steady climbing brought us to 18,500. Tair Shah sent tracker ahead to crest of ridge. Tracker crawled last few feet, peered across, motioned us to his side.

"Inched to crest and peered over. Quarter mile away, in snow meadow, were seven Marco Polo sheep—four ewes, three rams. Wind toward us, they unalarmed.

"*Ovis poli* has body large as donkey, great head, magnificent curved horns. World record head, taken nearby, had horns 75 inches around outside curve.

"Lay flat waiting for my gasping breath to smooth out. Inched rifle across crest, sighted, squeezed trigger.

"Grazing animals leaped as if propelled by springs. Hurtled straight up sheer rock wall. All but big ram. He motionless for second, then pitched down slope. Tair Shah fired. Young ram tumbled in mid-flight.

"Dead rams only quarter mile away, as bullet flies, but terrain so rugged it took trackers nearly two hours to return with carcasses. While they gone, I dozed.

"Tair Shah woke me when men dragged the animals in. Took one look and screamed. 'The heads,' I shouted in Urdu. 'Where are the heads?'

"Trackers had decapitated both animals.

" 'Why the heads?' asked Tair Shah. 'Horns are heavy, and you cannot eat them.'

"My Urdu too meager. Pointed to spot where rams had fallen, firmly repeated word for head. Tair Shah gave me a peculiar look, sent trackers back with orders bring heads to nearest village.

"Took *shikari* and me six hours to slide down to the village. Soon after trackers walked in, each carrying nearly 200 pounds of sheep. Neither seemed tired.

"My horns measured 47 inches around the outside turn.

"Napped rest of afternoon. Tair Shah set out after ibex. At nine that night, a knock on my door. Opened it to find *shikari*, trackers, and curious villagers. They had three ibexes slung over shoulders, each carried a head in his hand. They piled heads, with long, curving horns on porch.

" 'Sahib likes heads,' Tair Shah told Mirzah. 'Why? Does he cook them? Or is it only the eyes he likes?'

"Mirzah explained Western fondness for trophies. Tair Shah much relieved."


ONE SUNNY MORNING we attended a session of the Mir's council meeting. This one was held atop the old castle, although more often they are held in the garden before the new palace. The atmosphere was informal, with the council members and visitors sitting in a circle around the Mir.

Here to the court came Hunzukuts from villages above and below Baltit, dissatisfied either with the decision of an *arbab* or with a telephone discussion with the Mir himself. Each case was put to a vote of the council. By his own decree, the Mir's vote normally counts no more than any other. In a pinch he can veto his council, for he is an absolute monarch. But in actuality he rules almost entirely as a wise and respected mediator.

The problems that day mostly concerned water rights. An intricate system of canals irrigates most farms. The aqueduct is an engineering wonder, carrying some of the water more than sixty miles along sheer cliffs, and it is community owned and maintained. It is not strange that occasionally some member of the community thinks he deserves more water than his neighbor, and the dispute ends up in Baltit.

We saw two such arguments. In both contests the men argued long and loudly, forensic qualities appreciated by the audience. In each case the Mir suggested a compromise, immediately accepted. Each time the two men embraced, kissed each other on the cheek, and left arm-in-arm—probably to walk forty or fifty miles back to their adjoining fields, friends once more.

But one case involving a land inheritance ended less amicably. After it was put to a vote the losing litigant, his henna beard standing out in rage, waved his arms and shouted at the council. The loser was in no kissing mood and stomped off yelling his opinions to anyone who would listen. "That," said the Mir, turning to Franc, "is the Hunza free press."

Only one case involved a woman. She came to argue about the ownership of a copper stew pot which had belonged to her mother, but which her brother had inherited. The council decided in favor of the brother, and the woman went away furious. "She brings it up every year," explained the Mir, "although she knows she will lose. The woman dislikes her sister-in-law, and hopes the matter of the pot will embarrass her. Had it only been a breakable clay pot!"

We visited a farmer, Nazar Shah, near Baltit, to study his methods and his way of life. For centuries these people have

practiced crop rotation and have carefully replenished the soil
with compost. They are regarded by experts as among the world's
finest agriculturists. In "Thoughts on Feeding" by Dr. L. J.
Picton, an authority on nutrition, the Hunzukuts are summed
up as follows: "Somehow their life, seemingly hard and austere,
has endowed these people with a happiness I forbear to over-
state. They have achieved engineering without mathematics,
morality without moralizing, agriculture without chemistry,
health without medicine, sufficiency without trade. In the harsh
and uncompromising surroundings of the Hunza, mastery of the
art of life has been engendered by an unremitting agriculture."

Every Hunza farmer is almost completely self-sufficient. On a
bit more than two acres, Nazar Shah raised enough barley and
potatoes, the country's chief crops, and smaller amounts of millet,
wheat, gram, and fresh vegetables for his family of seven. His
orchard yielded apricots, pears, apples, and walnuts. Like every
Hunza farmer, Nazar Shah had eight or ten sheep, for milk and
wool. All his family's clothing was homespun. Except in December, when two sheep are killed for the feast, meat is rarely
tasted, but fowl and eggs are eaten the year around.

Like most Hunza houses, Nazar Shah's was spotless. Its two
floors were connected by a ladder. "All our houses are built like
this," he explained. "The lower room has only one small window
and is easy to keep warm. We live there all winter. But every
year, on the twenty-first of March, we and everyone else in Hunza
move upstairs—where we have a balcony with a view. There is
a Hunza saying: 'Better a home with no roof than one with no
view.'" Even the Mir and royal family move upstairs on March
21, the day of the spring equinox. Like a large-scale farmhouse,
the palace has duplicate apartments on two floors.

Nazar Shah showed us his storerooms, piled with dried apricots
and walnuts, jars of grain, and strings of pears and apples. A
special section of the storeroom held an emergency supply, reserved for neighbors who meet with misfortune. This was the
Hunza social security system.

After a pleasant visit and simple meal with Nazar Shah and his
wife, Soni Begum, we sent back Mirzah with presents—a Swiss
army knife for our host and a scarf for his wife. Ten minutes

later Nazar Shah's son appeared at our door with a plate of walnut halves. I thanked him, but still feeling obligated, sent Mirzah back to the farm with two small notebooks and a pencil. Back came the boy, this time carrying dried apricots and a mound of potatoes. Mirzah suggested that Soni Begum might like some aluminum foil for decorative purposes. I sent him with this, and most grateful thanks, praying that the flow would stop.

No such luck. Back came the farmer's daughter bringing me a Hunza lady's cap, and a rawhide quirt for Franc. I retaliated with some rupees and a can of shoe polish, and was looking around frantically for other gifts when Nazar Shah himself appeared. Somewhat wearily, I thought, he presented us with a platter of apples. After handshakes all around, and many more "thank yous," we allowed the amenities to subside. You can't get ahead of a Hunzukut in courtesy.

As promised, the Mir sponsored a polo game for our benefit, and I was asked to throw out the first ball. Up to that moment it was just like Meadowbrook—but then the riotous differences became apparent.

The play was wild and reckless, with the most daring horsemanship we had ever seen. There were no rest periods, no fouls, no penalties, and few rules that we could see. Play lasted until one side made a score of nine goals. Any player who caught a ball in flight could ride through the goal with it, but his opponents were allowed to use any means short of murder (it was even permissible to pull him off his horse), to prevent a score. Through the whole game drums and flutes beat out a martial tattoo. At the end we were surprised to see all the players still intact. I was as exhausted as they were.

Warlike polo is one of the few relics of Hunza's violent past. Peace has not always existed in the blessed valley. The Mir showed us a calf-bound volume detailing the history of his family for forty generations. Translated into English, it was written by the Mir's grandfather. "He was the first who *could* write it down," the Mir explained, "for until that time the Mirs spoke only the Hunzas' unwritten tongue.

The history was full of strange and gruesome tales, perhaps more legendary than historical, for until the mid-eighteen hun-

dreds history depended upon memory. There was one Mir who, according to legend, ate young children, and another who was abandoned in the river in a basket and recovered downstream like Moses.

But there was no doubt that the great-uncle of the present Mir was a bloodthirsty ruler who murdered his father, poisoned his mother, and tossed two brothers over a precipice. He later blandly reported the incident to his suzerain, the Maharajah of Kashmir:

"By the will of God and the decree of fate, my late father and I recently fell out. I took the initiative and settled the matter, and have placed myself on the throne of my ancestors."

That particular Mir took to raiding British stations in India, and an expeditionary force was required to drive him into exile. The present Mir's grandfather was placed on the throne, and Hunza has been peaceful ever since.

I wondered whether this peace could continue, for the Hunza Valley is of considerable strategic importance, and the rest of the world lives in uneasy truce. All one could do was hope, said the Mir. He had been frightened a few years before when a prospector thought he had discovered a rich vein of gold near Baltit. "For a time I was alarmed. But fortunately," the Mir added, "the ore turned out to be worthless."

It seemed hard to believe that anyone could be alarmed because gold had been discovered on his land.

"It would have meant the end of Hunza and our way of life," explained the Mir. "Had the strike been genuine, some gold-hungry country would have moved in on the pretext of protecting us."

In Hunza, Franc and I learned the true joy of leisure. There was no place to go, and no way to get there, except on foot. There were no movies and no television. Only the Mir possessed a radio and his family rarely bothered to listen. Yet we were never bored. We discovered the pleasures of sitting quietly on a hillside and absorbing the beauty of our surroundings, the terraced green fields and the racing white river below, and the Queen of the Snows above.

But modern man's sojourn in paradise must be brief. One

day the Mir brought us the Hunza guest book to sign. On its yellowing pages were the signatures of Sir Aurel Stein, Lord Curzon, C. P. Skrine, Sven Hedin, Theodore and Kermit Roosevelt. Proudly yet humbly, we wrote our names beneath these.

The next day we joined the Mir on his balcony, where he made a touching and friendly farewell speech, asking us to return and live for a year in the peace of his valley. "And, Mrs. Shor, the Rani asked me to present you with these." He handed me two exquisite pearl bracelets. To Franc he gave a Hunza robe, a choga of ibex wool such as only the Mir himself is privileged to wear.

Franc threw the robe over his shoulders, and I slipped the bracelets on my wrists, and we walked on reluctant feet to our horses. From the quarters of the shy Rani I could see a flutter of chiffon, and I waved. We rode off down the trail toward Gilgit. Were we returning to civilization—or had we left it?

In Gilgit we met Liaquat Ali Khan, Pakistan's soon-to-be-martyred prime minister, and with him flew to Lahore and Karachi. Thence an airliner carried us, in nineteen hours, to London—retracing a journey which it had taken us eight months to accomplish overland. Still, we felt, we hadn't done so badly. Marco Polo's round trip took twenty-five years.

But the fruits of our journey were not to be measured in terms of time or speed. We had set out to follow an ancient trail, and in that we had been partially successful. Along that trail we had found hospitality and human kindness, warm hearts and open hands, generosity from kings and merchants and yak pullers, each giving what he had to give.

There is in Arabic an ancient proverb which says that "Travel is the gate of hell." This it may be for those who count only the wearying marches, the steep trails, the sore feet, and the freezing nights. But such inconveniences are soon forgotten.

I have never stopped traveling. I hope I never shall. Somewhere in the world there are other people like the Shah of Iran, like Rahman Qul, like Mirzah Hussan. Somewhere, perhaps, there is another Hunza. And I, like Marco Polo, shall be ever hunting them—hunting with a hungry heart.

# IN THE FOOTSTEPS
## VENICE

Venice

ITALY

BLACK SEA

Istanbul

TURKEY

Ankara

Kayseri  Sivas

Mersin

Iskenderun  Erzurum

Mt. Ararat

Khoi

SYRIA  Tabriz

Haifa

Jerusalem

IRAQ

CASPIAN SEA

Tehran  Shahrud

Meshed  Mazar-i-sherif  Khanabad  Faizabad

Nishapur

Oregon  Isfahan  Maimana

SAUDI  IRAN  Herat  Kabul  Gilgit

ARABIA  Kerman  AFGHANISTAN

Kandahar

Bandar
Abbas

PAKISTAN

YEMEN

Karachi

INDIAN OCEAN